Australian

CFDs

FOR

DUMMIES®

Australian Edition

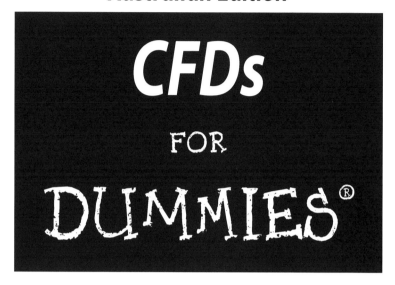

CFDs
FOR
DUMMIES®

by David Land

WILEY

Wiley Publishing Australia Pty Ltd

CFDs For Dummies®

Australian Edition published by
Wiley Publishing Australia Pty Ltd
42 McDougall Street
Milton, Qld 4064
www.dummies.com

Copyright © 2010 Wiley Publishing Australia Pty Ltd

The moral rights of the author have been asserted.

National Library of Australia

Cataloguing-in-Publication data:

Author:	Land, David
Title:	CFDs For Dummies / David Land
Edition:	Australian Ed.
ISBN:	978 1 74216 939 2 (pbk.)
Notes:	Includes index
Subjects:	Futures — Australia.
	Margins (Futures trading) — Australia.
	Stocks — Prices — Australia.
	Investment analysis — Australia.
	Finance, Personal.
Dewey Number:	332.63220994

Cover image: © Eric Hood/ iStock

Figures 12-1 and 12-2: © Bloomberg Finance L.P.
All other charts powered by MetaStock

Typeset by diacriTech, Chennai, India

MIX
Paper from
responsible sources
FSC® C013604

About the Author

David Land is Chief Market Analyst for stockbroker and CFD provider CMC Markets.

David has worked in the financial markets for well over a decade in a wide range of roles. Although his experience is diverse, he has always remained greatly interested in and focused on short-term trading methods employed across financial markets.

David started life in the financial markets working for a small Sydney-based stockbroker, before moving on to work for Colonial and the Commonwealth Bank of Australia. These roles led to an investor education role at the Australian Securities Exchange, which really improved his ability to relate to traders and investors from all sorts of backgrounds.

On the work front, these days David divides his time between writing analytical and commentary reports and providing education in trading to clients of CMC Markets. In addition, he lectures for Kaplan Professional and makes regular TV appearances providing market commentary.

David holds a Master of Applied Finance from Macquarie Applied Finance Centre.

He currently lives in Sydney with his wife and small white dog.

Dedication

I dedicate this book to all the people out there who take up the challenge of trading, investing and otherwise managing their own portfolio. While this can be time consuming, it is such a great challenge — I hope you find the rewards you are looking for. In addition, I must mention my wonderful family, without whom nothing I have done would have been possible.

Author's Acknowledgements

I have received so much help on this book for which I am immensely grateful.

First, I must thank all the team at Wiley who have been very understanding and supportive over the course of production. Thanks to Charlotte Duff and Bronwyn Duhigg, the commissioning editors, who provided a great deal of guidance in the development of the book. In addition, thanks to Gabrielle Packman, senior editor.

I also have a long list of editors to thank. Maryanne Phillips provided a huge amount of help in the book's initial stages. Caroline Hunter, Jenny Scepanovic, Robi van Nooten and Catherine Spedding were all fantastic in the support they provided in the book's production. Without their expertise, *CFDs For Dummies*, Australian Edition, simply wouldn't have happened.

My thanks to Ric Spooner, who provided excellent support in the checking of this book and is at all times a fantastic sounding board for ideas. Also thanks to Vincent McCartney and James Foulsham for their help on the technical side. Finally, thanks to Louis Cooper and Eva Diaz, who were great proponents of *CFDs For Dummies*, Australian Edition, from the outset.

Publisher's Acknowledgements

We're proud of this book; please send us your comments through our online registration form located at http://dummies.custhelp.com.

Some of the people who helped bring this book to market include the following:

Acquisitions, Editorial and Media Development

Project Editors:
Maryanne Phillips,
Caroline Hunter,
Jenny Scepanovic,
Robi van Nooten,
Catherine Spedding

Acquisitions Editor: Bronwyn Duhigg

Editorial Manager:
Gabrielle Packman

Production

Graphics: Wiley Art Studio

Cartoons: Glenn Lumsden

Proofreader: Pam Dunne

Indexer: Karen Gillen

Contents at a Glance

Table of Contents

Introduction

I've been lucky enough to have spent more than a decade working in a number of facets of the financial sector. While many people would consider that more of a punishment than a career, it has given me exposure to a lot of people, a lot of fascinating concepts and a lot of different ways in which people manage their investments. Over the last five years, I have worked full-time with CFDs and as a product I find them fascinating and powerful — while also requiring a great amount of careful treatment.

I know that investors generally are keen to take a more self-directed approach to their investments, so I was very keen to be able to help them do exactly that. At the same time, I wanted to produce a guide that was as upfront as possible in dealing with the mass of different considerations that CFD traders have to take into account when buying and selling positions. Most importantly, I hope after reading this book you will go away thinking about how you will include risk management as a key part of your trading process. Leverage is a powerful tool that needs to be applied with the greatest of care so be sure to consider that point as you go through this book.

CFDs have captivated the trading audience wherever they have been offered — and with good reason. They are a simple to understand and easy to use product. The thing that requires the most effort is learning how to manage your positions and how to fit CFDs into your wider portfolio. You are given so many different alternatives as to what to trade that it can seem a little overwhelming. By being patient and methodical in the way you approach any investment — and particularly CFDs — you give yourself a big advantage. There are no short cuts to successful CFD trading but you set yourself apart from the beginning by preparing yourself as well as you can for all the challenges that you will face.

A lot of people want to be short-term traders and that's a wonderful goal to have — just make sure that you're a short-term trader around for the long term. No matter who you are you should start small, remain conservative and be as methodical as you can be. Everyone wants to be wealthy and the markets can deliver that for you but they won't provide it for free, so be prepared for a long journey that will hopefully be rewarding and satisfying.

About This Book

CFDs are a wonderful product for traders. They offer incredible advantages, such as built-in leverage, low entry cost, a huge range of markets to trade and the ability to profit in a rising or falling market. From the perspective of attracting traders they are pretty much unrivalled in the market. *CFDs For Dummies* gives you the full picture of what this product is all about. This doesn't mean it tells you ten ways to become a millionaire — because you won't find any short cuts that way — but reading *CFDs For Dummies* will help you make a well-informed decision about how CFDs fit into your overall portfolio.

Once you are informed as a trader you can go about the task of building a strong trading methodology to follow. I applaud a 'have a go' mentality but CFDs are not the place for it. People may find trading satisfying but it's not a forum to just make a few trades and see what happens. I have built nearly all of the chapters around an awareness of the pluses and minuses of dealing in CFDs. Once you have properly recognised the risks you can take steps to dealing with them and trying to keep them to a minimum. Risk can't be eliminated but by planning to be successful over the long term you can deal with it effectively.

You shouldn't be afraid of making mistakes — just make sure they don't cost much money. I think the difference between the good trader and the bad trader with equal amounts of knowledge is the way each deals with losing trades. Put yourself in the good trader camp and keep your risk and your losses conservative.

How to Use This Book

CFDs For Dummies is designed so that you can jump in at any point and get the information that you need. This means that you don't have to read entire parts or every chapter to find what you're looking for. The table of contents gives a very detailed view of what can be found where so make good use of it, and then head straight to the point of most interest to you.

At the back of the book I include a handy glossary of terms. Don't let trading terminology put you off getting to know more about CFDs!

Foolish Assumptions

Although I wish everyone would buy this book I know it's not going to be that simple — if you're not interested in CFDs then *CFDs For Dummies* isn't going to be for you. Having said that if you're reading this, you've passed the first assumption — that you've heard about CFDs and you want to know more.

I've assumed that you have a working knowledge of markets and have as a minimum dealt in shares before. Derivatives (such as CFDs) are an extension of other markets so you need to be aware of the underlying market first in order to make sense of the derivative.

I've also assumed you want to take an active approach to your investing and are comfortable with the idea of applying a conservative amount of leverage to the trades that you take.

Perhaps my most important assumption involves risk management. Despite what you may have heard about traders, I've assumed you are not interested in the idea of getting rich quick and you understand that learning about the product is only the first step towards your trading future.

Finally, I've assumed that CFDs will only make up a very small portion of your overall investment portfolio, although they will most likely make up the more actively managed part of your portfolio.

How This Book Is Organised

This book is split into six parts.

Part 1: Getting Started

In this section you'll find out what CFDs are, the key points you need to consider when deciding who you will use as a provider, and how to place enter and exit orders. I discuss the difference between trading long and trading short, and start to look at leverage and how you should manage it. There are lots of providers, different CFDs and markets out there for you to consider. Take the time to consider here what these differences mean to you and make the decision you're happy with.

Part II: Touring the CFD Marketplace

In this section I introduce you to the main types of CFDs that are available, including shares, foreign exchange, indices, commodities and interest rate securities. All of these have their unique points that need to be understood before you make any trades. Once you understand them, however, there is sure to be a product suitable for you in this group, whether you are a short- or longer-term trader and whether you want to trade night or day.

Part III: Keeping Risk Under Control

This section is a must read for people who are new to the world of derivatives and CFDs. In this part I look at keeping a lid on leverage, applying stop loss orders and the merits of sensible position sizes. While it may be tempting to think only of the possible profits you can make from a trade, you should trade only when you have a keen awareness of the possible downsides that you may face. Any trading has risk attached to it but you put yourself ahead of the group if you manage yours carefully at all times.

Part IV: Trading Strategies

In this section I look at a number of different methods that you can use to start your trading journey, such as swing trading and trend trading. I look also at the core concepts of fundamental and technical analysis and show how these can be applied to your use of CFDs within your portfolio. The use of a strategy that is well thought out and personalised allows you to consistently trade according to this strategy, and this is what enables shrewd traders to pick up times when they could be doing things better. Taking a scattergun approach may be a lot easier but it's not going to help you be profitable over the long term.

Part V: Knowing Where You're Going

Happily this section is all about you. This is the part where I look at bringing together what you know, analysing your trading behaviour and turning this knowledge into a working trading methodology. As part of this I also look at record-keeping and some of the perils of not making good trading plans. Some people say that you won't know whether you've reached the end of your journey unless you know where you're going. Traders don't get that luxury because the journey never ends but you need to be sure you're moving ahead at all times and not losing money or opportunity without being well aware of it.

Part VI: The Part of Tens

This is the part where I look at a number of key considerations that can make life a lot easier for CFD traders — ten rules or thoughts that are there to make things go more smoothly. I take a look at mistakes made by beginners, strategies for better risk management and how to deal with leverage.

Icons Used in This Book

To help you use this book, there are a few icons that are used to mark special information. Here's what they mean:

This icon appears when I need to reiterate a key point that you should employ whenever necessary. Do whatever it takes to remember these points!

Look out for these little gems — they note ways you can do things more easily or more quickly, or strategies to keep you trading more successfully for longer.

When you see these icons, pay attention! Trading is easy to do but difficult to master so in order to keep moving forward you need to be aware of traps that ensnare the unwary.

This icon flags where you'll find descriptions of phrases or concepts that you may not be familiar with. This is usually good background or more advanced information on the market that you're dealing with — which may interest you, or may not. You can skip these icons if you choose without missing out on the main gist of the section or chapter.

The internet is the best friend of the trader so be sure to use it. As there is so much information out there, this icon notes site names that will be good reference points for the future.

Where to Go from Here

Where you choose to dive into the book is really up to you. If you are making a new venture into CFDs, Parts I and II are probably the ones to begin with. If you have some experience trading CFDs, you might like to just skim Parts I and II and then really sink your teeth into Parts III, IV and V.

Part I
Getting Started

Glenn Lumsden

'Greetings! I come from the future with an important message for Earth. But first, I'd like to open a CFD account.'

In this part ...

*B*efore you begin trading CFDs you need to understand the basics. In this part, I explain how CFDs work and why they're one of the most interesting products for traders. I help you work out whether trading CFDs is for you, and cover how to make the most of their best features.

Chapter 1

Deciding Whether CFD Trading Is For You

* *

In This Chapter

▶ Understanding where CFDs fit into the financial product spectrum

▶ Fulfilling your responsibilities as a trader

▶ Taking the preliminary steps to trading success

* *

A *financial derivative* is an instrument whose price is based on something else — such as a share price, a barrel of oil or any of a wide range of other products. CFDs (contracts for difference) are financial derivatives that are popular with traders because they're possibly the most simple of all derivatives and this makes them accessible to a very wide audience. This ease of understanding carries with it a tendency to create a false sense of security, however, which can lead to traders being overexposed and overlooking the fact that losses are largely unlimited in some circumstances (see Chapter 3 to find out how this occurs). When used properly though, CFDs enable you to trade a vast array of products very easily and very cheaply, which can greatly enhance your profitability.

In this chapter, I explain how CFDs work and how you can use them as part of your overall portfolio. I also discuss using CFDs to benefit from short-term price movements in a number of financial markets, including shares and foreign exchange. Finally, I start you on the journey of understanding how best to manage your risk as a CFD trader, since managing risk is critical to your success as a trader.

Grasping the Ground Rules

In this section, I look at the major characteristics of CFDs and some of the main points that you need to understand before starting on your CFD trading journey.

So what are CFDs, anyway?

A *CFD* is an agreement to pay the difference between two prices — the price at which the contract is opened and the price at which the contract is closed. The CFD's price is based on that of an underlying instrument, which varies depending on the particular CFD, but may be, say, a share or foreign exchange rate. A CFD is typically an OTC (over-the-counter) product. This means that it isn't traded on a centralised exchange or market like shares. Each contract involves only two parties: You (the trader, or buyer) and the CFD provider (the counterparty to the transaction, or seller).

When you open a CFD trade you do so based on current market prices. The same applies when you close the position. What makes CFDs unique when compared with many other categories of derivatives is the way that they're priced. Other derivative products use complex formulas to determine their prices (generally a variation on the Black–Scholes options pricing formula), but CFDs simply mimic the price of the underlying instrument that they track.

In essence, a CFD puts you in a position to make a profit (or loss) from changes in the price of the underlying instrument. For example, if you enter a long trade (that is, you purchase CFDs with the view that the price will rise):

- ✔ If the price rises between the time the CFD is opened and closed, the seller must pay the difference in value to the buyer (you). Provided costs are covered, you make a profit and the seller makes a loss.

- ✔ If the price falls between the time the CFD is opened and closed, the buyer (you) must pay the difference to the seller. In this case, the seller makes a profit and you suffer a loss.

CFD trading can be risky, especially when traders overuse leverage — I cover strategies for managing this risk in Chapter 8. However, CFDs also have features that make them very useful and the preferred instrument for many traders. These features include

- **Ability to easily and practically short sell shares and other financial instruments** — this increases your opportunity to make money from good trading strategies by allowing you to profit from falling as well as rising markets (see Chapter 3 for more information).

- **Ability to trade small positions** — you can purchase small amounts of CFDs and scale your position to suit your requirements.

- **Access to a wide range of products from all around the world.**

- **Access to cost-effective trading platforms that provide you with a wide range of analytical capabilities** — including real-time pricing, charting packages and financial news.

- **Leverage** — when you purchase a CFD, you don't have to pay the full price of the underlying product, but simply a smaller deposit known as an initial margin (see the section 'Paying margins' later in the chapter), so you pay only a small amount to control a much larger position.

- **No physical delivery or settlement of the full value of the underlying instrument.**

- **Simplicity of use.**

CFDs have become a very popular short-term trading product in a large number of countries. By 'short-term' I mean less than one month, but the duration can be shorter or longer than this, depending on the trader. By using CFDs, you're trying to capture short-term price movements in financial markets. If you establish a solid trading methodology, you can generate profits very quickly, but — and it's a *big* but — before you rush headfirst into CFD trading you must consider the potential downsides that exist when trading CFDs. The downsides include losing more capital than you invested and seeing large swings in your capital due to the over-application of leverage. Most of these downsides relate to risk management, which I discuss at length in Chapter 8.

CFDs are a product for sophisticated traders and you need to understand the mechanics of CFDs before placing any trades. I explain more about CFDs in general in Chapters 2 and 3.

To give you an idea of the different markets that CFDs track, in the following section I briefly discuss the main types of CFDs available to trade. These are discussed in-depth in Chapters 4 to 7.

Types of CFDs

A real highlight for CFD traders is being able to trade in a wide range of market types and geographic locations. At one time dealing in foreign shares was a big drama, but the internet has changed all that by giving traders online access to markets in different locations and in different time zones. CFDs take this one step further by allowing you to deal in products from all around the world from a single trading platform — which means you can build trading strategies for just about anything.

Here are the main categories of CFDs that you can trade:

✔ **Commodity CFDs:** Commodity CFDs have been around for some time, but have become more popular in recent years as the commodity boom has brought the world's attention to this investment category. Commodity CFDs enable you to trade products like crude oil over a long trading day, which makes these CFDs very convenient. Commodity CFDs also offer very good portfolio diversification for traders. I discuss commodity CFDs in Chapter 7.

✔ **Foreign exchange (FX, Forex) CFDs:** Foreign exchange CFDs are a very popular trading tool offered by most providers. In this market you're dealing in the relative value of two currencies (the exchange rate). The market is very liquid (meaning it's very easy to get in and out of trades). Foreign exchange CFDs are available to trade 24 hours a day, so you can trade at any time that appeals to you. In Chapter 5 I examine FX CFDs.

✔ **Index CFDs:** Index CFDs have become very popular because they allow traders to take exposure to the wider market in a single trade by buying a CFD over an index. This may be something like the S&P/ASX 200 Index in Australia or the Dow Jones Industrial Average in the United States. Index CFDs are typically available to trade all day and much of the night, and they're likely to be commission-free — depending on your CFD provider. I look at index CFDs in Chapter 6.

✔ **Interest rate CFDs:** Interest rate CFDs enable traders to access a market that most traders haven't dealt in before — the interest rate securities market, with a particular emphasis on short-term notes and longer-term bonds. While the underlying instruments may have a specific term (for example, ten years), this isn't an issue for CFD traders, who're only interested in capturing the price *movements*. Interest rate CFDs can offer real benefits to traders in the form of diversification. I discuss interest rate CFDs in Chapter 7.

✔ **Share CFDs:** For budding CFD traders share CFDs are likely to be the first step, because they're the most similar CFDs to a market you should already be familiar with — the share market. Share CFDs enable you to trade the price movements of domestic markets and most of the larger foreign markets. Share CFDs are available to trade during the same hours that the underlying market is open — so if you want to trade US CFDs, you're in for a late night. I look at share CFDs in Chapter 4.

Ownership

Ownership is a very easy part of the overall concept of CFDs to grasp, because buying a CFD gives you no right to do anything with the underlying instrument that you're trading. Keep in mind that the 'C' in CFD stands for 'contract' — and a contract is all you have. The contract states that the CFD provider will pay you if you're correct about the movement of the underlying instrument, and that you'll pay the CFD provider if you're incorrect. The contract mentions nothing about taking on ownership of the underlying instrument by paying the difference between your margin (the small payment you make to secure the CFD position) and the outstanding amount (the total amount you have exposure to).

Some traders see the margin that they pay to open a CFD position as part payment for the position, and wonder why they can't just pay for the rest of it. Once you understand how CFDs work, you may ask why you'd want to convert CFDs into the fully paid version of the underlying instrument. A CFD moves directly in line with the underlying instrument — but when holding the underlying instrument you're required to pay your financing charges for as long as you hold the position open.

Even though you can't do a direct conversion from the CFD to the underlying instrument, you can consider the price at which you open the CFD position as 'locked in'. This means that you can capture any price movements without the expense of having to buy the underlying instrument.

Example: Imagine that you buy 100 BHP share CFDs at $35.00, paying an initial margin of about 5 per cent ($175). The share price rallies to $37.00 but you don't have ownership of the shares — you can't convert your CFDs to shares. However, this doesn't mean that you miss out on the share price movements that have taken place. This is because the initial margin that you paid enabled you to lock in the price movement, so you capture the price gain anyway. Buying the shares isn't necessary because you have to pay the full value of the shares ($3,700) plus commission, and all you'll be doing is extending your original position for roughly the same profit. See Chapter 4 for more information about share CFDs.

CFD providers

There are two main categories of CFD providers in Australia (although some providers offer both categories):

- ✔ **Direct market access (DMA) providers:** Generally, these deal only in Australian shares and allow you to place your orders for CFDs directly into the underlying share market.

- ✔ **Market makers:** These offer a price to the market at which they buy and/or sell a given instrument. Many different financial products rely on market makers: Their purpose is to provide liquidity in a market. CFD market makers provide you with both the price and the market where you trade, which means there's no central exchange. The price they offer generally reflects that of the underlying market, but there can be some differences, which I look at in Chapter 2.

I discuss the main differences between these two types of providers and outline the various issues you need to consider when selecting the right type of provider for you in Chapter 2.

Unlike shares, CFDs aren't transferable to another provider. So, even though you can buy shares through one stockbroker and sell them through another, you cannot transfer CFDs to another provider. This is because the CFD contract is between you and the CFD provider — so it's not surprising that another provider won't be willing to honour it.

Coming To Grips With Trading Factors

Although many of the key features of CFDs are quite simple, you need to have a very firm understanding of the factors that you as the trader are contractually obliged to deal with. This means not only dealing with losses but also understanding how much money you need to open a position and the conditions under which you have to provide more money to your CFD provider. The better your understanding *before* you trade in CFDs, the less likely you are to receive a shock down the track.

Understanding commission charges

For most traders, CFDs make up only a small portion of their overall investment portfolio but a big portion of the investments that they consider to be short term in nature. A good deal of the attractiveness that is generated by CFDs is the fact that commission on CFDs is very cheap when compared to that on shares. CFD providers charge a low commission rate, starting at about the 0.1 per cent mark on share CFDs, which are subject to a minimum commission amount (say, $10). This is payable on both the entry and exit of your positions. You may see promotional rates somewhat lower than this, but it's more important to think about what your costs of commission will be on an ongoing basis.

Most providers charge commission on the *total exposure* that you take out — although you may think that you should be charged on the total exposure *minus* your margin payment, this generally isn't the case.

Paying margins

CFDs are the first product that many traders employ that requires payment of a margin. You may be familiar with margin lending, but there are really some very stark differences between margin lending and paying a margin on CFDs.

- With margin lending, you buy a number of shares but pay for only a portion of the amount that you hold (say, 50 per cent). The remaining amount is paid by the margin lender (such as a bank or broker) and you repay the margin lender over time. The amount of money that you put up initially acts as security for the loan, as well as being a part payment over the shares that underlie the loan.

✔ A margin in terms of CFDs is a percentage of the total position that you pay to your CFD provider to secure a holding — and this amount is returned to you after you close the trade.

Look very closely at your CFD provider's product disclosure statement (PDS) so that you understand exactly how margin is taken from your account. In general, the CFD provider takes margin payments from your trading account as soon as the trade takes place. Although you may prefer not to have to pay margin straight after the trade takes place, you do get the benefit of being able to use these funds as soon as the position closes.

Initial margin

The amount your CFD provider requires upfront in order to open your position is known as the *initial margin*. The contract that you enter into with the CFD provider requires you to pay the difference between your entry and exit price if you're incorrect in your judgement about the direction of the underlying instrument. So the initial margin acts as security for the CFD provider for any move against you that may occur. You can certainly think of your initial margin requirement as a deposit, because the amount is refunded to you when the trade closes.

CFD providers publish the initial margin requirements for all CFDs that they offer. You find that the more liquid the underlying instrument, the lower the margin requirement. So if the underlying instrument is very *illiquid* (not readily convertible into cash), the CFD provider wants a large part of the payment upfront. This is because liquidity (or lack thereof) is one of the risks that the CFD provider takes when entering into a CFD with a client.

Liquidity refers to the ease with which a position can be bought or sold in the market and the impact that this has on price. In an extremely liquid market like the foreign exchange market, you can buy and sell very large quantities without having any impact on the price. Conversely, trading shares in small companies in the share market readily affects price, even if the trade being made is relatively small.

The initial margin that you pay on different products varies greatly, from lows of around 1 per cent to highs of about 50 per cent. For example, you may pay an initial margin of about 1 per cent on products like index CFDs and foreign exchange CFDs. The initial margin for share CFDs starts at around 5 per cent and rises to a level of about 50 per cent for the smallest companies that the CFD provider offers.

Variation margin

CFDs are a *marked-to-market* product, which means that all profits and losses are settled at the end of every trading session and at the start of every session the slate is wiped clean for everyone. If you make a loss over the course of the trading day, you need to pay your CFD provider a *variation margin*. The variation margin is the unrealised profit or loss on your position and is equal to the dollar value movement in your position when compared against the current market price. You may like to think of your variation margin as the initial margin plus/minus the margin on the rise or fall of your position. In other words, if your position rises in value, you pay the variation margin to your CFD provider and if it falls, your provider pays the variation margin to you. This happens in real time.

Example: Say that you hold 1,000 share CFDs over XYZ Ltd and the share price falls in value by $0.10 during the trading day. Immediately, your CFD provider deducts a variation margin payment of $100 from your account (1,000 × $0.10). Conversely, if the share price rises by $0.10 during the trading day, your CFD provider credits your account with the $100 that this has generated for you.

Marking to market

Traditionally, for products that are marked-to-market, all profit and loss on the positions is settled at the end of the trading session. This occurs whether the positions are open or closed. The idea is to reduce *counterparty risk* — that is, the risk that one party won't be able to pay the other party when the trade eventually closes. By marking to market, the risk exists for only one day, whereas for many other products settlement is at the end of the contract and so counterparty risk is increased. Marking to market is commonly used on nearly every product that requires only a margin payment rather than full payment to open the position. CFD providers generally take this a step further and require this settlement in real time.

In other words, you need to put up more margin if the value of your position has increased, but you receive some margin if the value of the position has decreased.

In addition to the variation margin, most CFD providers debit and credit your account in real time as positions move in your favour and against you. Make sure that you have plenty of available funds in your account to pay for any variation margins that may be required and that you understand the conditions under which you have to supply more funds to your provider. (In Chapters 8 and 9 I look at risk management and position sizing, respectively, which can help you to avoid this type of trouble.)

Employing leverage

One of the most interesting elements of CFD trading relates to using margin payments as a means of increasing the size of your position — or, looking at the issue another way, not tying up as much of your capital in holding your positions open. CFD providers keenly compete to keep margins as low as possible, because this allows traders to open more positions with a smaller amount of their own capital.

The term *leverage* means making your capital work harder and amplifying the results of an investment by using borrowed funds to trade larger positions. Employing *leverage* is a really big component of trading CFDs, but you always need to be thinking about how you're managing your risk when using leveraged. That is, even if margin requirements are very low, rather than thinking exclusively about the exciting part of carrying leveraged positions you should be mindful of the amount of exposure you take to the market at any given point in time and the risk that this exposure carries. (I examine some risk minimisation techniques in Chapter 8.)

Having a low level of margin doesn't always have to imply that you're taking on a massive position in the market. For example, if you look at the index CFDs offered by market makers (see Chapter 6), these tend to trade at a minimum size of $1 per point, meaning that you make or lose $1 for each 1-point movement of the index. This type of contract usually requires only a 1 per cent margin, which means that if the index is trading at 4,500 points, you need to make a margin payment of only $45. So although this is a really highly leveraged position, because you're getting $4,500 worth of market exposure for a $45 margin, it doesn't give you a massive exposure in the market.

The main rule that you need to set for yourself relates to the amount by which you lever your overall account. An individual position may carry a large amount of leveraged, but how this relates to your overall capital base is more important. For example, if you had $4,500 in your account and paid a margin of $45 for a highly leveraged position, you wouldn't be levered at all relative to your available capital — which illustrates how margin requirements and the actual exposure that you have to the market relate to one another.

If you're so inclined, you can actually use CFDs as a means of gaining quick and cheap exposure to the market without using leverage at all. More commonly, though, traders want to apply leverage to their accounts. One of the principal advantages of CFDs over margin lending is the fact that with CFDs you can turn the loan on and off, depending on whether you have a position open or not.

I talk more about using leverage in Chapters 8 and 19.

Considering the effect of delta

CFDs have become very popular as a standalone trading product and traders use them to gain exposure to movements in the price of underlying instruments. CFDs track the underlying instrument more closely than other financial derivatives, which makes CFDs much more predictable. In essence, this means that if you can correctly pick the direction of the underlying instrument, the CFD moves in line with your prediction too.

One of the biggest considerations for traders is the closeness with which the derivatives they're trading track the underlying instrument. CFDs are possibly the simplest derivative to understand in terms of how they move relative to the underlying instrument. The underlying instrument for CFDs can be just about anything, but most commonly comprises shares, indices or foreign exchange. The closeness with which a derivative tracks its underlying instrument is measured using the Greek letter delta. If the derivative has a delta of 0.5, you expect the derivative to move 0.5 for every 1 movement of the underlying instrument. Happily for CFD traders, CFDs tend to have a delta of 1, which means that for a $1 movement in the underlying instrument you expect to see a $1 move on the CFD.

Capital is the trader's lifeblood

For years I've been hearing people say that you should trade only with money that you can afford to lose, and yet others say that you should invest in shares only with money that you can afford to lose. Anything you invest in gives you the potential to lose, but you can control how much you risk. My advice is

✔ Trade only with money that, if lost, isn't going to stop you paying your bills.

✔ Don't trade when in a position where you 'have to win'.

As you become more confident in trading, you get a better idea of what 'sensible risk' is. You shouldn't be thinking: 'I'll just take this one trade and if I lose my $1,000, then that'll be that.' My guess is that if you think this way and make money on the trade, you'll risk it all until you lose and become yet another person who says that you can't make money from trading.

Remember: If you risk all your trading capital again and again, you need to lose only once to be finished for good.

Although using delta sounds like a very simple equation for successful trading, beginner traders have a long journey in front of them coming to terms with the addition of leverage and the multiplying effect this has on the volatility of their trading. This is a really important issue, which I discuss in more detail in Chapter 8.

Pulling it all together

To open any CFD trade, you must have enough money in your account to cover an initial margin. While your position is open it is constantly revalued as the market fluctuates, and your account is debited and credited with losses or profits caused by these fluctuations. If you get the trade right, your profit will be the difference between the opening price of the underlying instrument and its closing price. But how does this all play out?

Example: Say you open a trading account with a balance of $10,000. You then buy 1,000 ABC share CFDs at a price of $10, with an initial margin requirement of 5 per cent. You close the position three days later at a price of $11. While the position is open there will be changes to the balance of your account as your position is revalued and as your margin obligation varies. Table 1-1 shows what your initial margins and account balance will be while you hold the position open, and what your closing profit will be. (Note that other costs for this trade would include commission and financing charges. For more on financing charges, see Chapter 4.)

Table 1-1	Example Share CFD Trade			
	Settlement price	Initial margin	Total Profit (Loss)	Account balance
				$10,000
Day 1: Buy 1,000 ABC CFDs @ $10	$10	$500		$9,500
Day 2	$10.50	$525	$500	$9,975
Day 3	$11	$550	$1,000	$10,450
Day 4: Sell 1,000 ABC CFDs @ $11		0	**$1,000**	**$11,000**

The example shown in Table 1-1 shows a good profit from a winning trade. Remember, though, that not all trades will move in your favour — or as quickly!

Managing Your Trading

As soon as you hear from your CFD provider that your account is funded and ready to go, you'll likely want to trade right away. Try to resist doing so, however, because opening your account is the easiest part of the trading process. Most people think the first step to trading success is to work out how best to choose your trades, but before you do this you need to:

✔ Understand the market

✔ Know how much you're going to buy and when you'll get out of a position if it moves against you (broadly referred to as risk and money management)

So, before trading a single cent, do your homework. Ask yourself:

- ✔ Do I understand the market?
- ✔ Can I control my risk in this market?

You need to be able to answer 'yes' to both questions before you begin trading in CFDs.

As you become a more experienced trader, you'll probably want to invest in some software to help you uncover potential trades and to maintain your records. You don't need to spend a fortune, but there are some very simple considerations that you should make before spending a cent.

Understanding the market

The question 'Do I understand the market?' is easy enough to resolve: Simply study the market you're interested in by reading relevant articles in the business section of the newspaper and online.

Although you need a good theoretical grounding before you start trading, understanding the practicalities of trading comes only by placing trades. You may spend a lot of time studying a market, but it's only after you make your first trade using real capital that you'll feel like you really understand the market. Many people think that paper trading has value (and it may do), but putting real money on the line teaches you lessons you won't soon forget — so start small. Chapter 9 has more information on position sizing.

Paper trading is a means of replicating actual trades without risking your money. It involves making hypothetical trades as if you were trading with real money, but without putting your actual money at risk. To get any value out of the activity, you must follow a very clear trading strategy (I discuss trading strategies in the section 'Developing your trading plan' later in the chapter and in Chapter 16). If you think that guessing what to buy and recording the results can help you learn about trading, you're wasting your time.

Controlling your risk and managing your money

The question 'Can I control my risk in this market?' requires a more in-depth understanding of the nature of the market. The characteristic of most interest here is the amount that the price in a given instrument moves over the time that you plan to trade it. For example, if the company over which you're planning to buy share CFDs moves on average 2 per cent per day, you may have more trouble trading this for a single day than a share price that moves an average of 5 per cent per day. The very short-term trader needs to be able to capture a reasonable price movement in order to make a decent profit. The longer the period over which you trade, the easier this becomes, because you have more time to capture the profits.

You have two very powerful weapons at your disposal to manage your risk:

✔ **Position sizing strategies:** One fundamental principle of trading is that the bigger your position, the bigger your risk. So, based on your available capital and the use of stop loss orders (see below), you can work out the position sizes that mean you lose only a small percentage of your capital on any trades in which you lose money. I talk more about using position sizing strategies in Chapter 9.

✔ **Stop loss orders:** A *stop loss order* is an order offered by CFD providers that enables you to elect the price at which you admit that you were wrong about a trade that you're in and close it down to preserve your precious capital. (I explain how to use stop loss orders in Chapter 2.) You should plan where to place your stop loss order *before* you open a trade, because doing so helps with your trade discipline (see Chapter 15 for more information on trade discipline).

Being consistent with your risk management is key to survival when dealing with an ever-changing market, so I strongly suggest that you familiarise yourself with Chapter 8, which deals with risk management in much more detail.

As an extension of this issue you need to know the minimum cost to you if you get closed out of a trade. Not all CFDs are equal when it comes to how much a one-increment movement in the price impacts on the value of the position you hold. Some CFDs can seem very conservative, but others are anything but.

All discussions of what constitute reasonable costs for trading are quite relative. For example, traders with a high risk tolerance (who're comfortable with the potential for large percentage swings against them in the short term) can cope easily with the trading of volatile positions, whereas traders with a small capital base or a low tolerance for volatility won't cope so easily. Spend time getting used to a product to find out whether it's suitable for you.

I recommend trading very small when you get started, irrespective of how much capital you have to play with, because you may be surprised by how much a market can move if you don't.

Developing your trading plan

'Failing to plan is planning to fail.' If you're like me, you can't stand expressions like this — pieces of wisdom that are breathtakingly easy to dispense but infuriatingly difficult to put into practice! Obviously, if you have no planning in place then life will be much more difficult for you. However, having a plan won't work wonders for you if that plan is ineffective or you don't follow it consistently.

In very general terms, your *trading plan* represents your guide to helping you know what to do in a wide range of situations — some of which may be very unpleasant for you from a trading perspective. Your trading plan should cover the following issues:

- ✔ Why you want to trade
- ✔ What you're going to trade
- ✔ How you decide what to buy
- ✔ When you want to sell, and how much risk you take on with each trade

Pretty much everything else should be derived from these important aspects of trading. I give you tips on developing your trading plan in Chapter 16.

Finding a method in the madness

A commodities trader named Richard Dennis once created a group known as 'The Turtles' whom he trained to trade using a very specific set of rules. All the group members had to do was follow the rules that they'd been given. They did so and some became very successful, accumulating huge profits. Dennis commented that he'd happily publish his methodology in the *Wall Street Journal* because he knew no-one would follow it anyway.

Although you may scoff at this comment, following someone else's method is tougher than it sounds. Many people believe that if only they can be told what to buy, everything else will fall into place. But if you're following someone else's advice, doing the right thing is easy — until you have a losing trade, or a string of losing trades. Then life becomes a bit trickier. You need to have confidence and a firm understanding of what you're doing, otherwise you can't respond to the changing market conditions and, more importantly, to changes in your account balance.

Choosing your software

Using software to help you make trading decisions is really standard these days, but the range of products available can make choosing the best software a challenge.

The following sensible considerations should help with your decision:

✔ Many of the features of very powerful software (which tends to be expensive and allows for extensive customisation) aren't necessary unless you're an extremely advanced analyst. Start with the cheaper software, because then you have less sunk costs working against you. As long as you can use common indicators (for example, moving averages, which I explain in Chapter 13) and draw trend lines and support/resistance lines (which I also explain in Chapter 13), you're ready to use software to start trading.

✔ The cost of charting software doesn't have a large correlation with your effectiveness as a trader. In other words, a good trader can be successful using cheaper software. Cheaper software limits the amount of customisation that you can do, but this isn't likely to be an issue until you're a more advanced trader.

I examine software options in more detail in Chapter 14.

Record-keeping

You need to think quite carefully about the record-keeping that you undertake. Naturally, you want to know whether you're winning or losing over time, but this isn't the only issue you need to consider. You need to think about how often you're winning compared with how often you're losing. And you also need to look at the average size of your wins compared with the average size of your losses. Such factors help you to develop the fullest appreciation of your trading success. I outline how to keep track of your progress in Chapter 17.

Chapter 2

Setting Yourself Up for Success

In This Chapter

▶ Getting to know the providers

▶ Understanding how to place orders

*B*efore you can start trading, you need to select a CFD provider. The CFD market is a very competitive environment for providers, so you need to consider your choice of provider carefully. There are many similarities between providers, and you may find that it's the small differences that make the differentiation for you and the trading you plan to do. After you select your provider, before you can start trading you need to examine the types of orders that you can use as part of your trading plan.

In this chapter, I examine some of the fundamental differences between the two main types of CFD providers and what these differences mean to you in terms of selecting a provider. I also look at the different types of orders that you can use to best implement your trading strategy.

Choosing a CFD Provider

Few feuds in finance between two competing strategies of doing business are bigger than the competition between the two main types of CFD providers: Market makers and direct market access (DMA) providers. Yet like many such divides, the majority of issues between the two types of provider come down to some fairly minor differences. You need to understand these differences before you can find the most suitable CFD provider for you.

The upside of market makers

Although you may read negative things about market makers in the press (such as market makers being on the other side of the trade to the trader — that is, they win when you lose, and vice versa) the case against market makers isn't an open and shut issue. One of the best things that market makers do is add more volume to the market than would otherwise exist if the market was left solely to the other market participants, meaning that there may be more volume available to you than in the underlying market (so you may get a better price).

One major difference between market makers and DMA providers is the range of products available. DMA providers generally deal only in Australian shares. Market makers offer CFDs over a much wider range of underlying instruments.

There's no reason why you can't have accounts with multiple providers, so don't feel that you're stuck with having just the one provider.

Understanding how the different providers operate

The differences between market makers and DMA providers aren't as huge as the terms suggest. For instance, both types of provider allow you to access the market using margin and both charge a lower rate of commission than you pay using most stockbrokers.

Major differences

The major differences between the two providers boil down to the following:

- **Filling your order:** DMA providers may fill your order at several different prices if there's not enough volume on the nearest bid/offer to fill your order. Market makers requote to fill the whole volume at a single average price.

- **Following your order:** When you use a DMA provider, you can see your order in the stock exchange queue — meaning that you can see what's happening with your order, as you would when placing an order for actual shares. Although this won't improve your execution price, you may find it of interest as a trader.

✔ **Partial fills:** DMA providers give you 'partial fills' of your order if there's only enough volume of buyers or sellers to fill a portion of your order. Market makers fill all of your order — or none of it.

✔ **Placing orders inside the current bid offer spread:** If there's a gap of more than one price increment between the bid and offer prices, DMA providers allow you to place an order within that space. Market makers don't allow you to do this.

✔ **Pre- and post-market auctions:** By dealing in Australian share CFDs through a DMA provider, you can enter the pre- and post-market auctions, which enables you to place a buy or sell order outside of market hours (although not 24/7) to deal up to a specific price level that you nominate. With some market makers you can use a *stop-to-enter order* (which is executed if the price moves higher than the price at which it closed in the previous session) or a *limit order* (which is executed if the market moves lower than the previous session's closing price). The converse of this would apply if you wanted to trade on the short side. The key difference is that the DMA provider places the order in the market, whereas the market maker holds the order — but the net result for you is the same.

The Australian share market uses a system referred to as the *auction*, which enables all overlapping buy and sell orders that are placed prior to the opening and closing of trade to receive one price. (By overlapping I mean buy prices that are greater than or equal to some of the selling prices and selling prices that are less than or equal to some of the buying prices.) This happens because all the overlapping prices are allocated a weighted average price and that is how the opening and closing prices are calculated. The auction system comprises pre- and post-market auctions. In the pre-market auction, before trade begins each day all the overlapping buyers and sellers have their trades executed at one price. This one price is a weighted average of all the buy and sell prices that overlap each other and forms the opening price for the day. In the post-market auction in the afternoon, the overlapping buyers and sellers again have their trades executed at one price, to make the closing price for shares for the day.

- ✔ **Pricing:** Market makers sometimes give you fills at better prices than DMA providers because market makers can add the volume from other clients to what's available in the underlying market.

- ✔ **Trading platforms:** Market makers usually offer proprietary software, whereas DMA providers usually offer modified software used for dealing in shares.

  Depending on your provider, you may receive the software for free or pay a fee. Most DMA providers charge for the software, because they need to pay the company that provides them with the software. However, charges are often negotiable and depend on how much business you do with the provider during a month. The more trades you make, the less software charge you pay.

- ✔ **What goes on behind the scenes after you place your order:** DMA providers always go immediately to the underlying market and purchase the same number of shares that you purchased as CFDs. In this way they hedge their exposure to the market from providing CFDs to their clients. This also explains why you won't receive *requotes* from DMA providers: DMA providers don't allocate CFDs that they can't hedge immediately in the underlying market. (A requote occurs when insufficient shares are available in the underlying market to fill your order.)

  Market makers, on the other hand, don't necessarily hedge their exposure immediately in the underlying market.

No matter what a provider's marketing spiel tells you, there are clear advantages to both the market maker and DMA models of doing business. I've seen plenty of surveys in which traders state that they prefer one model over the other but can't say why. I can — they've been taken in by the marketing and not by a solid assessment of what they really need as a trader. Keep in mind that both market maker and DMA CFDs are over-the-counter products. You're dealing in CFDs and not the underlying market.

Yet more to think about

The type of provider you choose doesn't affect your access to the market because you're still buying CFDs and the end product you receive doesn't change whether or not the provider goes straight to the market to buy or sell the physical shares. So, these points of 'difference' may not give you much to go on when choosing between the two types of providers.

To help you make your decision, you may also want to consider the following issues, all of which should be readily answered on the provider's website:

✔ **Margins and commission rates:** The market has become incredibly competitive in recent years regarding the amount of margin required and the amount of commission payable. Traders are really benefiting from this competition, getting ever-better deals. Generally, market makers charge the lowest commission rates and have the lowest margin requirements. The reason for this probably comes down to scale of operation: Market makers are generally larger than DMA providers.

My advice, though, is not to get too wound up about margin requirements. As I explain in Chapter 8 you always want to have plenty of spare capital in your account and not use it all up on margin payments.

✔ **Product range:** One of the more clear advantages of dealing through a market maker is the range of products that market makers make available to their traders. Many market makers provide access to CFDs in the following markets: Foreign exchange (FX), indices, commodities, treasuries and equities (foreign and domestic). Conversely, DMA providers tend to offer only domestic share CFDs. Access to a wider range of products is becoming an increasingly important issue for traders as index and FX products gain in popularity.

✔ **Software and data fees:** Some DMA providers require you to pay a fee to use their software each month. Since these fees vary, you need to check with potential suppliers as to how much you need to pay. In addition, both market makers and DMA providers charge an ASX data feed fee, which covers the live price data for Australian equities. Often your provider waives the software fee if you undertake more than a certain amount of trades in a calendar month.

Your provider may be willing to waive the costs of your data feed fees if you complete a certain amount of trading over the course of a single month. Check with potential providers for their terms and conditions.

Considering other points of differentiation

As part of the growing competition between providers for traders' business, providers are now offering numerous benefits that are peripheral to the actual dealing function, but that may be very useful to you as a trader. Such offerings also help you to differentiate between providers:

- **Funds on deposit:** Ask potential providers what happens to the funds that you have on deposit with them. You need to establish how safe these funds are with the provider and what happens to any interest you earn. CFD trades settle immediately and for this reason you need to have funds available in your trading account at all times, both to deal and to provide margin to your CFD provider. CFD providers detail in their product disclosure statements (PDSs) what provisions they have in place to look after your money and how your funds are segregated from theirs, but make sure that you're happy with the proposed arrangements.

- **Integration of services:** Some providers enable you to deal in both CFDs and the physical share market, thus enabling you to deal using a single trading account.

- **Interest:** Check whether you earn interest on funds on deposit. Usually you need to have more than a certain amount in your trading account before you earn interest, with something like $15,000 being the likely minimum threshold.

- **Ongoing trader education and market research:** Some providers offer trader education in the form of courses or printed material, and market research such as market updates and trade strategies.

- **Volume discounts:** You may qualify for volume discounts on the commission that you pay if you're trading frequently or in large amounts. Such discounts can make a pretty significant difference to you as a trader if you do trade frequently or in large amounts. Keep in mind that commissions are one of your biggest costs of doing business, so aim to keep them as low as possible.

Placing Orders

After you decide which type of provider fits the bill for you, you need to examine the ways in which you can manage your account and your trades. One of the main areas of CFD trading that new traders often find a bit of an eye opener is the wide range of different orders available. An *order* is an instruction from a trader to the provider to buy or sell a specified item in a market. Compared to share investments where market orders and limit orders are the most common orders, CFD trading offers a much wider range of orders as part of the standard offering. By using these CFD orders properly you can take much more control over your trading and plan ahead how you'll execute your trades.

Different providers offer different types of orders, so check what your chosen provider has available and be sure that the offering meets your needs.

CFDs are generally a *non-advisory product*, which means that you're totally responsible for making all of your trade decisions and placing all of your orders. I strongly suggest that you set yourself a routine for placing orders, such as always reading your order back to yourself twice or even saying the order out loud, to ensure that you aren't buying 10,000 when you want to buy 1,000. Such a huge error takes the fun out of your day very quickly indeed!

Market orders

A *market order* is an order to buy or sell immediately at the current market price. Market orders are probably the most commonly used orders because they allow you to get in and out of the market immediately. If you're buying CFDs, you buy from the lowest-priced seller; if you're selling CFDs, you sell to the highest-priced buyer.

Stop orders

A *stop order* is an order to buy when the price has climbed to or above a specified stop price or to sell when the price has dropped to or below a specified stop price. The stop order is one of the most important orders available to traders because you can use this order to manage your risk by selling automatically when the price reaches a level that you nominate.

Stop orders can also be used to automate the entry of breakout trades, which occur when the price moves through a support or resistance level (see Chapter 13 for more information on support and resistance levels).

A *stop loss order* does exactly what the name implies — it stops your loss. The reason a stop order isn't always a *stop loss order* is because you aren't always going to use the order to stop a loss — you may also use the order as a stop entry order.

Your CFD provider places limits on how close to the current market price you can place a stop order. For example, if you're currently in a long position (meaning you expect the price to rise) and you place a stop loss order to limit your loss, the order may be executed as soon as the bid price matches (or is less than) the price you nominated — although some CFD providers wait until the market actually trades at this level before they execute the order. You may think that getting out before the market actually trades at your level sounds like a bad deal, but if you think about it your CFD provider doesn't know what's going to happen next, so it will close out the position as soon as possible.

Stop orders are available from market makers only. DMA providers offer something similar but different in execution: These are known as contingent orders (see the section 'Contingent orders').

Being able to use stop orders is a critical component of being a successful trader, because of the ability that stop orders give you to manage your risk. The key issue is to work out before trade opens where to place your stop. If you're not sure about where to place your stop orders, check out Chapter 8 on risk management strategies.

If you're dealing in the share market, stop orders are normally triggered when the price trades at the level that you nominated rather than the bid price (or the offer price if you're short) hitting that level. With FX, stop orders are triggered on the bid price because there's no published traded price to go by.

Contingent orders

A *contingent order* is executed only if another order is executed first. Contingent orders are available through DMA providers (and some stockbrokers) and are used in a similar way to stop orders. By using a contingent order you're saying that if the market trades at a certain price, then a market order is automatically placed — which is how a contingent order behaves in a way similar to a stop order. If your provider offers this type of order instead of stop orders, you can use it as your primary means of managing your risk.

Stop orders versus contingent orders

In many ways stop orders and contingent orders perform the same task: Allowing traders to cap the downside that they may otherwise have been exposed to. Potentially, however, stop orders may be superior to contingent orders in the event of a significant price gap occurring in the market, as follows:

- ✔ If such a gap occurs when you're using a stop order, the market maker will still close the position at the first available price and you'll be out of the position — although this may be well below your originally nominated stop loss level (an issue known as slippage).

- ✔ If such a gap occurs when you're using a contingent order and the contingent price that you nominate isn't traded at (meaning that no trades occur in the underlying market at that price), the position remains in place. As a result, unless you have access to your trading platform to close the position yourself, you'll still be in a trade that you'd rather not be in.

Limit orders

A *limit order* is an order to buy at no more than (or sell at no less than) a specified price. You use a limit order if you want to deal at a price below the current level (that is, if you want to go long — meaning to benefit from a rising price) or above the current price (that is, if you want to go short — meaning to benefit from a falling price). This means that you trade only if the price moves to the level that you nominate.

Limit orders are a popular means of trading for people whose strategy relies on the price coming to them, and not the other way around. Generally, there's a limit on how close to the current market price you can place a limit order: Check your provider's PDS so that you know how the provider handles the issue.

You may be tempted to think that using limit orders is always a good idea and in some ways getting into a position as cheaply as possible makes good sense. Be sure that you're using the limit order for the right reason, though, because in a sense what you're saying is something like 'I believe that this position is going to go up, but I won't buy it until it goes down'. One of the worst outcomes of trading like this is that you end up chasing the price higher but always put in the order at a lower price until you get the position — by which stage the price is already heading lower and will keep going that way.

Requotes

A *requote* occurs when there is insufficient volume available to fill your market order at the current price. While a requote isn't an order type in itself, it's something of a subset of orders. You receive a requote only when dealing with market makers — not DMA providers. The market maker sends you a requote if insufficient volume is available to fill your order. This is because market makers use a 'fill-or-kill' order system, which means that your whole order is either filled or cancelled — the order cannot be partially filled. So, if not enough volume is available to fill your order at one price, the market maker offers you a requote to trade at the next level up, or a volume-weighted average price requote over more than one level.

When you place an order online and insufficient volume is available to fill your order, a separate box pops up on your screen, explaining that the price at which you wanted to deal at isn't available anymore. Instead, you're offered a quote at a different price, although this new price won't be as good as your initial price.

You can choose whether to take the new trade or not — but you generally have only a few seconds to decide!

✔ If you accept the trade, your order is filled at the new price that the provider offered you.

✔ If you reject the trade, you can wait to see what happens to the available volume and perhaps try to place the order again at a later time.

If you use a DMA provider, you may receive several fills at different levels of price. Although this may be no better or worse than receiving a requote, it may be easier to visualise as a trader.

Guaranteed stop loss orders

Using a *guaranteed stop loss order* (GSLO) from a market maker, you can manage your risk even more effectively than with a regular stop order because you pay extra to ensure that if you get stopped out, you know at exactly what price it will occur. The benefit is that even if large price gaps develop (perhaps triggered by a large fall in the US market overnight) you have the assurance of knowing where you'll get stopped out.

The downside to using a GSLO is that you have to pay a premium upfront whether the order is executed or not. This premium differs from provider to provider (as do policy conditions like whether you can move the order without extra charge), so check your provider's PDS for clarification.

If-done orders

An *if-done order* is an advanced order type that allows you to connect two different orders together, such as a limit order and a stop order. As the name implies, if one order is done, the other order is placed. Using an if-done order enables you to plan much of the order set-up ahead of time and then execute the order automatically when certain conditions are met.

Example: Say you start with a limit order that's below the current market price: You plan to buy if the price retraces to a level that you have chosen. When you first place this order you say that *if* it's executed, you want to automatically place a stop order $0.20 below the limit entry. This leaves you with a long CFD position and a stop order $0.20 below the price at which you entered the trade. In other words, you've got into your position and placed your stop order to manage your risk all in one step, using an if-done order.

One cancels other orders

One cancels other (OCO) orders are designed to let you have two connected orders (to get you out of the market) surrounding a position that you already have. Most commonly this allows you to either stop your loss (if the price moves against you) or take your profit (if the price moves in your favour). OCO orders are a really important order type for many traders, but if you plan to trade a 24-hour market like foreign exchange, then they're essential.

Example: Say that you are long 1,000 XYZ CFDs and want to take the profits if the share price rises by $0.30 but close out the position if the price falls by $0.15. You can place both of these orders and link them together as an OCO order: If one of the orders is executed, the other order is automatically cancelled.

An OCO saves you from having to be glued to your trading screen to manage your orders because the order removes the risk that a second order will be executed before you get a chance to cancel it. *Note:* There is generally a minimum distance the two orders need to be apart.

Chapter 3

Making the Most of CFD Trading

*W*hen you start dealing in CFDs the number of different products and strategies to choose between can be a bit overwhelming. The key is not to carry too many preconceived notions about how you're going to trade and instead focus on keeping your risk low and devising strategies that follow the trends in the market. In other words, look to the direction of the overall market and the individual instruments that make up the market (for example, a share index and the individual shares that make up that index) and trade in line with the way they're trending. Simply, this means being primarily on the long side when the market trends up and being short when the market trends down.

In this chapter, I look at dealing on the long and short side of the market — having this amount of choice to benefit from rising and falling markets will be unfamiliar to many traders who are new to CFDs. I also look at some of the key issues you need to understand about market conditions and then examine how you can adapt your trading strategy accordingly.

Examining Long Versus Short Trading

So often the things that appeal to traders about CFDs are factors like leverage and small commissions, because you can take on large positions very cheaply, but an amazing (although not unique) strength of CFDs is that they allow you to trade very easily on the long and short sides of the market.

- ✔ Trading on the long side (*long trading*) means buying with the view that the price is going to rise and selling at a higher price in order to make a profit.

- ✔ Trading on the short side (*short trading*) means selling with the view that the price is going to fall and then buying back at a lower price in order to make a profit.

Since many people are comfortable with the concept of long trading but have difficulties with the concept of short trading, I concentrate on short trading in this section so that you can be completely at ease with the process.

Benefiting from a price that goes down

One of the first questions that beginner traders ask concerning short trading is: 'How can I sell something that I don't own?' The answer is really simple, because with CFDs you don't own anything anyway — even if you're buying to go long. Remember that a CFD is simply a contract between you and the provider, so instead of thinking about ownership, just remember that buying and selling determine only whether your contract value rises or falls as the price rises or falls.

Many people continue to look past short trading even after they understand the concept because they feel that it's a step too far for them. Others are happy dealing on the long side, because it's more akin to dealing in the share market. Of course you need to be comfortable with your trading strategy, but make sure that you consider some of the potential advantages of short trading before closing the door on short trades for good.

A closer look at short trading

One of my colleagues used to tell a brilliant story illustrating how short trading works, which I've been dining out on for years — so another rendition can't hurt. Imagine that you're at work and you need to go up the road to buy your lunch, but it's raining outside. You borrow an umbrella from a colleague and head off. In the doorway to the building, you're approached by someone with a mass of paperwork who offers to buy the umbrella for $30. You agree and take the money. Then you head across the road to the umbrella store and buy an identical umbrella to the one you just sold for $20, grab your lunch and head back to the office. When you get back to the office you return the umbrella to your colleague.

This scenario is very similar to a short trade because you sold as your opening trade and then bought back to close the trade. You pocketed the difference, which in this case was $10 and is your profit to keep, because all parties were returned to their original state.

Yes, I realise that you need to get rained on for this example to work, but hopefully you can look past that!

✔ Markets spend a lot of time heading lower, and trading on the short side of the market is the best way to take advantage of this. Over the long term, even though the share market historically has risen quite consistently, it has spent not much less than half the time going down and the average magnitude of the down days is only a little smaller than the average up day. This means that in bull (generally rising) markets and bear (generally falling) markets you have plenty of opportunity to find positions that are falling in value, which give you opportunities beyond those that would be available if you are only dealing on the long side of the market.

✔ Most markets tend to fall faster than they rise, so if you're keen to find some very short-term trading opportunities, the short side of the market may be just the place for you. The good thing is that you can use most of the same analysis as you would for trading on the long side — you just have to reverse your thinking. (Check out some of the methods mentioned in Chapter 13 on technical analysis.) Basically, methods such as a support/resistance breakout or a moving average crossover are the same whether in a rising or falling market — you just approach the analysis from the opposite direction.

✔ You may be able to reduce the volatility of your overall portfolio (that is, sharp movements in the value of the positions) by maintaining a combination of long and short exposure. A big part of this reduction comes from not relying so heavily on market direction as a driver of your profitability, which is a significant benefit for traders who prefer to see fewer up and down swings in the value of their portfolio.

You may have read that 80 per cent of share movements follow movements in the index. This concept doesn't really make sense, since the index value is calculated using the movement of the shares, and not the other way round. Nonetheless, the overall market is a major driver of the broader market moves that are seen on a day-to-day basis, and being caught up in the wider up or down movements of the market can be difficult to escape. However, if you're not quite unidirectional in the make-up of your portfolio and carry a portion of long *and* short positions, these movements may improve your portfolio — or at least make it less volatile, which a lot of traders really like.

Understanding that FX trading has built-in short trades

If you choose to trade foreign exchange (FX), you need to be comfortable with trading on the short side. This is because FX doesn't have any inherent directional bias and has as much opportunity on the long side as it does on the short side. More importantly though, you can't trade on just one side of the market in FX, because to buy one currency you must sell an equal-sized amount of another currency. This means that you go long in one currency and short in the other. For more on FX trades, see Chapter 5.

Keep in mind that the maximum downside to trading short is actually worse than the downside to trading long. The reason is that there's no limit to how high something can go in value but it can't go any lower than zero. This is worth remembering, but within reason. An author whose name eludes me once wrote that he'd seen many stocks go to zero but he hadn't seen any go to infinity, so you can make your own judgement on this concept.

Your most likely concern is a takeover bid being made for a company while you're short, making a large gap upward in the price of the shares — with very little you can do about it.

Recognising the Costs and Benefits of Doing Business

Financing charges are the costs that your CFD provider charges to you if you have long side exposure (long trading) to the market. You can think of this cost as interest on a loan that's been made to you by your CFD provider to allow you to take on this exposure to the market. Most providers charge financing based on your total exposure to the market (that is, the number of share CFDs you have, multiplied by the price of the CFDs) rather than your exposure minus the margin that you put up.

Margin isn't part payment for a position: It acts as security for the CFD provider.

Conversely, your CFD provider pays you financing payments on short positions. I examine how this works for different types of CFDs in Chapters 4 to 7 but the main thing to note here is how the payments are calculated and how much the provider pays you. The standard method of calculation is to add or subtract from the official cash rate in the country in which you're dealing. For example, for short positions in Australia you may receive the RBA rate minus 2 per cent (and for long positions you may pay the RBA rate plus 2 per cent). (If the cash rate is less than 2 per cent, you will be charged for the short mode.)

Although you're unlikely to earn a huge amount of money from your short position financing, the payments provide an interesting offset for you if you carry long and short exposure. In fact, if you were equally long and short in the market, then using the example of the RBA rate plus/minus 2 per cent your overall financing charge would be 4 per cent, regardless of what happens to the RBA rate. This may not necessarily be the most realistic outcome for you, but it does go to show how short positions can benefit you beyond capturing falling prices.

Exploring the Pros and Cons of Trading in Different Markets

One of the simultaneously most exciting and most daunting aspects of trading CFDs is the large variety of different CFDs that are available to trade. In fact, some several thousand different instruments are available, so you could be forgiven for being a little unsure about where to start trading! However, in actual fact most beginner traders are fairly sure where they want to begin — for most people the choice is share CFDs, but for others it may be FX or commodities. There are no right or wrong choices, and you certainly don't need to feel like you have to trade everything that's on your provider's product list. How many traders do you think trade lumber CFDs? Very few, I suspect.

One way that many people decide between different types of CFDs is to weigh up whether they're worth trading or not based on commission charges. This is why traders often focus on commission-free products like indices and FX.

The goal of trading CFDs is to make money for you, not for your provider. Your provider makes money on commission-free products through the spread that he or she charges when you buy and sell. There's no such thing as a free lunch, so trade the most appropriate product for you, not the one that seems cheapest to trade.

Even if commissions are small, keep your portfolio turnover as low as you can, because commissions can quickly add up.

One of the things about CFDs that has always captivated me is the idea that a person can run something that closely resembles a hedge fund from his or her personal computer. This is because with CFDs you can trade both long and short, as well as across a massive range of different products — enabling you to take a view on a range of different markets. Although you may think that this is too much for a beginner trader to take on, this isn't the case for someone who's willing to dedicate a reasonable amount of time to trading.

Coping With Market Trading Conditions

You don't need to view your CFD portfolio in isolation from the rest of your investment portfolio — and, indeed, you can create quite a bit of interactivity between the portfolios. For example, you can use your dealing on the short side with CFDs to hedge the market exposure you have with physical shares — and even to potentially reduce the overall volatility of your portfolio. Similarly, you may find that because of the wide range of asset categories you can gain exposure to with CFDs, you may get diversification benefits that otherwise would be difficult to achieve.

Getting fancy: Hedging your bets

One of the huge upsides that comes from dealing in CFDs is the fact that trading on the short side can offer strategic opportunities. One such opportunity is *portfolio hedging*. Typically in the past the main form of defence that traders have undertaken for their portfolios has been diversification. This tactic relies on spreading money widely enough so that a fall in the value of a small number of positions should be offset by rises in other positions. The main problem with diversification occurs when the wider market falls heavily — the benefits of diversification are then seriously limited.

In such a falling market a more direct defensive approach — hedging — can yield greater benefits. When you hedge your position you take on exposure to another instrument that moves in a different direction to the investment you already hold.

Example: Imagine that you're long 1,000 XYZ shares. You've held these shares for a long time and although you believe the company to be very sound, you expect a short-term downturn in the share price, which you want to defend against. With hedging, you simply go short 1,000 XYZ share CFDs, so that for every cent the share price moves down, you lose $10 of your floating profit on your XYZ shares but gain this back exactly on your XYZ share CFDs. You can see that CFDs offer a great deal of precision in the way they deliver the hedging benefit.

If you were feeling a little more adventurous you could go short 2,000 XYZ share CFDs, so that you go from being net long 1,000 XYZ shares to being net short 1,000 XYZ share CFDs. Note that you still hold your original shares, but you switch your exposure to being short in order to benefit from the falling share price.

Many products are available to help you with hedging, among which options are the most notable, but with CFDs you can be a lot more direct with this type of method because the underlying share price and the price of the CFD precisely offset one another, which is an ideal situation when hedging. In Chapter 1, I briefly look at the concept of delta and how it helps you to determine how one instrument is likely to move in relation to another instrument.

Although a hedging strategy seems like a relatively harmless way of dealing in the market and it does defend the downside that you'd otherwise be exposed to, hedging has its disadvantages:

- ✔ You receive no benefit if the underlying share price rises.

- ✔ Even though you earn financing payments on the short CFDs, this strategy doesn't pay for itself because the money that you have tied up in the physical shares isn't earning anything for you.

Such considerations must remain in your mind at all times when dealing in CFD trades. Remember, there's no such thing as a risk-free trade, and for every reward there must be a risk attached.

Coping with FX volatility

You need to have a keen understanding of the nature of the markets that you're dealing in. For example, if markets are inherently volatile, you need to ensure that your strategy evolves to cope with this volatility. In this section I explain how to deal with volatility and how allowing for volatility is a necessary skill that you need to adopt in order to avoid the frustration of being stopped out frequently on trades that would eventually have gone in your favour.

The FX market is one of the most volatile markets but it's also the market where your risk management can be the most effective. This is because the huge volumes that are traded mean that you're very likely to be able to close out your losing positions at precisely (or very close to) the level that you nominate, even in times of high volatility — which is something you won't see in any other market.

Importantly, though, just like in any other market, you need to take account of the prevailing level of volatility and adjust your expectations accordingly. So, if the market is volatile you need to set wider stop losses to avoid getting stopped out too quickly and unnecessarily. There are several ways that you can judge volatility. The average true range indicator is a good option and I explain this in more detail in Chapter 13.

In addition, you find that although the FX market frequently offers good trending opportunities over periods of weeks and months, in the short term (which often seems attractive to new traders) there can be periods of high volatility and largely directionless trade. In order to illustrate this concept, consider Figures 3-1 and 3-2.

Figure 3-1 is a five-minute chart showing the value of the Australian dollar against the US dollar. The chart provides a new price candle every five minutes (a *candle* shows the open, high, low and close for that period; see Chapter 13 for more details). In the space of about four hours the value of the Australian dollar ranges from 0.8710 to 0.8670 and then back again. Most CFD providers offer a minimum position size of US$10,000, which means that each tick (smallest movement in price) the price of the currency rises or falls costs you as the buyer US$1. Although you may not think that this cost sounds too bad, you have to consider its impact on your overall risk and reward:

✔ If you're happy to take a 40-pip profit (a *pip* being the smallest price movement of an FX rate) — which equates to US$40 if you deal on the smallest position size — you can't reasonably risk more than about one-third of this profit amount on each of your trades.

✔ You need to consider the spread your provider charges on the risk side of the proposition because it costs you money. This is a cost that you can't avoid and it impacts you as soon as you open the trade.

Figure 3-1: Short-term directionless trade.

Figure 3-2: More time can equal more profit potential.

In other words, if you're always looking for small profits, you need to be even more aware of the risks and costs of doing business because you have fewer gains to offset them against.

Now look at Figure 3-2, an hourly chart of the Australian dollar/ US dollar relationship. This chart has a significantly different time scale to that used in Figure 3-1. The hourly chart shows a significantly greater range or volatility being achieved, but it also illustrates that your profit potential is significantly higher, which means that on a winning trade you expect significantly bigger profits. Of course, the opposite also applies, because in general terms you need to be able to take larger losses in order to generate larger profits.

In adapting to a given set of market circumstances you must look to the expected volatility of a position and set your stop losses accordingly. If you were to look at any FX chart and aim to take a profit of 100 pips but place your stop loss 5 pips away (which is about as close as any provider will allow), very likely you'd be stopped out of your position before the position has any reasonable chance to be successful. Although you may think that stopping your loss if the price moves against you even a little bit sounds perfectly reasonable it actually isn't very sensible, because you're very unlikely to be able to pick the precise moment to get into an FX trade such that the price only moves higher from that moment on.

Wiggle room: Allowing the market to move

I've often heard traders say: 'I always put my stop x points away on all my trades.' While being disciplined enough to use stops is certainly a plus for such traders, the resulting plan of attack may not be as effective. As an example, if you're dealing in a $50 stock and a $1 stock and you always put your stop $0.10 away, then your stop is almost certainly too close in the case of the $50 stock (it absorbs too little volatility) and too far away for the $1 stock (it absorbs too much volatility). Some people refer to allowing the market enough room to move against you in order to absorb normal market volatility as *wiggle room*, and while you want to keep your downsides small, you don't want to get taken out of positions only to have them move in your favour afterwards. Recognising that you need to let the market move against you a sensible amount takes a little while to digest, but you can see that different trading methods are available to help you find the right mix of return and volatility absorption. The average true range indicator is great at measuring this (see Chapter 13).

Dealing with slippage and gaps

Depending on the markets that you trade, you may see a great degree of slippage and gaps in prices. *Slippage* means having an order executed at a price worse than the order you placed, while *gaps* are movements in prices where no trade occurs — for example, if one trade occurs at a price of $1.00 and the next trade occurs at a price of $1.10, the market has 'gapped' $0.10.

This high degree of slippage and gapping in prices occurs for two main reasons:

- ✔ Conditions changing when the market is closed, such as economic news being released
- ✔ Low volumes, which sees prices move more erratically than in high-volume markets

Because the FX market has a high turnover and trades 24 hours a day, it has the lowest likelihood of slippage and gapping. To reduce your risk in this market, you can use stop losses. The reasons that stop losses work so well in managing your risk are twofold.

Big volume for low slippage

The FX market is the most liquid of all markets. This is particularly notable when you're looking at the more liquid currency pairs such as the EUR/USD. As a result of this liquidity, there's a much lower likelihood of slippage taking place on your trading.

Slippage usually occurs when your order is too big for the buyers/sellers to absorb, but it can also occur in times of high volatility. Happily, because the FX market has so much turnover, slippage is less likely to be an issue in this market than in any other market.

Index CFDs trade in both day and night sessions, but the night sessions see significantly lower volumes and as a result have a much greater likelihood of slippage occurring. So, if you trade large volumes in index CFDs in a night session and a ruction occurs in the market, you may get slipped quite aggressively. This doesn't mean that you shouldn't trade at night, but if you do you must exercise greater caution. However, if you trade large amounts, you may be best avoiding night-time trading altogether.

If you get slipped on a position that you're trading, the natural temptation may be to blame your CFD provider. However, although sometimes CFD providers are to blame, make sure that you know the characteristics of the product you're dealing in before racing to the conclusion that your CFD provider is at fault. CFD providers generally give you no more volume to trade than is available in the underlying market, so if you're quickly trying to unwind a large position in an illiquid market, you'll certainly experience some slippage.

Frequent gaps in prices

Gaps in prices occur as the market absorbs new information. In Australia (and indeed in most countries) traders focus on events in the United States overnight and these events have a major impact on the local market when trade begins. A big move higher or lower in the US market may see companies locally 'gapping' higher or lower. The frequency with which gaps occur depends on the market. For example, the share market closes every night, so each day when it opens 'gaps' may occur, whereas the FX market closes only once a week and so has fewer opportunities for gaps.

No trading takes place in these gaps and if your stop loss is placed within the gap, you won't get out at the price you hoped to. This is one of the most common examples of slippage that occurs.

Gapping occurs regularly during trading sessions in low liquidity instruments, so I suggest you stick to the more liquid products. I'm not trying to dissuade you from any type of trading that you want to get involved in, however, so if you prefer illiquid instruments make sure that you thoroughly plan ahead how to handle the gaps in prices that occur. You need to recognise that when trading in less liquid markets, more frequent slippage is essentially an additional cost of doing business. When you trade in the longer term, slippage is less of an issue because you're trading less frequently. In other words, the more you trade, the more of an issue slippage becomes.

Part II
Touring the CFD Marketplace

Glenn Lumsden

'I'm betting that the Zimbabwean dollar will rise from a gazillionth of a cent based on the fact that there is no number lower than a gazillionth.'

In this part ...

*T*he range of CFDs that you can trade provides an easy way to diversify your portfolio and gain exposure to markets all around the world, 24 hours a day.

In this part, I cover the different categories of CFDs that allow you to trade in different markets. You can buy CFDs that trade over the price of shares, foreign exchange, indices, commodities and interest rate products.

Chapter 4

Exploring Share CFDs

Share CFDs have a large number of similarities with their underlying market and these similarities can ease your transition from trading in the share market to trading share CFDs.

In this chapter, I describe how shares and share CFDs relate to one another and how you can incorporate share CFDs into your trading portfolio. I also examine how trading share CFDs on both the long and the short side can help balance your trading portfolio while dealing in the inherently volatile share market.

CFDs are a derivative product and should make up only a small portion of your overall investment portfolio because of the high degree of leverage they carry. If you need a refresher on derivatives, refer to Chapter 1.

Understanding How Shares and Share CFDs Differ

A big part of the overall difference between shares and share CFDs comes down to ownership. Perhaps you've noticed that sometimes after the company name on share certificates you see the letters 'FPO': These letters stand for Fully Paid Ordinary. This basically means that you have nothing left to pay on the shares and that ownership of the shares gives you certain rights, such as a right over company dividends and the right to vote on matters concerning the company.

Share CFDs never allow you to take ownership of the underlying instrument. So, unlike holding shares, share CFDs don't entitle you to vote at the company's annual general meeting. Some CFDs do pay dividends; see the section 'Dividend payments' later in this chapter.

Other derivatives such as options, warrants and futures allow you to take ownership of the underlying instrument, but that's because different maturity features are built into these products.

When you open a share CFD position, you make a margin payment, but this payment doesn't give you ownership of the underlying shares — it isn't like a margin loan, which provides a part payment of the shares. Rather, this margin payment acts as security for your CFD provider, ensuring that you can pay for any losses that occur due to normal market activity. (At the time of writing some CFD providers were looking at allowing traders to use CFDs to buy the underlying shares, but as yet this isn't possible.)

The easiest way to think of a share CFD is as a derivative that mirrors the price of the underlying shares. This means that if ABC Ltd shares increase in value by $0.50, so too do ABC Ltd share CFDs.

Traders in share CFDs are interested in only one thing: Capturing movements in price. CFDs are not designed to be a long-term investment.

Accounting for Dividends and Other Corporate Action

Several common occurrences in the share market move the price of shares and in turn the price of share CFDs. It's very important that share CFDs reflect these share price changes because otherwise the ability of CFDs to mirror the price of the underlying shares breaks down — and this mirroring is the reason that CFDs are so popular in the first place.

Dividend payments

The most important time for both share CFD holders and shareholders in a particular company is the ex-dividend date. On this date the value of the dividend is removed from the value of the shares. So, if on the day prior to the ex-dividend date the share price is $5.00 and the company pays a $0.20 dividend then, all other things being equal, when trade begins on the ex-dividend date the share price starts at $4.80.

No problem, you may say: Why not go short share CFDs the day before the dividend is paid and collect a very likely profit? Unfortunately, CFD providers didn't blow into town yesterday and things work a little differently for share CFD holders:

- ✔ If you're trading long share CFDs into the ex-dividend date, you *receive* the dividend.

- ✔ If you're trading short share CFDs into the ex-dividend date, you *pay* the dividend.

If you think that it sounds great to be long share CFDs on the ex-dividend date and lousy to be short, the story isn't quite that simple either: The payment of dividends offsets the movement of the share price whether you're long or short.

Example: The best way to understand what's actually going on is to look at Table 4-1, which shows two traders in XYZ share CFDs: Trader A, who's long, and Trader B, who's short. In this example, XYZ Ltd is trading at $3.00 and is about to pay a $0.10 dividend. On the ex-dividend date the share price falls from $3.00 to $2.90. Yet, as you can see from the table, both traders end up in the same overall position. How come? Trader A, who's long, sees a benefit from the receipt of the dividend but loses on the falling share price; and Trader B, who's short, loses on the dividend payment but benefits from the falling share price.

If dividend payments weren't handled in this way, traders would just go short before the ex-dividend date, which wouldn't be fair to either the traders on the long side of the market or CFD providers.

Table 4-1	The Impact of Dividend Payments	
	Trader A: Long 1,000 XYZ Share CFDs	*Trader B: Short 1,000 XYZ Share CFDs*
Value before dividend payment	$3,000.00	$3,000.00
Dividend payment	$100.00	–$100.00
Profit and loss due to share price movements	–$100.00	$100.00
Net position	$3,000.00	$3,000.00

In general terms, franking (imputation) credits aren't paid on the dividends received by share CFD holders or by traders who're short, but in certain instances they may be paid. This depends on the conditions set by the individual CFD providers: Check your provider's product disclosure statement (PDS) or contact your provider to find out more details.

Share bonuses and splits

In general terms, whatever happens to shares happens to share CFDs. For example:

✔ **Share bonus issue:** If one new share is issued for every five shares held, as a share CFD holder you receive one new CFD for every five CFDs you hold.

✔ **Share split:** If three shares are issued for every one share held, as a CFD holder you receive three CFDs for every CFD you hold.

As with dividend payments (see the section 'Dividend payments' earlier in the chapter), share CFDs adjust to share bonuses and splits so that traders on the long or short side of the market don't get an unfair advantage.

Familiarise yourself with your CFD provider's PDS and use the PDS as a point of reference. Although the PDS is a long document, it provides full details about the way in which your provider does business with its clients, including

- ✔ How prices are struck

- ✔ The conditions under which positions can be opened and closed

- ✔ The rights and obligations that you have as a client

Financing Charges

The difference between trading shares and trading share CFDs is that when you buy shares you have to pay the full amount in order to take out the position, whereas when you buy share CFDs you pay financing charges in order to replicate the cost that share buyers incur on purchasing the position. In other words, financing charges are what you pay in order to take out CFD positions with only a small amount of cash upfront (your margin payments). Because a margin payment is only a small percentage of the overall market exposure that you're receiving, you can apply a great deal of leverage to your CFD position.

Your CFD provider almost certainly charges you financing on the total exposure that you have in the market and doesn't take your margin payment into account. You may think this doesn't sound right, but you mustn't see the margin you pay as part payment for your position. Your margin acts as security for your CFD provider to allow for any losses that you may have. I look at the margin payment mechanism in more depth in Chapter 1.

Providers of share CFDs calculate financing charges differently, but usually they take the local cash rate (in Australia this is the official interest rate published by the Reserve Bank of Australia) and add what's known in the trade as a *haircut* — an addition to the cash rate that's generally in the region of 2 to 3 per cent. This premium is the way providers make additional profit above the cash rate. So, if the cash rate is 4 per cent and your provider charges a 2 per cent haircut, you pay 6 per cent per annum in financing charges.

Note that financing charges apply *each night* that you hold the position open. This is one reason many traders like trading intra-day with CFDs, because then they don't pay any financing — but you wouldn't want to turn to intra-day trading based on this one factor alone.

On short positions you *earn* financing payments on the positions that you hold. In this case, though, the haircut works the other way round: You earn the cash rate minus 2 to 3 per cent.

Although this is unlikely to be a big earner for you, it can make all the difference when you use hedging strategies (which I look at in Chapter 3). Keep in mind that if interest rates are really low, you may not receive any financing payments for short positions. Check your provider's PDS for the exact details.

When you deal in foreign share markets, the financing charge that applies is generally based on the cash rate of the country from which the shares originate. This means that if you're dealing in a French company, you're liable for the Euro zone interest rate plus the CFD provider's extra clip, and if you're dealing in a US company, the finance charge is based on the US Federal Reserve cash rate. The rates in different countries can vary significantly. For more information on financing charges when dealing in foreign exchange, see Chapter 5.

Dealing in Foreign Share Markets

With the advent of online trading, investors could more easily gain access to different share markets around the world by opening an account with a foreign stockbroker. Unfortunately, this involved sending cash overseas to settle your trades. However, using the right CFD provider you can now gain exposure to international share markets from a single trading platform, so you can monitor prices and positions very easily. In addition, your CFD provider allows you to trade using a single currency (normally your local currency), so you don't need to worry about exchanging currency upfront.

Normally, when people talk about the benefits of dealing in foreign share markets, they consider points such as the diversification of industries and the potential for growth beyond what's available domestically — and these are valid points. When it comes to short-term trading, though, a potentially bigger consideration is *opportunity*.

Proficient traders look for the same characteristics in each and every trade that they make. Say you have a really good trading strategy but this strategy offers you only one trade a week in your home market, which is too infrequent for you. By looking outside the limited opportunities that you have in your home market you may be able to use your trading strategy in foreign markets and so take advantage of greater opportunity.

On the edge

Many trading books refer to a trader's 'edge', which is the way in which a trader's methodology allows him or her to consistently make money. If you have an edge, obviously you try to apply it as widely as you possibly can.

The best example of using an edge is a casino, because all the games that you can play have the odds stacked in the casino's favour. As a result of this stacking, the casino doesn't have just one table open for people to play on, it has as many as it can possibly fill — because even though players often win, the casino always wins more.

The casino's actual edge may be only a couple of percentage points over the players, but over thousands of rolls of the dice this small percentage really pays off for the casino.

I'm not suggesting that you open a casino so that you have the best trader's edge! But I recommend developing your edge and then exploiting your advantage in the market — or across many markets. For more information check out Chapter 16, in which I outline ways to develop your trading plan.

Foreign market trades are generally denominated in the currency of the country in which the company trades. Here are a couple of things to be aware of regarding trading in foreign currencies:

✔ **The difference in value between two currencies can be very high, so ensure that you take extra care with the number of CFDs that you buy.** If you underestimate the exchange rate and buy too many foreign share CFDs, you may receive a nasty shock when you see how much market exposure you actually have, as this may mean that you're risking a lot more than you originally anticipated.

Current exchange rates are easy to find either through your CFD provider or online (try Yahoo! Finance at au.finance.yahoo.com), so be sure to check the current exchange rate before taking the plunge.

✔ **The movements in the exchange rate between your home country and the country where you buy foreign share CFDs affect foreign market trades.** For example, if you buy a US stock that rallies 5 per cent but at the same time the Australian dollar rallies 5 per cent against the US dollar, your profit reduces in real terms by 5 per cent. This is a reasonably extreme example, of course, but it underlines the fact that you need to be aware of the impact that currency moves can have on your profitability. Keep in mind that currency movements can work the other way too: If the Australian dollar falls by 5 per cent in the same time period, your profit increases by 10 per cent.

As is the case with many aspects of CFD trading, individual CFD providers often approach things differently when it comes to settling trades involving a foreign currency. Check out the following with your CFD provider before making any trades:

✔ **Does your CFD provider calculate profits and losses in the local currency or foreign currency?** With share CFDs you're most likely to be left with a profit or loss in your trading account in the currency in which the shares are denominated.

Some providers convert any profit or loss back to the local currency at the end of each trading session, using the prevailing exchange rate at the time. Other providers keep a cumulative balance of foreign currency in your account that you can convert at a time of your choosing.

While you allow foreign currency to accumulate in your account, the value in your local currency is fluctuating as exchange rates change — this may be to your benefit or detriment depending on which way the currency moves.

You may try to time the point at which you convert your exposure back to Australian dollars — this actually involves taking on a separate trade. I suspect that sometimes you benefit from these currency movements and sometimes you lose, but these gains and losses likely average out over time.

✔ **Does your CFD provider charge the commission payable in the foreign currency that you're dealing in?** For example, if your provider charges commission in the foreign currency, you may need to cough up an additional payment of, say, US$10.

When you start dealing in foreign share markets, you most likely want to look at markets in a similar time zone, as this makes monitoring easier. Be aware that some share markets still take a lunch break and may close for an hour or more in the middle of their session. Make sure that you know whether the market you're interested in takes a lunch break before you make any trades, otherwise you may not be able to buy or sell at the time you planned to do so.

Trading Over Different Time Frames

With share CFDs you can trade from the very short to moderate time frames. By very short, I mean less than one day and by moderate I mean several months. You can hold share CFDs for longer than several months, but if you're thinking about doing this you may want to look into whether using margin lending rather than CFDs is a more effective trading strategy (primarily from a tax perspective). The choice of using margin lending may become particularly important if you're looking to obtain large amounts of franked dividends in your portfolio, because franked dividends aren't generally available on CFDs.

Whatever time frame you prefer for your share CFD trading, be sure to stick with your strategy. Each type of trading requires a very different skill set and you certainly won't reach the required skill level for proficient trading if you're constantly chopping and changing your market strategy.

Trading over the longer term

The almost universal rule of trading is that the longer your time frame, the bigger your profit potential, but this statement needs to be qualified. If you're looking at a stock with a share price that is consistently rising and decide to buy that stock, there's a good chance that the price uptrend will continue, but remember that the price won't only move upwards. Over a period of a month the price may go up for 13 sessions and down for seven. In all probability, however, making as much money from several short trades on the down days compared with holding your long position all through the trend (particularly when you incorporate paying multiple commissions) is almost impossible.

Trading over a longer time frame also helps you benefit from several features of CFDs:

- ✔ **CFDs attract lower commission charges.** Traders like CFDs because the commission charges are very cheap. Compared to the brokerage charged by stockbrokers, you can expect to pay a CFD provider somewhere between half to one-third of the price charged by a cheap online broker. However, this discount is wiped out if you end up turning over your portfolio frequently. Trading frequently can be even worse than it seems if the gains you make on your share trades are significantly greater than your share CFD trades because you were holding the shares through much bigger swings in the market. I don't want to rain on your CFD trading parade, but just because you turn over your portfolio very frequently doesn't mean that you're going to make a lot of money — your CFD provider certainly will, though.

✔ **CFDs are a marked-to-market product (refer to Chapter 1).** Compared with trading shares, by trading CFDs you get paid for your gains (and you pay for your losses) even without closing the position. When you trade shares you need to sell your shares in order to crystallise any gains that you've made. So, if you intend to live on your trading gains, you need to regularly close out your positions in order to turn them into cash. However, with marked-to-market products, each day of trading sees the slate wiped clean, with you paying your CFD provider for any losses and your CFD provider paying you for any gains. This means that you don't need to have any more cash tied up than is required to pay for the margin.

Trading over the short term

There are, of course, pluses to short-term trading. One of the most distinct advantages is that you tend to be exposed to less market risk — that is, the risk that the market as a whole will fall in value. One experience you may be familiar with in the Asia–Pacific region is waking up in the morning and looking to see what the US market has done overnight (the rationale being that this movement is one of the key leads for other world markets on any given day). If the US market has fallen 4 per cent overnight, then in all probability you're in for a very 'ordinary' session on local markets. Generally speaking, very short-term traders can avoid this overnight exposure and simply deal with the subsequent trading session. Of course, day trading does require you to time your trades very precisely and to make profits from potentially very small market movements.

If you're willing to monitor your positions carefully, another advantage to day trading is that you may be able to carry more highly leveraged positions, because they're not exposed to as much chance of slippage. This doesn't mean that you can be any more relaxed with your risk in this case, though, because your chances of picking the correct market direction are lower over such a short period of time.

You can also reduce your overnight financing bill by trading in and out on the same day. However, keep in mind that this is generally a pretty weak reason to trade frequently, because any reductions in financing charges are always outweighed by share prices making a decent move in your favour.

Prospective traders often have romantic ideals about day trading: The idea of making potentially large amounts of money very quickly is very attractive. However, you need to always remember that to generate greater returns, you have to take bigger risks. This rule applies across the world of finance, so never assume that because an investment is short term in nature that somehow the risk reduces itself. The roadside of trading is littered with folk who were looking for a quick turn of profit but instead discovered how the potential for a quick profit can turn into an even quicker loss.

Capturing trend moves

If you're new to CFD trading, I suggest that instead of opting for either short- or longer-term trading you focus on capturing trend moves in the market. The downside of trend following is that you have to be willing to absorb more volatility — a trade-off that you'll have to make repeatedly throughout your trading journey. However, you certainly won't have to spend all day looking at the market, and trend trading done well is arguably the most profitable method of trading, so you won't be losing out on the profit front either.

Perhaps you're thinking that trend following may cost you a lot in financing charges? Imagine that you hold a $5,000 position. If interest rates are 4 per cent and your CFD provider adds a 2 per cent haircut, your financing charge is $0.82 a day. This cost would prove inexpensive if, by holding the position, you were able to secure a much larger percentage gain over the next few months.

Example: To understand trend following in action, take a look at Figure 4-1, which shows a consistent upturn in AOE company's share price over several months. From mid-January 2009, the company's share price rose from around $2.00 to a high of around $4.00 over a period of 130 days — a gain of about 100 per cent. (I'm certainly not suggesting that all your CFD purchases are going to generate absolute returns of 100 per cent! But in the right trade you can easily exceed the cost of carrying the position resulting from financing charges.)

Figure 4-1: Trend following with CFDs.

Here's how the profit and loss break down over the 130 days (note that in order to make these calculations I averaged the gains over the time frame):

Opening exposure to AOE (2,500 share CFDs at $2.00 per share)	$5,000
Initial margin payment (5 per cent)	$250
Days in position (130)	Interest rate 4 per cent + haircut 2 per cent = 6 per cent
Approx. average daily financing charge	$0.82
Approx. total financing charge	$107
Commission payments	$20
Closing exposure to AOE (2,500 share CFDs at $4.00 per share)	$10,000
Gain after costs	$4,873

As your position grows, of course, so too does the cost of financing the position.

The most important thing to take away from this example is that it's definitely possible to carry a position for several months and remain profitable, so long as you're capturing a decent trending move. Although this example delivers a very large gain in share price, you can see that even a relatively modest gain can easily outweigh the cost of financing the position each day.

Now consider Figure 4-2, which shows AOE's share price movements on an hourly basis. The share price has traded over quite a modest range during the course of the session ($0.05). On its own this trade doesn't sound like a lot and represents less than a 2 per cent movement on the share price, but that gain may be enough for the short-term trader. However, to capture this price movement you would have to be either extraordinarily precise in your timing or very lucky!

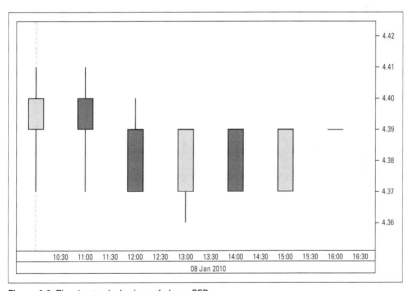

Figure 4-2: The day trader's view of share CFDs.

Dealing with Different Time Zones

You can look to markets all around the world in an effort to gain exposure or diversification, or to exploit your trading edge. However, if you become serious about following share trading in foreign markets, managing your life and getting a decent night's sleep can be tricky. Although trading 24/7 sounds great, working all hours doesn't make for a contented home life or a socially well-adjusted human being. You need to find a happy medium.

Some tricks you can use to ensure your life is well balanced include dealing in sympathetic foreign markets and employing some tactics so that your orders are executed automatically when your specific price targets are met. Using such tactics requires you to plan your trades carefully in advance and to place orders to be executed if your expectations are met.

Checking out sympathetic markets

As the sun moves around the world, share markets open and close. *Sympathetic markets* are those that are relatively easy to fit into your trading schedule. For Australian traders the Asian markets are a natural starting point. The best example in Asia is the Japanese market, which not only is one of the biggest share markets in the world (meaning it's very liquid with many listed companies) but also opens at the same time as the Australian share market (or one hour later, during daylight saving).

The European markets are quite sympathetic for Australian traders because they start to open in the early evening; the North American markets (the United States and Canada) are the last to open for business at around 11 pm Australian Eastern Standard Time. The North American markets are the most difficult markets to trade in if you're looking for day trading opportunities, due to the late hours required.

Making use of stop and limit orders

If the foreign markets you're interested in are open during your own normal business hours, then monitoring foreign share CFDs is no more difficult than monitoring Australian share CFDs. For times when you can't be in front of your computer screen and you're buying into a share, use stop orders (if you want the price to rise before entry) or limit orders (if you want the price to fall before entry) to enter your positions. (Refer to Chapter 2 for more information on these different types of orders.)

However, if you want to enter a position during the night and open the trade with a buy order, I recommend that you use a stop order to enter, rather than a limit order. The reason for this is as follows:

✔ If you use a stop order, the trigger price will be above the market price (from the previous session's close). This means that for the order to trigger, the share price initially at least has to rise, which is what you want to happen.

✔ If you use a limit order and the market falls very heavily on opening, your CFD provider will still open the position for you, even though now you may not be so keen to hold the position.

Conversely, if you want to go short (that is, open the trade with a sell order), you need to place the 'stop to sell' order *below* the market price.

 Always tie your entry order to an if-done order (see Chapter 2 for more information on if-done orders). The if-done order automatically adds a stop order in when the entry order has been triggered (for more information on placing stop orders, see Chapter 2). **Remember:** Manage your risk first and worry about taking profits second.

Foreign companies are everywhere

I find it interesting that many traders aren't comfortable with the idea of dealing in foreign shares or foreign share CFDs, citing that they feel they know Australian companies better than foreign companies. Take a look around your house: I bet you're surrounded by products from overseas, produced by foreign companies trading on foreign share markets.

If you're not sure which offshore companies may be good investments, your CFD provider may be able to offer you some starting points for researching different foreign companies. You can also dig up plenty of free information about foreign companies online using your preferred search engine.

Chapter 5

Taking on the World of Foreign Exchange

*T*he foreign exchange (FX) market is the world's largest financial market — although, interestingly, it isn't really a market in the conventional sense because it has no central meeting place for buyers and sellers beyond the computers into which they place their orders. The prices paid for currencies are struck by banks and huge corporations dealing with one another around the world, and because these groups have the most money in the world the FX market is the most liquid trading environment on the planet, with plenty of volatility too. Not surprisingly, the market attracts huge volumes of traders trying to take advantage of this remarkable trading environment.

In this chapter, I outline how you can apply trading techniques you may already be familiar with to the popular FX market. One of the great features of the FX market is that it is open for trade day and night, which means that you can trade foreign exchange to suit your schedule no matter who you are. Although the FX market is renowned for short-term trading, I also describe how you can capture and profit from larger trending moves in the market. In addition, I explain how information that's released into the market can impact the market and your trades.

Understanding Foreign Exchange CFD Trading

Foreign exchange CFD trading has some key differences from any other financial products that you trade. Essentially, the main difference is that in the FX market you never trade just one product, in this case currency — you always trade one product (currency) against another product (currency). To understand this concept, consider the way in which prices are displayed on currencies: You always see the price of one currency quoted against the price of another currency. If you're interested in buying the euro (EUR), for example, you need to sell another currency in order to pay for the euro. You may see the price of the euro expressed as EUR/USD 1.3467, which means that 1 euro buys 1.3467 USD (US dollars). So, if you want to buy 1 euro, you need to sell 1.3467 US dollars.

Grasping FX terminology

You need to fully understand several key items of terminology before you can begin trading FX CFDs:

- ✔ **Currency quotes:** You may have noted that the price of a currency is quoted to four decimal places. The fourth decimal place is important in FX trading because almost all currencies show prices to the fourth decimal place (with the notable exception of the Japanese yen). A movement of one increment in the fourth decimal place is known as a pip.

- ✔ **Currency pairs:** The two currencies combined in any currency quotation are known as a currency pair. The first currency in the pair is the *terms* currency and the second currency is the *commodity* currency. So, in the example EUR/USD, the euro is the terms currency and the US dollars is the commodity currency.

  The quotation depicts how many units of the commodity currency can be bought by one unit of the terms currency. Thus in the quote EUR/USD 1.3467, 1 euro buys 1.3467 US dollars.

  However, I find it easier to think of the first currency in the pair as *fixed* and the second currency as *floating*, because you can think of the first currency as always representing 1 and the second currency as representing however many that 1 unit buys you.

✔ **Spot price:** The price quoted in a currency quotation is known as the spot price, which simply means the price that you can buy and sell that currency for at that particular moment.

In addition, to complete your understanding of FX terminology, you need to become familiar with the terms 'spot rates' and 'cross rates'.

I remember hearing British comedian Ben Elton doing a skit on TV where he spoke about the words 'cross rates' on the evening news being a signal to go and make a cup of tea. For many people spot and cross rates are unexciting, but as a trader you need to understand them.

✔ A *spot rate* refers to the price of an FX contract at any particular moment in time.

✔ A *cross rate* is any currency quotation that doesn't include the US dollar.

That wasn't too difficult, was it?

If you compare the charts of currency pairs such as the EUR/USD, GBP/USD and USD/CHF they often look quite similar because they all trade against the US dollar. In contrast, cross rates such as the EUR/GBP look quite different. There can be a real diversification benefit for traders using cross rates because they allow you to trade currencies without being impacted by movements of the US dollar.

One final word on cross rates: They're so-called because you need to *cross* two different US exchange rate quotations in order to work out a separate rate — because you can only trade the spot rates directly. So, to work out the value of the AUD/NZD rate you need to compare the value of the AUD/USD rate and the NZD/USD rate.

Example: If you buy AUD/USD (which means buying AUD and selling USD) and sell NZD/USD (which means selling NZD and buying USD), then your overall position is long AUD/NZD (which means buying AUD and selling NZD). The USD is taken out of the equation because you buy it in one transaction and then sell it in the other.

Don't worry — you won't have to put a cross rate together: Your CFD provider does this for you automatically. Still, at the very least you can impress your friends by showing that you know what a cross rate is.

Starting small

Most CFD providers set their smallest trade at US$10,000 exposure. This may sound like quite a lot of money, but it's not quite what you think. For a start, the margin requirement on FX CFD trades is generally no more than 1 per cent, so for a trade of US$10,000 you pay a margin requirement of US$100. Second, for US$10,000 exposure your profit and loss are US$1 per pip movement in price.

Although the minimum exposure of $10,000 means only $1 profit or loss for you for each pip movement, you shouldn't think of this profit or loss as a trivial figure. Foreign exchange prices can move several hundred pips in some sessions, which even on the smallest exposure can mean a loss of US$300 or more. I don't say this to put you off FX CFDs but to make you realise why you don't want to start out with position sizes generating profits and losses of US$20 per pip.

I generally suggest that even experienced traders start out at the minimum position size of US$10,000 exposure to FX CFDs until such time as they become more familiar with dealing with FX CFDs.

Settling your trades

Different CFD providers have different ways of accounting for your outstanding profits and losses from your FX CFD trades. In many cases, when you're dealing in foreign exchange CFDs your trades are automatically settled in US dollars. Some providers automatically convert this back into your local currency at the end of each session, whereas others let the foreign currency you earn from your trades accumulate in your account. Check with your provider's PDS to see how your accounts are handled.

You can leave the foreign currency you earn from your FX CFD trades to accumulate in your account for as long as you want: Its value will rise and fall with the currency market. However, unless you have a particular reason for expecting the currency to change in your favour, so increasing the money in your account,

I suggest you regularly (monthly or thereabouts) convert your trades to your local currency — sometimes you'll convert at a good rate, sometimes at a lesser rate, but the gains and losses should average out over time.

Dealing With a 24-Hour Market (and Getting Some Sleep)

One of the most interesting features of the foreign exchange market is the fact that it trades from early Monday morning all the way through to Saturday morning in Australian time. Throughout this period the market has peaks and troughs in terms of the volume traded and its volatility, but it's always on the move and open for action. Even keen and inspired traders have to sleep some time, so you need to have a plan in place for managing your trade while you sleep.

Building in stop orders

Much can change in the FX market in a very short space of time, so you always need to look at ways to protect yourself in order to minimise your risks and losses. One of the best ways to manage your risk is to set up stop loss orders, which you place with your CFD provider. A *stop loss order* is an order to sell when the price drops below a specified price: The order kicks in automatically, even if you're asleep, so you don't always have to have one eye on the market. (You can also use stop orders to buy new positions as well. I talk more about using and placing stop orders in Chapter 2.)

One of the things that beginner traders frequently note about the FX market is its huge volume of turnover. This volume is an advantage not only for entering and exiting positions (because you're much less likely to experience any price slippage) but also when using stop loss orders. With such huge amounts of volume on offer, even in times of high volatility you should be able to get stopped out of your position at — or very near to — the price that you request on your order, because so many traders are willing to buy or sell all the time.

 If your chosen trading strategy requires you to be in front of the trading screen all the time, you may think that stop loss orders aren't necessary. But when it comes to trading FX CFDs, it's better to be safe than sorry. Like all trading strategies, you need to know where you're going to get out *before* you get in. If you know where to get out, it really shouldn't make any difference whether you close out the position manually or your CFD provider closes the position for you automatically via a stop loss order.

Even if you plan to always keep an eye on the market, remember that using a stop loss order has two advantages to closing manually, because your CFD provider's trading system:

✓ Won't be tempted to give the position the benefit of the doubt, as you may do, leaving the position open

✓ Has reflexes a lot faster than your own

If you plan your trades well, you'll get the best outcome when you let the technology manage the execution for you.

By using your CFD provider's trading platform in the form of various orders you can execute many (if not all) of your transactions without being in front of the trading screen day and night. This means that you can sit down with your charts well in advance and determine where to enter trades, where to place your stop loss orders and where to take profits. You can accomplish all this planning by linking orders that execute the trades when the appropriate price level is reached. I talk more about the various types of orders that you can execute in Chapter 2.

Make room for volatility

When you're deciding where to place your stop loss order, you may be very tempted to place your order extremely close to the point where you enter a position. The downside to this strategy is that you're much more likely to get stopped out of the position before the trade has an opportunity to move in the right direction. So, whether you're trading on the five-minute chart or on the daily chart, you need to allow for a reasonable amount of volatility. Several indicators can help you determine volatility, but one of the best is the average true range (ATR) indicator, which is specifically designed to help you factor the recent volatility of an instrument into your determination of where to place your stop loss order. I explain the ATR indicator in Chapter 13.

Placing profit target orders

If you aren't trading based on trending movements, you're probably looking to earn specific profit targets. To avoid having to trade 24/7 to keep an eye on the market and maximise your profits, you can ask your CFD provider for a *one cancels other (OCO) order* to link two orders on your position. As the name 'one cancels other' suggests, the OCO order automatically cancels one of the two orders if the other order is executed.

For example, you may want to link a stop loss order and a take profit order on a position. If the trade drops, you want your stop loss order to be executed; and if the trade rallies, you want your take profit order to be executed — but you don't want both orders to be executed or you could lose money. An OCO order is a good option because it cancels orders that you no longer need in the market and so reduces your potential losses and risks. By using an OCO order to link the two orders, if the stop loss order is triggered, the take profit order is automatically cancelled.

Consider what could happen if you place two orders — one to stop loss and the other to take profit — that *aren't linked* in a volatile market: You may easily end up in a position where the stop loss order is triggered, followed by the take profit order. The stop loss order sees you out of the trade and the take profit order puts you back in — but in the opposite direction and losing money!

Charting Methods for Short- and Medium-Term Trading

Don't make too many assumptions about the time frame over which to make your FX CFD trades because the FX market has opportunities for all sorts of traders. You can choose to trade for less than an hour or for several weeks with the right FX position, so don't fall into the trap of thinking you have to trade in and out every few minutes.

Short-term trading

The FX market is one of the best markets for short-term trading. Here are some points to consider if short-term trades are your goal:

- **Charting methods:** Look at charting methods that incorporate charts with a time value of less than one hour per bar (I explain charting methods in Chapter 13). Using this time period you can isolate short-term trends as well as support and resistance lines to trade with (see Chapter 13 for more about support and resistance strategies). However, you need to be careful of getting *too* short term with your charts (such as time values of five minutes or less), because managing the inherent short-term volatility in FX trades is very difficult.

  Alternatively, you may choose to incorporate oscillating indicators (such as the Relative Strength Indicator (RSI), the Stochastic Oscillator or MACD Histogram as a means of looking for changes in market direction, but I suggest that you start with support and resistance lines because they're easily identified while still allowing you powerful trading opportunities.

- **If-done orders:** You can incorporate if-done orders to enter the market when the market reaches the optimum price point (that is, the price where you determine it's best to enter your trade), because no matter how keen you are, you can't stay in front of the trading screen all the time. I examine if-done orders in Chapter 2.

In Figure 5-1 I've marked a resistance line that has been respected a number of times — meaning that the price has touched the line and then reversed itself. Short-term traders can either wait for the resistance to break or assume that the resistance will hold and trade accordingly. In either case, you can place your stop order close to the resistance line. By so doing you can potentially set yourself up for a solid risk/reward trade because your risk is very small.

Figure 5-1: Support and resistance strategies can make excellent trade set-ups.

Numerous authors suggest that support and resistance lines may not be very effective in foreign exchange CFD trading because every trader can identify where support and resistance occur and can use this knowledge as an opportunity to unload the position if the support or resistance line is broken. (When a line is 'broken' this means that the price suddenly moves through a previous support or resistance level — this is referred to as a breakout.) Certainly plenty of evidence supports this theory, but not always. Your best option is to form your own opinion of support and resistance lines by studying a wide selection of charts, using either those available on your CFD provider's platform or your own standalone charts. I explain support and resistance lines in more detail in Chapter 13. A firm understanding of support and resistance strategies is a key skill for any trader to have, so I wouldn't ignore their benefits.

Medium-term trading

Although very short term trading may carry certain appeal for traders looking to make quick profits, taking a slightly longer-term approach to FX trading has its advantages:

- You don't need to watch your trading screen the whole time.

- You can capture some of the bigger moves that occur in the market over time (that is, by trend following).

One of the great characteristics of FX trading is that consistent trends often appear in prices over weeks and even months, which means that like share CFD trading, FX CFD trading offers you the possibility of significant gains over the duration of a trade.

Figure 5-2 is a daily trending chart that shows quite a consistent increase in the value of the Australian dollar against the US dollar, driven largely by the expectation of strengthening commodity demand. As the trend progresses the traffic certainly isn't all one-way, but there are plenty of gains to be captured.

Of course, you have to consider the amount of volatility that needs to be absorbed over the course of a medium-term trade. Even if you trade the smallest amount, you can easily see swings in the value of your position of +/– 300 pips (or US$300 at the minimum trade size), which means it won't be all one-way traffic for you. For some traders this amount of money isn't significant, but for others such a loss may stretch the risk tolerance of their account beyond the reasonable limit.

For the most part, you don't want to risk more than 2 per cent of your capital on any given trade. This is referred to as a fixed percentage risk model.

Figure 5-2: Bigger trends can mean bigger profits.

As an alternative to a fixed percentage risk model you can place a stop loss order within the appropriate range allowed by your maximum percentage loss. This strategy involves working out how many pips against you your account can stand and then placing your stop accordingly. I'm against this type of strategy because you're taking a fairly random approach to the placement of your stops, and common wisdom suggests this isn't the most sensible approach because you give no consideration to the behaviour of the individual instrument that you're trading.

I discuss different position sizing strategies in Chapter 9.

In medium-term FX CFD trading, you need to find a balance between trying to capture trending effects and absorbing volatility.

- ✔ Absorb too much volatility and you may get stopped out of a position too late, causing you a very large loss.

- ✔ Absorb too little volatility and you won't give a position enough room to move which makes a small loss very likely and a large profit very unlikely.

Be mindful of the risks that you take on all your trades and try to ensure that any risk isn't too big for your available trading capital. I talk more about managing your risk in Chapter 8.

Exploring the Impact of Currency Differentials

Like all CFDs, when trading FX CFDs you're required only to put up a small percentage (margin) of your exposure, which you need to pay for one way or another. However, the interesting thing about FX CFD trades is that as well as paying financing you can actually *receive* some financing too.

The amount of financing you pay or receive on FX CFDs is based on the *interest rate differential*, which is the difference in official interest rates between the currencies of the two countries in which you're dealing. Whenever you deal in foreign exchange you buy one currency and sell the same value in another currency.

For the purposes of financing, you receive interest on the currency that you buy and pay interest on the currency that you sell. So:

- ✔ If the currency you sell has a higher prevailing interest rate than the currency you buy, you *pay* financing.

- ✔ If the currency you buy has a higher prevailing interest rate than the currency you sell, you *receive* financing.

Example: Say you buy $20,000 worth of Australian dollars and sell the equivalent amount of US dollars at a rate of 0.7500 (US$15,000). If interest rates are 5 per cent in Australia and 3 per cent in the United States, then the interest rate differential is 2 per cent. Because you're buying the higher interest rate currency, you receive $1.10 each day that you hold the position open (0.02 × $20,000/365 = $1.10).

Your CFD provider likely has information on its website to help you find the prevailing cash rates for different currencies. Alternatively, you should be able to find the rates quite easily by searching online.

When the interest rate differential becomes really big, the trade that people undertake on currency transactions to benefit from the differential and collect financing is known as a *carry trade*. The most popular example of a large interest rate differential in recent times (2006–2008) was on the NZD/JPY currency pair — at the time New Zealand was offering a very high interest rate and Japan was offering essentially a zero interest rate.

Many people find trading on large interest rate differentials exciting, but keep in mind that the potential for capital loss on such transactions easily outweighs the potential gains that you can make from the financing benefit.

Following the Big News: Data Releases

One of the most interesting times when you're observing foreign exchange movements is the release of key pieces of financial information, called data releases. *Data releases* usually relate to financial and economic news, but may also cover measures of sentiment and policy statements. Measures of sentiment include items such as consumer confidence and in Australia are shown in economic data released by the Australian Bureau of Statistics and some private companies. Government and non-government institutions, such as central banks and statistics bureaus, and large financial institutions, regularly release different types of data. Often this data presents news that the market expects, such as economic forecasts and interest rate decisions, but sometimes unexpected shifts in government or central bank policy are announced.

Traders pay attention to data releases because the announcement of new information can have an impact on prices in a market. Of the data released, economic news is the most watched category in the market and, given the country's place at the top of the economic ladder, news that comes out of the United States is easily the most important. Traders usually pay less attention to measures of sentiment, policy statements and more minor economic data.

Before data is released, the market often predicts what the announcement may be, based on a consensual forecast from various sources. When the data is released, if the difference between the forecast figure and the actual figure is huge, the market tends to move very quickly to buy or sell currency to accommodate this news. This is because the market 'prices in' expectations about what the future holds into current FX values. *Pricing in* means working out what a financial instrument should be worth based on expectations. When expectations are shown to be incorrect, the market very quickly changes its expectations and buys or sells currency, depending on whether the information makes the currency worth more or less than was previously thought.

The FX market can get very volatile very quickly as news is announced, so some people use data releases as a trading opportunity. Traders often place limit and stop orders just before data is released (for more on these orders, refer to Chapter 2) in order to capture sharp swings in the market. Although news trading can be profitable, it's a highly speculative way to trade because during data releases a currency pair can swing sharply one way and then the other before you have enough time to react.

Some experts warn that you should never trade in the FX market during data releases, because the way in which the market responds to the new information can be very violent and unpredictable. However, such advice needs to be qualified:

✔ If you're a short-term trader then I couldn't agree more with holding off trading until the dust has settled after an announcement, because during the data release your risk can become very difficult for you to manage. There's the potential for you to make a great gain — but also the potential for you to make a significant loss.

✔ If you're trading for weeks or months with the goal of capturing a trending movement, you have little choice but to trade during data releases such as interest rate decisions — such releases are hard to avoid, because financial announcements are made every day somewhere in the world.

Keeping advised of the latest data releases is important. Your CFD provider should give you details of upcoming economic releases and may also send you electronic alerts when the data is released. I suggest that you also search the internet using key words such as 'Economic data releases'. Your search should reveal a number of good news sources such as Bloomberg (www.bloomberg.com) and MarketWatch.com (www.marketwatch.com).

Figure 5-3 shows the type of data that is released in the United States over a period of one week. Not all of these releases are watched very closely, but some are very important. Probably the most-watched news items from the United States are Federal Reserve interest rate decisions and the Nonfarm Payroll (NFP; this gives the major US employment data). As I note in the section 'Grasping FX terminology' earlier in the chapter, all currency quotes either directly follow the US dollar or are derived from it (cross rates), which explains why US economic data has such a widespread impact on all the currencies around the world: When newly released economic data impacts the value of the US dollar, the US currency in turn affects all currencies that are priced relative to the US dollar.

Region: North America				**Country: United States**		**Type: Economic releases**			
Date 07/12/09				**11:43:23**		**United States: Economic releases**			
	Date	**Time**	**A**	**M**	**Event**	**Period**	**Survey**	**Actual**	**Prior**	**Revised**
106	08/06	22:30		📷	Continuing Claims	JUL 26	—	—	—	—
107	08/07	01:00		📷	ICSC Chain Store Sales YoY	JUL	—	—	–5.1%	—
108	08/07	22:30	🔊	📷	Change in Nonfarm Payrolls	JUL	—	—	–467 K	—
109	08/07	22:30		📷	Unemployment Rate	JUL	—	—	9.5%	—
110	08/07	22:30		📷	Change in Manufact. Payrolls	JUL	—	—	–136 K	—
111	08/07	22:30		📷	Average Hourly Earnings MoM	JUL	—	—	0.0%	—
112	08/07	22:30		📷	Average Hourly Earnings YoY	JUL	—	—	2.7%	—
113	08/07	22:30		📷	Average Weekly Hours	JUL	—	—	33.0	—
114	08/08	05:00		📷	Consumer Credit	JUN	—	—	–$3.2 B	—
115	08/11	22:30		📷	Nonfarm Productivity	2Q P	—	—	1.6%	—
116	08/11	22:30		📷	Unit Labor Costs	2Q P	—	—	3.0%	—
117	08/12	00:00	🔊	📷	Wholesale Inventories	JUN	—	—	–0.8%	—
118	08/12	00:00		📷	IBD/TIPP Economic Optimism	AUG	—	—	—	—
119	08/12	07:00		📷	ABC Consumer Confidence	AUG 10	—	—	—	—
120	08/12	21:00		📷	Bloomberg Global Confidence	AUG	—	—	—	—
121	08/12	21:00	🔊	📷	MBA Mortgage Applications	AUG 8	—	—	—	—
122	08/12	22:30	🔊	📷	Trade Balance	JUN	—	—	–$26.0 B	—
123	08/13	04:00	🔊	📷	Monthly Budget Statement	JUL	—	—	—	—
124	08/13	04:15	🔊	📷	FOMC Rate Decision	AUG 13	—	—	0.25%	—

Data derived from Bloomberg.

Figure 5-3 A week of US economic data releases.

US data releases aren't the only announcements to have a big effect on FX values. Australian data releases such as the unemployment data released by the Australian Bureau of Statistics also affect FX trading locally, although often such news doesn't have as widespread an impact on currency values globally. You can check websites such as Bloomberg (www.bloomberg.com) to find out what consensus expectations are for a particular data release: If the actual results are different to expectations, currency markets will react quickly.

The chart in Figure 5-4 shows just how swift market reaction can be when a data release contains a surprise. In this case, unexpected news about unemployment data caused an immediate change in the AUD/USD exchange rate, which moved from 0.8050 to 0.8200 in less than a day.

Of course, such a data release doesn't only impact the AUD/USD rate: It can also affect other currencies such as the NZD and GBP. You'll see this same sort of impact when other countries release data as well.

Figure 5-4: Economic data can rock the market.

By watching how a short-term chart responds when data is released, you can learn an awful lot about how FX markets behave. The best example in the Australian time zone is the release of interest rate decisions by the Reserve Bank of Australia. After most interest rate decisions are announced, you see some very swift price changes in the market, which gives you a good idea of how volatile the FX market can be. And simply watching the market reaction is good fun, because you have no money at risk.

Chapter 6

Following the Big Guns: Index CFDs

*O*ne of the first instruments that many beginner traders find out about in financial markets is an index. In market terms, an *index* is a way of tracking and measuring broad movements that occur in a particular market. There are major indexes, called indices, for currencies, commodities, bonds, property and shares; but in this chapter, I talk only about share indices. Numerous share indices are followed in Australia and around the world: Each index is made up of a 'basket' of shares and given a value. When the average value of the basket moves higher, so too does the index value, and vice versa. The real value of indices for traders is that they can use the indices to track broad movements in a related set of shares.

By trading index CFDs you can track the value of a whole index, rather than one or several individual shares. Such a strategy can be very valuable as a means of hedging to reduce risk or speculating to make profit. Many traders use index CFDs exclusively, which underlines what a powerful and flexible product they can be.

In this chapter, I describe the key features of index CFDs and detail how you can use index CFDs in your trading portfolio. I also explain how you can apply many of the technical analysis techniques that you would use with other tradeable products in trading index CFDs. In addition, I outline some of the key considerations you need to be aware of if you want to trade foreign index CFDs.

Understanding the Basics of Index Trading

Index trading is all about taking a broad view of future movements in a particular market. Even though all traders and investors track market movements, they mostly trade shares and share CFDs to try to profit from their view of a market. By trading index CFDs instead you're taking a much simpler approach, because you're speculating simply that a particular market *as a whole* will either rise or fall in value over the period in which you trade — you don't have to specify which individual shares you think may rise or fall. Like share CFDs, you have the opportunity to trade index CFDs from all around the world, which means that you have additional opportunity to speculate for profits or spread your risk.

All countries that have shares listed on an exchange offer an index (or several indices) over a basket of shares of the biggest companies so that investors can track changes in value that occur over time. Many countries have only one index that can be traded.

For example, in Australia the main index of interest to traders on the share market is the S&P/ASX 200 Index. The basket of shares for this index is the top 200 companies listed on the Australian Securities Exchange (ASX). The index was started on 31 March 2000 with a value of 3133.3 and traders track movements in the basket of shares by monitoring changes in the index value. The very largest companies make up a big portion of the index: 20 per cent of the index's value comes from the four biggest banks in Australia, and the top 10 stocks account for half the value of the index. In addition, the largest company in Australia, BHP Billiton, makes up 13 per cent of the index.

In the United States, the world's biggest market, the focus is mainly on three indices: the S&P 500, the Dow Jones Industrial Average and the NASDAQ.

When you trade index CFDs you take immediate exposure to the market in a single trade. If you couldn't do this, potentially you'd have to buy hundreds of individual shares to get the same market exposure. So trying to replicate this exposure with individual shares or share CFDs is hugely unfeasible.

Looking at your share portfolio, you may notice how similar its movements are on any given day compared to the movements in the S&P/ASX 200 Index as a whole. This is hardly surprising considering the index value derives from the value of individual shares.

Getting a Grip on Index CFDs

Index CFDs, like other CFDs, derive their price from an underlying instrument. However, in the case of index CFDs the underlying instrument isn't an index itself, but rather a futures contract on the index. Why a futures contract? CFDs track only tradeable underlying instruments (that is, instruments that can be sold). An index itself isn't tradeable, because the index value derives from the value of a *basket* of shares, not one individual share — so it's just a number. However, a futures contract is a tradeable instrument, which is why the underlying instrument for index CFDs is a futures contract on the index. The futures contract tracks the value of the index, and the index CFD tracks the value of the futures contract.

Different CFD providers price their index CFDs slightly differently. Some providers offer CFDs that directly follow the futures contract, whereas others offer CFDs that track a recalculation of the contract. This recalculation is often the index value minus the fair value (the *fair value* is the value of upcoming dividends on shares within the index). Both pricing methods follow the index, but the method that directly tracks the futures contract is a little more transparent because you can more easily see the underlying price.

Not all CFD providers offer index CFDs, but for those that do index CFDs have proven to be one of their most popular products, and there are a number of good reasons for this being the case.

Understanding price spreads

A *price spread* is the distance between the price the highest buyer is willing to pay and the price the lowest seller is willing to sell for. The buyer's price is referred to as the *bid* and the seller's price is referred to as the *ask*, or offer. How does the price spread affect you as a trader? Simply, the closer the price spread in a market, the smaller the price move required in your favour before you start making money on a position.

Imagine that you want to trade an index CFD over the S&P/ASX 200 Index and the current price of index CFDs is quoted as 4,280/82. The first figure in the quote is the bid price and the second figure is the ask price, which means that you can buy the CFD at $4,282.

However, as soon as you enter a position you see a loss, which in this example is $2. Why a loss? Because the price you can sell at is 4,280, which is 2 points *below* the price you entered the trade. In order for you to break even, the price needs to rise by 2 points.

Another way to look at this loss is to think of it as paying $2 commission per contract. However, instead of the amount being shown separately, as is the case with share CFDs, it's incorporated into the price at which you deal in the market.

Sometimes the price spread is determined by the market, such as you may see with shares where the difference between the buyer and seller isn't artificially inflated — it's simply the price at which people are willing to buy and sell.

Most CFD providers charge a certain price spread during market hours (essentially daytime business hours) and a higher price spread after market hours. In general terms expect to pay a 2-point spread during market hours and a 4-point spread after market hours. This difference arises because after market hours the underlying market has less liquidity and price spreads will likely increase — so CFD providers increase their spread to account for this increase.

The importance of futures

Futures contracts are one of the most important (and often misunderstood) types of derivatives (financial instruments). A *futures contract* gives the holder the right to buy (or sell) a set quantity of a commodity at a set price in the future. Futures contracts usually cover physical commodities like wool, corn and soy beans, but they can also cover financial commodities such as government bonds and indices. Just as a share CFD tracks the price of a share, an index CFD tracks the value of a futures contract.

Depending on the type of futures contract that you're trading, settlement may be in cash or physically.

✓ Commodities like gold or oil are settled physically: At the expiry of the futures contract, the final holder purchases the commodity at a set price.

✓ Index futures are settled in cash: The holder pays in cash the difference in value between the price at which the contract is opened and closed.

Taking advantage of commission-free trading

One of the main reasons many traders are attracted to index CFDs is the fact that these CFDs are almost always offered free of commission. CFD providers waive the commission in order to attract traders to this product. Note, however, that your CFD provider will add extra spread to the underlying market in order to make its money, so you're by no means receiving a free service.

Commission-free trading is hugely attractive because it helps you to limit a guaranteed cost of doing business — this is how you need to think of commission payments. However, you mustn't get complacent with your trading and throw caution to the wind just because a product is commission-free. Remember:

✓ Whether you're paying commission or not, you should take a trade only if it fits in with your overall market strategy.

✓ You need to be able to limit your risk appropriately on each trade, even if you aren't paying commission. You can be sure that there's more capital at risk on the trade itself than there is capital spent on commission, so remain cautious about your trades at all times.

✔ You pay a higher price spread on most commission-free products. The price spread is the difference between the buy price and the sell price. For the implications of this for your trading, refer to the section 'Understanding price spreads' earlier in the chapter.

Following market movements

The value of an index CFD is determined by the current trading price multiplied by the number of contracts that the trader buys or sells. The amount of exposure is easy to calculate because each CFD is worth $1 per point in the index, so the dollar value of the CFD is the current index value multiplied by $1. Thus, if the S&P/ASX 200 Index is trading at 4,400 points, one CFD gives you $4,400 worth of exposure. To work out how many contracts you need to buy to cover your required market exposure, you simply divide the total market exposure you require by the dollar value of the CFD, which in this example is $4,400. Following on with this example, if you want immediate market exposure of $50,000, you need to buy $50,000/4,400 = 11.36 contracts, which rounds up to 12 whole contracts.

Index CFDs are a popular choice for traders because you can trade broad market movements in a single trade, which is easier and cheaper than trying to replicate the index by purchasing all the shares individually. This means that if you believe the market as a whole will rise or fall over a given time frame, you can go either long or short on the index, respectively. You can carry an index position for as long as you like, but short-term movements are likely to prove most attractive for traders. In the section 'Short- and Long-Term Trading' later in this chapter, I explain how you can use index CFDs to *reduce* your exposure to the market by trading on the short side of the market.

Examining sector trades

Sector CFDs are a more specific type of index CFD that allow you to take exposure to a broad (but nonetheless similar) category of shares in an index, rather than all the shares in the index, in a single trade (saving you commission charges and fees). Most of the larger market sectors are dominated by several large companies, and companies within the same sector are likely to be heavily correlated, so in many cases it makes sense to take exposure to them all rather than trying to pick several of the best companies.

For example, you may want to concentrate on only finance sector shares covering banks and insurance companies. So, instead of trading all 200 shares in a CFD covering the S&P/ASX 200 Index, you can use a sector CFD to trade only the 10 or so largest shares in the finance sector of that index.

You can also use sector CFDs along with index CFDs to undertake the hedging strategy of index stripping. *Index stripping* generally involves being long the index (taking the view that the value will rise) and then going short on the sector that you believe will underperform (taking the view that the value will fall). Since the index is an average of share price performances, if you can remove the underperformer(s), then naturally your returns should improve.

Trading Local Index CFDs

In general, the index market doesn't quite trade for 24 hours a day. For example, the Australian S&P/ASX 200 Index trades in two blocks each 24-hour period:

- ✔ 9.50 am to 4.30 pm
- ✔ 5.10 pm to 7.00 am

Importantly, unlike the share market, the index market isn't asleep when you are. This means that when you wake up, any new information that's been released overnight may have impacted on the value of your index CFDs, so how your profit and loss statement looks before you go to bed may be quite different to what you see in the morning. In this section I describe some of the factors you need to be aware of at these times to help you deal with changing market conditions.

Taking care when volumes are low

One aspect you need to consider if you let your positions run overnight is that at night the volume of trade goes down and the volatility goes up, which increases your risk at a time when you don't have your eye on the market. If you're trading only one or two CFDs at a time this risk may not be a particularly significant issue for you, but if you're trading multiples of ten CFDs this becomes much more important.

Example: Say you're trading 20 CFDs overnight and a major move in the market sees the price move over your stop loss such that you experience a 10-point slippage — *slippage* happens when no trade occurs at the price you nominate as your stop loss, and can result from volatility or low liquidity, or both. Your trade will be executed at the next available price, which means you make an additional loss beyond what you anticipated based on where you placed your stop loss of $200 (20 contracts × $10 per point). Although this may not sound like an overly large amount of money, many people trade in volumes far outweighing 20 CFDs and so would experience greater losses in such a situation.

Trading overnight can be beneficial, because you can respond immediately when news is released in other parts of the world, whereas daytime traders cannot respond until trade begins the next day. This isn't always an advantage, though, because short-term movements may reverse themselves by the opening of trade the following day!

I know several traders of index CFDs and SPI (share price index) futures (see the sidebar 'SPI futures') who don't allow their positions to run overnight because they find it too difficult to manage their risk in the event of an increase in volatility. You don't necessarily have to follow the same rule, but you do need to be aware of the potential outcomes of leaving your positions open overnight. To improve your understanding of coping with risks see Chapter 8.

You can see that there isn't a single easy answer for traders, so you need to be very thoughtful about the strategy that you employ and be sure that it's suitable.

Putting in stops

A lot can change in the index market in a very short space of time, so as with other types of CFDs you always need to protect yourself and this means using stop orders with your index CFDs. However, just as you need to be mindful about not throwing caution to the wind when you aren't paying commission (see the section 'Taking advantage of commission-free trading' earlier in the chapter), so you need to avoid being careless with where you place your stop orders.

Putting your stop orders as close as you can to your entry price in the hope of reducing your risk isn't a good idea, because:

✔ You'll very likely get closed out simply due to normal market volatility and so miss out on the opportunity to make bigger profits. This is a very real risk beyond more obvious things like major market announcements.

✔ Although your loss may be relatively minor, there's a much better chance that you'll lock in more losing positions overall because you'll likely have a smaller number of winning trades.

I talk more about how to place stop orders to reduce your risk in Chapter 8.

SPI futures

A very closely related product to index CFDs is SPI futures. They're close relatives because their prices are determined by the movements of the same underlying index — the S&P/ASX 200. In Australia SPI futures trade with a value of $25 per point movement — the equivalent of 25 index CFDs. So you can see that even on the smallest trade size, with SPI futures it doesn't take a very big market movement to make or lose $100. Although there are advantages to trading both CFDs and SPI futures, one of the key advantages of trading index CFDs over SPI futures is the fact that you can take on smaller and more manageable positions from as little as $1 per point.

Trading Foreign Index CFDs

Trading foreign index CFDs gives you the same advantages as trading Australian index CFDs but over different baskets of shares: You can take on immediate exposure to baskets of shares in the United States, the United Kingdom, France, Germany, Hong Kong and Japan among others. Trading different baskets of shares has two specific advantages:

- ✔ You gain new trading opportunities, which increases your chances for making profits.

- ✔ You may increase the diversity of your portfolio, which can reduce your risk in the marketplace. Keep in mind that there's often very strong correlation between different share markets on a day-to-day basis, so these diversification benefits may not be as great in the short term as you may hope.

Before you rush to your trading screen to make a foray into the foreign index market, there are a couple of distinct issues you need to be aware of relating to the times at which these markets are open and the currency in which you trade.

Timing your trades

Most indices trade an extended session (by which I mean almost 24 hours) that is broken down into a day session and a night session. Invariably, the day session offers higher volumes, which tends to make trade less choppy; and the night session trades lower volumes, which tends to increase volatility.

- ✔ **Day trading:** To trade during the day in Australia you may want to focus your energies on the Hong Kong and Japanese index markets, as these two countries are in a similar time zone to Australia. In addition, some European indices offer good short-term opportunities and are suitable for Australian traders because these indices start their sessions in the early evening local time.

- ✔ **Night trading:** If you're a bit of a night owl and want to trade at night in Australia during a foreign market's day trading session, the S&P 500 Index in the United States is probably the most popular index in the world to trade and should offer you plenty of opportunity. Other large markets of note are the FTSE index in the United Kingdom and the DAX in Germany.

Always check with your CFD provider to see what indices it offers and what times it trades.

Knowing which currency to use

When you buy an index CFD based in another country you make your margin payments in the currency of the country that the contract is based in. In addition, any profits or losses that you make are paid in that currency.

Example: Say that you want to buy an index CFD representing the Dow Jones in the United States and the Dow Jones index is trading at 6,500 points. As with local index CFDs, the points value of the CFD tells you how much exposure you get, but the amount is in foreign currency not your local currency. In this case the CFD exposure is US$6,500. If the relevant margin requirement is 1 per cent, you pay 0.01 × 6,500, or US$65 for this CFD.

However, you need to pay with Australian dollars, not US dollars, so you have to consider the exchange rate between the Australian dollar and the US dollar. Say that one Australian dollar buys 0.70 US dollars. One CFD has a value of US$6,500, which equates to A$9,286 (6,500/0.7). This means that buying one CFD with a 1 per cent margin requirement costs you 1 per cent × 9,286, or A$92.86.

Each time the price of the CFD moves higher or lower, the impact to your account will be higher because the price is quoted in a more valuable currency. In fact, if the Australian dollar is trading at 0.70 US dollars, then each tick (movement in the smallest increment of the currency quote) up or down is worth A$1.43 (which at this exchange rate is the value of US$1). This means that if you're willing to tolerate a loss of, say, $100 each time you have a losing trade, you'll be able to risk fewer points than if the index CFD is priced in a less valuable currency, because you'll reach your maximum risk in the local currency after fewer points of movement against you.

Refer to Chapter 5 for some important lessons on how best to calculate the impact of different currencies and currency movements on your trading portfolio.

Guarding Against Bad News and Market Catastrophes

The announcement of major business, economic or disaster-related news can turn a trading position on its head — whether this is your index CFD position or your trading position in general. Some news announcements you can plan for, but others you can't foresee. In the last 30 years two market events stand out due to the speed and severity of their impact:

- The share market crash of 1987

- The shock to the markets that occurred after the terrorist attacks in the United States on September 11, 2001

In retrospect, I think there was some early warning about the 1987 share market crash (due to the extraordinary increase in share values that had been seen in the lead-up to the crash), but of course there was no economic precursor to the September 11 attacks.

So how can you manage your positions with these potential drops in market value in mind?

To answer this question you need to balance how much potential damage a catastrophe can do with the potential gains you'd miss out on if you didn't invest when the market wasn't in full-blown catastrophe mode. On the Australian share market, through most market conditions the index rises and falls on about 50 per cent of trading days. This means that through bull markets (with an upward trend) and bear markets (with a generally downward trend), there is an even chance of prices rising or falling. With that in mind you cannot expect the market to go your way every session.

The only way to defend yourself completely against drops in market value is to invest entirely in risk-free assets (that is, cash), but such a strategy won't get you returns that are particularly exciting. At a more extreme level, you can see that it's also impossible to defend against very large scale events without damaging your returns when there isn't a catastrophic event occurring.

To manage your risk against such market shocks, I suggest you carry no more leverage than you can manage to cover immediately with the cash that's in your trading account. Say that you have $10,000 in your trading account and are fully levered using index CFDs. CFD providers charge a 1 per cent margin for index CFDs, so this means you're carrying $1,000,000 worth of exposure to the market ($1,000,000 × 0.01 = $10,000). If there's a 1 per cent movement in price against you, it'll cost you $10,000 and you'll have no money left in your account; if there's a 2 per cent movement in price against you, your account won't cover your debt and you'll be left owing your CFD provider $10,000 on top of the $10,000 you lose from your account.

A conservative measure is not to lever your account by more than three times — that is, if you have $10,000 in your account, you shouldn't have more than $30,000 exposure to the market.

See Chapter 8 for more information on risk management.

Mentally stress test your positions on index CFDs (in fact, your whole trading portfolio) by looking at the current value of your positions, wiping off 20 per cent and then determining what you'd do next. After drying your eyes you'd need to take action, but would you sell out, wait it out or buy more? This is the type of decision that you'd face in a severe market shock.

A survivor's tale

Renowned US hedge fund manager Paul Tudor Jones became a market icon following the 1987 share market crash. While most traders around him were taking a hammering, Tudor Jones was carrying a large short index position (which means he'd sold short a number of index futures contracts) and a large long bonds position (which means he'd bought a lot of treasury futures). Both of these strategies benefited from the collapsing share market and allowed him to make an extraordinary profit in what proved to be a dire time for the vast majority of investors.

What made Tudor Jones even more remarkable was that in order to make these trades he had to be in a position contrary to the majority of other traders, who were riding a very exuberant bull (rising) market at the time. His success serves to illustrate that while following the prevailing direction of the market can be beneficial to traders much of the time, there's likely to be episodes where you need to go your own way.

Short- and Long-Term Trading

Many traders think that index CFDs are aimed at a very short-term time frame. There is good reason for thinking this, because index CFDs are a liquid trading instrument that can be accessed over long trading hours. However, you don't have to approach index CFDs as short-term trades only, because you can incorporate them into your overall portfolio to perform such functions as reducing your total market exposure.

Short-term strategies

The charts that your CFD provider gives you update in real time and enable you to make trading decisions in the short term. Many of the trades you're likely to deal in the short term arise as a result of what you see on your charts. I suggest that you look towards support and resistance lines as a starting strategy in index trading. This strategy involves looking for prices that are hitting the same price level repeatedly and then reversing. Support and resistance points are useful because they're easily identified and allow you to clearly set profit targets. For more information about support and resistance lines refer to Chapter 13.

When you're looking at your charts you often see prices trading between two distinct areas of support (the lower horizontal line) and resistance (the upper horizontal line). Commonly, traders take long positions if price moves above the resistance line or short positions if price moves below the support line — this is referred to as a breakout and is an opportunity for traders because it shows price moving in a new direction. These trades often see sharp price movements. I explain more about these support and resistance strategies in Chapter 13.

Long-term strategies

There are several different approaches to long-term trading strategies for index CFDs. Some approaches are quite conventional, but others are more unusual and involve modifying your exposure to the market by adding or removing exposure. By 'removing exposure' I mean offsetting other exposure that you have to the share market. For example, if you have a diversified share portfolio that is all 'long' side (that is, you benefit if the price rises), then going short on an index

CFD will reduce your market exposure in line with its value (the number of index points — such as 4,800 × the number of contracts you have).

Here are two long-term trading strategies:

- ✔ **Capturing trending movements in the overall market.** This is one of the more conventional ways in which you can approach trading the index. If you have a view of a specific market (such as the Australian share market), you can try to time your entry into the trending movement. For example, if you think the market is going to rise (that is, it's bullish), you may buy index CFDs to reflect this view and then hold them for as long as you believe the market will remain positive. The benefit of this type of approach is that you maintain your exposure to the market continuously: One of the things that can be quite frustrating about trading is missing moves in the market due to lack of exposure or having the wrong exposure.

- ✔ **Hedging against falls in share value.** Such a strategy would have been difficult for many retail traders to implement before the advent of CFDs. Given the fact that index CFDs give you a relatively small amount of exposure, you can use them to hedge against falls in the value of even a small share portfolio or share CFD portfolio. If you have a well-diversified portfolio, chances are it'll be quite highly correlated to movements of the index. For this reason, if you believe that a downturn will occur in the market in the short term, you may choose to hold your share/share CFD positions and simply short the index as a means of defending value within the rest of your portfolio, which simply would be eroded without your short index CFD exposure. Index CFDs won't provide a perfect hedge for your portfolio, but they can go a long way to defending against falls in the market.

Although hedging strategies are often discussed quite lightly, they're very serious and you need to plan your strategies carefully before you execute them. Even though the downside to your hedging strategies will be limited, the risk lies in the potential opportunity cost that you may lose: If you hedge your long share portfolio and the market surges, you'll receive little to no benefit from that movement. For this reason, you should implement hedging strategies sparingly.

I explain more about hedging strategies in Chapter 3.

Chapter 7

Venturing into Commodities and Interest Rate Products

Commodities are physical products that investors buy or sell, usually via futures contracts. The main commodities that are traded are oil, gold and agricultural products such as grains and livestock. In addition, financial products such as interest rate products are also traded. Because traders don't want to transport the actual products that they trade, they instead trade futures contracts on the commodities or financial products, which are agreements to buy or sell the products at an agreed price on a nominated date.

Traditional commodities, such as gold, oil, wheat and oats, are some of the more interesting products around because they have a more tangible quality — that is, you can picture what they look like.

In this chapter, I look at the major types of commodity CFDs that are available for trading and some of the main factors that may impact on the price of these CFDs at any given point in time. I also look at some of the main characteristics of interest rate products and the factors that impact on the value of these tradeable instruments. You will see that both commodity CFDs and interest rate CFDs are affected by different factors from those you'd normally be exposed to in other financial markets.

Understanding the Terminology: What Are Commodities, Anyway?

In general terms, you can think of commodities as valuable natural products that are the same no matter who produces them. For example, oil is oil no matter who produces the oil, and gold is gold no matter who produces the gold. Virtually anything that can be grown or taken from the ground is thus a commodity. Commodities cover a broad range of products but basically fall into three groups:

- Agricultural commodities
  - Grains and legumes
  - Meat and livestock
  - Softs

- Energy commodities
  - Gas
  - Oil

- Metal commodities
  - Base metals
  - Precious metals

Sometimes, financial products such as interest rate products like bonds and treasuries are traded on the same exchanges as these types of commodities and for this reason you may occasionally see such financial products referred to as commodities. However, I think it's clearer simply to define commodities as natural products such as metals — otherwise, the term starts to lose its meaning. I deal with financial products in the section 'Interest Rate Products' later in the chapter.

Although the commodities market has witnessed something of a decline lately due to the slowdown in the global economy, the overall interest that traders are taking in commodities has been greatly enhanced, and in recent years a number of commodities, such as gold, have shown a great deal of strength.

Agricultural commodities

Agricultural commodities are basically anything that's grown — or anything that a farmer makes and sells. Agricultural commodities include grains and legumes, such as wheat and soy beans, and livestock, such as cattle and hogs (pigs). So, unlike money, some agricultural commodities *do* grow on trees! However, not all commodities are traded on an exchange and of those that are traded only some have CFDs available to trade over them. You need to check with your provider which commodities it makes available for trade.

Agricultural commodities form a very important part of the financial world, from enabling farmers to lock in the prices at which they can sell their goods in the future to providing trading opportunities for speculators. You can assume that many of the food products that you eat have had some part of them bought through commodity markets. Another big user of agricultural commodities is the major processors, which include groups such as flour millers and textile mills. These companies use commodities to hedge the future costs of products that their businesses require. Traders and speculators (who don't want the end products) add liquidity to the market, which makes buying and selling of commodities easier for everyone.

Check out where they're traded

A number of different exchanges around the world quote different types of commodities, and their websites should be a stop on your journey to maximising your knowledge of commodities and commodity CFDs. Try starting with the websites of the following commodity markets:

✔ Chicago Mercantile Exchange (CME): www.cmegroup.com

✔ Intercontinental Exchange (ICE): www.theice.com

✔ London Metal Exchange (LME): www.lme.co.uk

If you spend time researching more about commodities, you'll see that a number of interesting factors go into their production, such as methods of sowing and harvesting. Sometimes such information can be quite useful and give you a good idea of how harvests can be impacted, which in turn can impact on price. The standard rules of supply and demand apply in the commodities market, but you'll see them expressed in different ways. For example, if a cold snap in the weather destroys large amounts of wheat, then supplies will likely be lower, which will drive prices higher. This explains why traders of agricultural commodities often take a huge interest in the weather. Some traders even deal in weather futures to defend against negative impacts caused by the weather!

One of the fascinating things about the commodities market is the fact that its products impact on the daily lives of virtually everyone, because people rely on them in order to survive. In the following sections I outline the main agricultural commodities.

The best-known commodities

The following commodities are likely to be well known to everyone. I briefly examine some of the key characteristics of these commodities so that you know exactly what you're trading.

- ✔ **Grains and legumes:** Some of the most widely traded grains and legumes, such as corn, oats, soy beans and wheat, are used in foods for both human and animal consumption.

    - Corn is used widely for human consumption, as the carbohydrate part of a balanced diet. Corn also makes up a very large component of animal feed. In the United States, corn is used to make ethanol fuel, and although you'd expect this extra demand on the product to reduce supply (and therefore drive up prices), instead farmers are planting more corn crops, taking advantage of the new source of demand.

    - Oats are something that most people are familiar with — as porridge — but this valuable cereal is also used widely in livestock feeding.

    - Soy beans and their derivatives are used in products such as tofu, soy milk and soy bean meal (a high-protein animal feed) and soy bean oil, which can be used as a vegetable oil.

- Wheat is grown in a large number of regions around the world and is used widely for human consumption, with flour being the most notable product.

✔ **Livestock:** The main animal products that are traded on the commodity market are cattle and pigs (listed as hogs on the market).

- The cattle market falls into two categories: live cattle and feeder cattle. The key difference between the categories lies in where the cattle are in their life cycle when they're sold: Live cattle somewhat paradoxically are slaughter-ready, whereas feeder cattle are still being fed and are sold to different farms to be grown out ready for slaughter. This feeding takes place at feedlots, which fatten cattle for sale.

  The best place to find out more about cattle and hogs is the Chicago Mercantile Exchange website (www.cmegroup.com).

- The pig (or hog) market is divided into lean hogs and pork bellies. *Lean hogs* are whole carcasses of a specific grade. *Pork bellies* are the parts of the carcass that are used to make bacon.

The softs: Coffee, cocoa, cotton and more

The other category in the agricultural market is known as the softs and includes sugar, coffee, cotton, lumber (timber), orange juice and cocoa. Some people think of the softs as breakfast commodities, because the category includes orange juice, sugar and coffee. This categorisation falls down a bit, though, because it omits key products — unless perhaps you think of cotton for your PJs and timber for the breakfast table!

Energy commodities

Energy commodities cover a relatively narrow band of product categories, the major ones being crude oil, natural gas, heating oil and gasoline. Of these products, crude oil is the most actively traded and is possibly the most politically sensitive instrument traded anywhere in the world — you've no doubt already noticed that when any major political upheavals happen in the world (particularly in any country that produces oil), there's a response in the oil price. In addition, vast amounts of the world's oil supply are controlled by a relatively small number of countries. Some of these countries make up the Organization of the Petroleum Exporting Countries (OPEC). The OPEC cartel aims to influence oil prices around the world by controlling the level of supply that goes to market.

Crude oil is one of the most important commodities in the world because it's universally used by consumers: Few consumers can escape its grasp. Even if you cycle everywhere and never use a car or bus, you'll use products like plastics that are made from oil derivatives.

Oil prices are said to have an inflationary effect because for consumers everywhere, higher oil prices mean having less money to spend on other things. Furthermore, higher oil prices may lead consumers to defer spending in other areas of the economy in order to fuel their cars — people who drive to work may have no other choice. Thus other areas of the economy, such as retail and tourism, may suffer as a result of increases in the oil price.

Oil markets can be very active and very liquid (no pun intended) — key characteristics that traders should be looking for. You can trade CFDs on oil from all over the world, such as Brent from the United Kingdom and West Texas Intermediate from the United States. The various contracts available worldwide have their differences in terms of standard viscosity and sulphur levels, which you can investigate simply by looking online. However, the CFDs from the United States and the United Kingdom are likely to be of most interest to you, given their great liquidity (meaning fewer gaps in the price) and long trading hours.

The contract that's most actively traded is the US West Texas Intermediate: You can check out this contract at www.cmegroup.com as a great example.

In addition to crude oil, in the US exchanges (where the most popular energy commodity CFDs are traded) the following contract sizes are available for the other major energy commodities:

- ✔ Heating oil: 42,000 gallons
- ✔ Natural gas: 10,000 million British thermal units (MMBtu)
- ✔ Unleaded gasoline: 42,000 gallons

Oil: Sweet crude stuff

It's worth understanding a little more of some of the terminology that's used when describing oil because you'll see these terms in the name of the contract when you trade the CFD. Often you see the words *light* and *sweet* used to define oil, as in light sweet crude.

✔ *Light* simply refers to the viscosity of the oil — the lighter, being better.

✔ *Sweet* (or sour) refers to the sulphur content of the oil — the less, the better.

The lighter and sweeter the oil, the less refining it needs, which means the less it costs to turn the oil into other products like diesel and gasoline.

As with any CFD, you don't pay for the full amount — expect your margin requirement to be in the region of 3 to 5 per cent. In addition, the size of the CFD may be a lot smaller than if you were trading the actual futures contract. For example, the WTI Crude Oil contract trades in Chicago at 1,000 barrels of oil per contract, whereas CFDs are generally traded over 100 or even single barrels of oil. The price moves in the same fashion, but CFD traders have less exposure per contract than futures traders.

Metals: All that glitters

The prices of metals commodities clearly reflect the overall state of the global economy and dictate just how much expenditure in areas such as housing and infrastructure is likely to cost.

Two important subsets of metals commodities are industrial (base) metals and precious metals. You'd be largely correct if you said that the difference between the two is the price, but that isn't entirely accurate. The actual difference is that *industrial metals* react with oxygen whereas *precious metals* don't react with oxygen.

Precious metals

The main precious metals that traders are interested in are gold, silver and platinum.

Gold is the most important precious metal and not just because it looks nice. It actually has a wide range of industrial uses, particularly because it conducts electricity very well — significantly better than copper, in fact. More important still, though, is gold's use as:

- ✔ **A store of value:** Given that gold never corrodes, you know that any value you hold in this metal will stand the test of time.

- ✔ **A hedge against inflation:** Because you have to trade dollars (generally US dollars) to buy gold, the gold acts very well as a hedge against inflation. This is because as the US dollar falls in value, the price of gold conversely rises in value — which is extremely useful for investors keen to defend the value of their money. This isn't a guarantee, though, because if you buy gold when it's highly priced it won't prove to be a good hedge against inflation at all.

Gold's characteristic as a hedge against inflation is the reason many people refer to gold as a currency unto itself — in fact, CFD providers often list gold in with the currencies.

Platinum and silver also have important applications in the industrial world. In addition, a big part of demand for these metals comes from jewellery manufacture, so low prices and a strong global economy can see a very sharp upswing in prices due to increased buyer demand.

Industrial metals

The industrial metals include copper, zinc, lead and aluminium. Many industrial metals are heavily traded in both the United Kingdom and the United States.

It's important to note that demand for industrial metals is fairly representative of the overall state of the general economy. Copper is often one of the most interesting from this perspective, because of the large amount of copper used in the construction of new buildings (in wiring and plumbing). For example, in the late 2000s the copper market saw a big swing downwards as the US housing market started to fall away and demand for one of the key uses of this metal started drying up.

Getting Ready to Trade in the Commodities Market

Once upon a time traders took exposure to the commodities market either by investing in managed funds or more indirectly by buying the shares of listed companies that dealt in commodities — for example, buying a copper mining company to gain exposure to the changing value of copper. Although these types of investment can be a very effective way of investing in specific commodities, they're not nearly as direct as many people would otherwise like. For example, a gold company's earnings are impacted by movements in the price of gold as well as factors such as the wider movements of the share market. This means that even if you can predict the price of gold correctly, the gold company's share price may not reflect the gold price itself, because other factors influence the share price. CFDs take the best parts of the futures market (that is, direct exposure to the price movements of commodities) and convert them into products that are much easier for traders to deal with because they can be traded at a much smaller size, which makes risk easier to control — gold, silver and oil are examples of the most popular CFD commodities to trade.

I believe that a big part of successful trading involves having good mental aspirations of what you want your trading to achieve. This doesn't mean simply daydreaming in the hope that big profits will come your way — you need to think about something inspirational that can give you actual goals. Try watching the 1983 John Landis film *Trading Places*, primarily for a chuckle but also for the brilliant backdrop of the commodities market, which should get your mind racing with the possibilities of commodity CFDs.

While a big part of trading relates to trying to predict price movements and managing your risk, you shouldn't underestimate the importance of understanding the fundamental characteristics of the market you're dealing in.

Asking questions of your CFD provider

One thing I must stress is that if you don't understand how a product operates, a condition under which a product trades or anything else to do with CFDs, call your CFD provider and ask for a clear explanation. Your provider should be more than happy to help you with any questions you have. Don't assume that you're asking something silly — you'll simply be the latest in a long line of people who have trouble understanding the same issue. In fact, the more people who ask about a particular issue, the more likely your provider is to make changes to the way it explains the issue in the future.

Sadly, watching a movie doesn't count as a rounded education on the commodities market! So here are some other things you need to know to help with your understanding of the workings of the commodities market:

- ✔ **Cost structure:** You probably won't have to pay commission or financing on commodity products, because like foreign exchange CFDs the provider adds an extra spread to the price instead (see Chapter 5). However, you need to know how much each tick of the price (that is, movement of the smallest price increment) will cost you if you buy the smallest amount of CFDs that your provider will allow. This is sensible regardless of what you're trading, because otherwise determining your risk is impossible.

  For example, if this cost is $1 per $0.001 movement, you may have difficultly managing your risk if you want to put your stop $1 away, because this equates to 1,000 ticks, which may be more risk than you want to take on a single position.

- ✔ **Expiry of the underlying futures contract:** CFDs track the price of an underlying instrument and in the case of commodities that instrument is a futures contract. There's a mismatch here, though, because futures contracts expire and CFDs don't: Commodities have underlying futures contracts that expire at certain times during the year. Some expire five times a year — for example, in March, May, July, September and December — while others may expire quarterly or monthly.

So how can you ensure that your CFDs keep trading? The answer is simple: Your CFD provider automatically rolls over each CFD near the expiry of the underlying futures contract. However, in real terms this means that your CFD stops tracking the price of one futures contract and starts tracking the price of the next futures contract in line.

When your CFD is rolled over, the value of your exposure changes — for better or for worse. You need to be firmly aware of when the rollover will occur to assess the impact it will have on the value of your holding. You may even prefer to close out your position rather than rolling it over.

Your CFD provider's PDS should outline how your provider handles the rollover of futures contracts from one expiry period to the next. In general terms you always deal in 'front-month' contracts, which are the next contracts to expire and are also the most liquid of the contracts available for you to trade.

✔ **'Limit-move' rules:** Several specific trading rules impact on each session in which the commodities market is operating, but one of the key rules is the 'limit-move' rules. The *'limit-move' rules* stop the underlying market (such as the New York Metals Exchange) from changing by more than a specific value (up or down) from the close of the previous session — the exact value is dictated by the particular market. The idea is that in times of very high volatility, the market will simply stop trading, limiting price swings that may otherwise occur. This means that if the underlying market locks limit up or limit down (meaning that trade is halted during the normal hours of a trading session), you won't be able to exit your position. There's great academic debate as to the benefit of the 'limit-move' rules (many argue that imposing the rules just saves up volatility for another day), but nevertheless you should expect your CFD provider to follow the rules.

Before you make a single trade in commodity CFDs, check the underlying market for the specific value that the 'limit-move' rules place on the different commodities.

✔ **Liquidity:** One of the key criteria that you need to consider about trading commodity CFDs is liquidity. *Liquidity* refers to the ease with which you can enter or exit a position without impacting adversely on the price of that position. If you trade very illiquid positions, getting in and out of trades can become difficult, which in turns makes your risk management more difficult because you may not be able to get out at your stop loss price (I discuss risk management in more detail in Chapter 8). Some commodity CFDs trade quite infrequently (to find out which ones, check the charts provided by your CFD provider), meaning they may not trade on a given day. This is something many traders want to avoid, because the major downside to infrequent trading is that price movements can be very erratic, making risk management very difficult.

✔ **Trading on the floor:** Like a lot of futures contracts, commodity CFDs trade on the floor as well as electronically. *Trading on the floor* refers to the time when contracts trade in their home country during business hours using what's known as an open outcry system, where traders deal face-to-face with one another — this is the time when contracts are most actively traded. In the United States, exchanges combine open outcry and electronic trading during the day (for four to eight hours) and use electronic trading at night, although many exchanges worldwide operate electronically for all trading sessions. Generally, your CFD provider offers trading during the same hours as the underlying market. Unfortunately this timing is very inconvenient for many traders around the world because it corresponds with when they need to sleep. Luckily, with electronic trading contracts can be traded almost around the clock.

Of course, you also need to look into the characteristics of the product you're trading before actually dealing in the product. The section 'Understanding the Terminology: What Are Commodities, Anyway?' earlier in the chapter outlines the basic commodities that CFD traders are interested in trading.

Interest Rate Products

Interest rate products represent one of the most important products within financial markets because they're a major way with which entire economies borrow funds — generally speaking, this is done in order to fund a deficit. *Treasuries* are debt obligations undertaken by national governments, usually in the form of government bonds. In exchange for this revenue, governments promise to repay the money lent plus interest. Since treasury bonds are guaranteed by government, they're extremely low risk — as long as they're issued by a government with a strong economy (there have been some occasional — though big — government defaults in history). Some traders hold the bonds until they mature, while others sell them on to other investors on the open market.

Because of the huge amounts of money involved, the treasury market is one of the biggest markets in the world. Happily for CFD traders, interest rate products give you another string to your trading bow, because often you find that interest rate products move in an entirely different way to other asset classes, such as shares, because they're impacted by other factors, such as interest rates and the expectation of interest rate movements in the future.

A vast number of interest rate products are available throughout the world, but not all are available to trade using CFDs. In fact, the main offerings for CFD traders come from the United States, the United Kingdom, Europe and Japan. This restriction on offerings isn't likely to represent too much of an issue for you, though, because the greatest liquidity lies in these four markets (traders like liquidity as it makes for less erratic price movements, meaning that they can easily get into and get out of positions).

You can trade CFDs over interest rate products issued for the short term all the way out to long-term bonds. A good starting point in the CFD interest rate products market is the Eurodollar contract, and US Treasury bonds and notes.

The Eurodollar is a highly liquid contract that is based on a 90-day debt issue, with the term actually referring to any US dollar-denominated fixed-interest investment made outside of the United States — not just Europe.

European contracts also offer very high levels of volume, which makes them popular with short-term traders, with the Euro-Schatz, Euro-Bobl and Euro-Bund being some of the best known products. The term structure of each of these is progressively longer, meaning that the underlying interest rate product has a longer and longer life span. In the United Kingdom, the Short Sterling and the Gilts are the main short- and long-term offerings, respectively.

In simple terms, a *note* is generally an issue that's short term in nature, whereas a *bond* is much longer term — some bonds run as long as 30 years. You don't have to worry about a treasury maturing, because you aren't planning on holding onto it that long. However, you do need to consider the impact that rollover at maturity of the CFD will have on the value of your trade. The prices of these instruments move up and down as economic expectations change and as market emotions drive prices higher and lower, so when your current contract rolls over automatically, you may pay a higher price for the new one. This rollover isn't the same as the maturity of the bond, though, which occurs at the end of the 30-year life span.

The key thing about interest rate CFDs isn't the products themselves but what they represent for the market. When investors buy shares, they don't expect a set level of payment when they sell those shares, but with interest rate products traders know upfront the amount that they'll be paid in the future if they hold the product until maturity. So, although returns on interest rate products aren't usually as high as returns on shares, interest rate products are more certain. As a result, in times of economic uncertainty you may see a rush of investors moving into interest rate products. Conversely, if the wider market has a growing risk appetite, you may see money flowing out of interest rate products and into higher paying but more risky instruments.

Prices and yields

The price and yield of interest rate products are said to have an inverse relationship, meaning that as the price falls, the yield rises, and vice versa. Here's why. If a bond starts life priced at $100 and pays a coupon (the term used to describe how interest is paid) of $10, then the interest rate is 10 per cent per annum (10/100 × 100).

If prevailing interest rates are expected to fall, investors will lock in existing high interest rates, which may drive the bond price higher to, say, $110. The bond still pays a coupon of $10, but the yield has fallen to a little over 9 per cent per annum (10/110 × 100).

Yield is a way of expressing what investors will earn in interest if they buy the bond at the current price. If the price moves higher or lower, the yield changes too. Yield is calculated as coupon/price multiplied by 100 (to make it a percentage).

Following Important Economic News From Around the Globe

No matter what products you're trading, you always know that their price is determined by the balance of supply and demand.

- ✓ **Demand.** For many commodities, like wheat, demand remains consistent, because people need it all the time. For other commodities, like copper and aluminium, the level of demand reflects the strength of the global economy (or the outlook for it). This means that your view on the outlook for the economy can have a large impact on your view of commodities that are impacted by economic growth levels.

- ✓ **Supply.** You can often find information online to help you determine supply levels of various commodities. For example, the exchanges themselves may give 'warehouse reports' and organisations such as OPEC give their own expectations for oil supplies. If demand increases and supplies remain constant, prices will rise. As an illustration, if no more copper is mined but demand for copper grows (for example, due to huge numbers of houses being built), then the price for copper will rise. Similarly, even if demand for some types of crops remains quite consistent, expectations of falls in supply due to drought or unseasonable weather destroying crops may cause prices to rise. Alternatively, if crop harvests are very good, supplies will be high and — all other things being equal — prices will fall.

Agricultural commodities are heavily influenced by seasonal conditions. This is why large differences in CFD prices occur at different times of the year. For instance, cattle prices may be relatively cheap in December if there's a drought, but much more expensive the following June if the drought is expected to break and farmers are holding onto stock to rebuild their depleted herds. Conversely, grain prices will be high if there's a drought due to lack of supply, but prices will be lower in the future if the drought is expected to break and the next harvest is expected to be large. It's always more interesting to perform analysis if you can visualise a story around what's happening in the market you're interested in.

When you start dealing in commodity CFDs, you need to develop an understanding of how money flows through the national and global economies. The wonder of commodities is that you get a great feel for cause and effect. For example, when a long drought strikes in a certain area of the world (such as Australia) you may see wheat prices in Chicago going higher because global supplies are lower.

Here's another example of cause and effect in commodities: If inflation and inflationary expectations are on the rise, people may wish to defend the value of their assets by buying gold and pushing its price higher. The same expectation may be held of movements in oil. A series of ructions in the Middle East may cause concerns about a drop in supplies of oil, which in turn pushes gasoline prices higher and drives up inflation. Traders may again turn to gold to defend the value of their funds.

For more information on broader economic factors and how causes and effects can move prices, see Chapter 10.

The following roundup highlights some of the key market and economic factors that traders look at when considering whether to buy or sell commodities and interest rate products.

- ✔ **Energy stocks:** Nothing moves energy prices more quickly than geopolitical tensions. The market will immediately assume that supplies are going to be limited, so prices rise.

  Several regular reports impact the market when they're released, particularly the US Department of Energy inventory report. This report outlines the status of US supplies: If supplies are lower than expected, this tends to have an upward impact on prices.

  Seasonality broadly impacts on prices too, particularly the northern hemisphere winter. If the weather is colder than expected, demand for heating oil rises, pushing prices higher. OPEC decisions also impact oil prices. The general rule is that when OPEC reduces supplies, prices go higher; and when OPEC increases supplies, prices go lower.

- ✔ **Grains:** Much of the wider price impacts on grain prices come from the stocks that are available at the end of the growing season. The lower the stocks, the higher the price. Crop reports are released regularly to help with estimates. Not surprisingly, the weather impacts on prices, too, with less-conducive growing conditions increasing prices due to shortness of supplies.

- ✔ **Industrial metals:** In general terms, the higher the overall level (and expected future levels) of global economic activity, the more demand there'll be for industrial metals.

When you consider that industrial metals are used in such a wide range of applications, you may wonder how economic growth can be achieved without them.

A good specific measure of how supply and demand for industrial metals are balancing against one another is to look at the warehouse supplies at COMEX (the Commodity Exchange in New York) and the London Metals Exchange (LME). If stock levels are high, either production is very high or demand is very low. When COMEX and the LME release such data, you'll find plenty of market commentary available: Check out sites like Bloomberg (www.bloom berg.com) to find out what the consensus opinion is saying.

✔ **Livestock:** Some of the same factors that affect the grain market impact on the livestock market. A colder season can see cattle gaining less weight, which makes them less valuable to farmers. In addition, a bad growing season for corn and soy beans may see prices for feed climb, and if cattle prices are not high, farmers may prefer to sell their cattle cheaply rather than pay for expensive food — which can negatively impact cattle prices.

✔ **Precious metals:** Demand for precious metals can come from the industrial side of the market, the retail side of the market and from investors looking to store value. Some of the key holders of gold looking to store value are the central banks around the world. When central banks choose to buy or sell gold, this can naturally have a large impact on supply and demand. The state of inflation globally can also have significant impacts on gold prices as other participants in the market try to hedge against weakening currencies.

✔ **Treasuries:** Inflation is one of the major factors that impacts on the yields paid by treasuries. Essentially, yield means the return. In most treasuries, the interest payment is a fixed amount, say, $4 per $100 bond: The yield is simply the return expressed as a percentage (in this case, $4/100 \times 100 = 4$ per cent). This relationship means that as price increases, yield decreases, and vice versa: This is referred to as an inverse correlation. If you hold a treasury that pays 4 per cent per annum and inflation is running at 3 per cent per annum, you're making a real return (the return you receive minus the rate of inflation) of 1 per cent. If inflation rises to 4 per cent, your real return is 0 per cent. As inflation — and equally importantly, inflationary expectations — increase, so too do treasury yields to compensate for the negative impact of inflation.

Inflation can also impact on future interest rate expectations: If inflation is high, the market may consider that interest rates are more likely to rise. You'll see interest rates on existing interest rate products move higher in anticipation of this type of change in expectations, because as people sell the existing bonds (which are now less attractive) the yields rise. This movement in the value of bonds generally is why the market watches the central banks for guidance on future interest rate movements, as well as combining guidance with the broader economic picture (determined by analysts and economists) for a better lead on overall expectations.

The main measure of inflation is the consumer price index (CPI), which I discuss in Chapter 10.

Part III
Keeping Risk Under Control

Glenn Lumsden

*'I still say that stop orders
are for sissies.'*

In this part ...

*T*rading CFDs allows you to access a wide range of markets around the world. However, managing risk, which I focus on in this part, is one of the most important aspects of CFD trading.

You have a great trading tool in CFDs, but if you don't understand the downsides of using leverage, or you don't apply stop losses effectively and manage your position sizes, you're sure to get burnt.

Chapter 8

Managing Risk Is Your Key to Trading Survival

*U*sing leveraged trading products is easy and fun up until the point when you begin losing money and realise your trek towards financial security is even further away. One of my favourite Homer (Simpson) quotes illustrates this: 'After years of disappointment with get-rich-quick schemes, I know I'm going to get rich with this scheme ... and quick!' This is funny, but don't ever let anyone tell you that trading is a sure-fire way to get rich quick.

A good friend of mine rides a motorbike and when he was learning to ride, his instructor told him that he always needed to be wary of reaching the point where he felt comfortable on his bike — he'd relax, then go faster, and then have an accident. Think of your trading in the same way. Just when you think you've mastered it, you're usually about to get a lesson in humility. The one thing that makes for successful trading — more than any other factor, such as picking the right position — is your ability to manage risk.

In this chapter, I explore some of the major issues surrounding risk management and look at how you can start managing your own trading portfolio based on a carefully thought out plan that involves the use of stop loss orders and other risk-reduction strategies. I talk about the special care you need to take when trading foreign exchange CFDs and how to use diversification and exposure to minimise risk. And I also discuss how you can get too cocky and start playing with CFDs rather than being conservative and planning. Dreaming about winning trades is fun, but you're better off spending time thinking about how you manage the losing trades in order to survive.

Keeping a Lid on Leverage

Managing risk varies depending on the type of product that you're trading because some trades are inherently more volatile than others, and some trades are more liquid than others. You need to take these factors into account when considering the overall leverage (see Chapter 1) that you're willing to apply to your CFD portfolio.

When you're trading in CFDs one of the things to remember is that you can employ a lot of leverage. When I say a lot of leverage, I really do mean *a lot*! A line I've been using for years in reference to trading parallels life: 'Just because you can do something doesn't mean that you should'. This line rings true for leverage too. No hard and fast rules dictate how much leverage is too much, but you should exercise caution and minimise your risk.

 Before you buy CFDs you need to decide the maximum amount of leverage that you are willing to apply to your capital. This is one of the best ways that you can manage your risk. I suggest that you incorporate no more than 3× leverage for the majority of your CFDs trading. At this level you're still attaining significant leverage on your capital without being overly aggressive.

These days a lot of share CFDs only require a 3 per cent margin payment, so if you put all of your capital into CFDs with that requirement then you would have 33× leverage. To calculate how much leverage you're currently employing, take the total *exposure* that you have to all markets in your CFD account and divide it by the amount of cash that you have in your account. Simple, right? Exposure is simply another way of referring to the total value of all the positions that you hold with your CFD provider and can act as a fantastic guide to tell you if you are carrying too many positions or positions that are too large.

Example: If your account has $60,000 worth of positions (trades) and you have $20,000 cash in your account then you have applied 3× leverage (60,000/20,000) to your money.

Avoid falling into the trap of thinking that if you apply a huge amount of leverage to your account you only need a small move in your favour to make a lot of money. Instead, consider that, at 33× leverage, you only need a 3 per cent move against you and all your money is gone!

Using more moderate amounts of leverage also provides returns, but allows you to absorb a lot more movement in the share price against you.

Table 8-1 outlines the way in which the application of leverage can have a negative impact when prices move against you. The table shows leverage applied to an account of $1,000. The figures in italics illustrate where the total loss of your trading account has occurred and you actually owe money to the CFD provider. If you fully lever on a CFD that requires a 3 per cent margin, then the share price moves against you by 3 per cent, your money is all gone. Each column shows the application of leverage growing the returns in both directions — you can see that when you apply a lot of leverage it doesn't take a lot for you to lose all of your money, no matter how much you have.

Why luck doesn't figure

Some people adopt a 'have a go' approach to CFD trading. Simply having a positive attitude isn't enough — a lack of planning inevitably leads to losses. The most likely outcome is that you'll lose money and stop trading after becoming very frustrated. You may decide to have another go down the track but you'll simply make the same mistakes.

Don't let yourself be lulled into thinking that trading involves some magic strategy or the need for a lot of luck.

If you think that you only need a few wins in a row to get ahead you're in for a shock if you've been sharply increasing your position sizes with each winning trade. When you make the inevitable losing trade you'll end up right back where you started because the big loss at the end wipes out the smaller profits you accumulated along the way. See the sidebar 'Messing up with martingale', later in the chapter, for information on betting strategies and the weaknesses inherent in doubling up your losing positions.

Table 8-1			Applying Leverage to Trades			
Share Price	*1x*	*3x*	*6x*	*10x*	*20x*	*33x*
0.95	–50	–150	–300	–500	*–1,000*	*–1,650*
0.96	–40	–120	–240	–400	–800	*–1,320*
0.97	–30	–90	–180	–300	–600	–990
0.98	–20	–60	–120	–200	–400	–660
0.99	–10	–30	–60	–100	–200	–330
1.00	1,000	3,000	6,000	10,000	20,000	33,000
1.01	10	30	60	100	200	330
1.02	20	60	120	200	400	660
1.03	30	90	180	300	600	990
1.04	40	120	240	400	800	1,320
1.05	50	150	300	500	1,000	1,650

CFDs are generally a non-advisory product, so no-one is going to stop you from making a very large trade like some of those listed in Table 8-1, especially the 10×, 20× and 33× columns.

Whatever percentage margin you pay (for example, 2 per cent or 5 per cent), if the share price moves against you (falls), you'll lose your margin payment. How much margin you pay is up to you, and you decide your margin by determining your position size (see Chapter 9).

Using Stop Loss Orders

A *stop loss order* allows you to close out a losing position to minimise the loss of capital. It allows you to plan ahead with your trading so that you know when your trade has failed and the position has moved too far against you (refer to Chapter 1).

Although you don't need to place a stop with your provider when entering into trades, I recommend that you do. Experienced traders sometimes prefer to close out the position themselves when their perceived stop loss point is reached. However, I don't suggest that new CFD traders do this, even when you're constantly monitoring the trade. Stopping a trade this way requires a higher degree of discipline. Often, in a situation where a position reaches the point where it needs to be closed, the trader does nothing and waits to see what happens next. If the position continues to slide then the trader may find it even more difficult to close it out.

Depending on what you're trading, you need to allow a decent amount of wiggle room when placing a stop loss. The industry expression *wiggle room* refers to the room that you give a position in order for it to survive minor downward movements. Although you should use stop loss orders every time you trade, don't place them too close to your entry point.

Putting your stop loss order only a few cents away from your entry point may seem like a good idea, but the problem with doing this is that you greatly increase your chance of getting stopped out if the price drops slightly. Sure, every trader's aim is to enter a position and see it move immediately in their favour (rather than downwards towards the stop order), but this won't happen all the time.

Don't give losing trades legroom

Some people are inclined to want to close out winning positions quickly and give losing positions the benefit of the doubt. Why do traders do this? I suspect that these decisions reflect the way that people mentally account for things. If you close out a winning position then you can add another tick to the wins column, regardless of how big the win might be, right? If you let a losing position continue to run then as long as it remains open it could come good. Yes? If you leave losing trades open then they 'might' come good again. Get into the habit of closing the losing trades quickly; they might come back but the ones that don't can significantly weigh on your capital.

If you were asked: 'Will the next move of the share price be up or down?' what would your answer be? You might respond that there isn't enough information for you to answer. What if I let you look at a chart? Or last year's earnings report? Or a broker recommendation? All of these things might help with your predictions of future movements, but they won't help you work out the problem in front of you. No matter how talented the trader, picking the next movement of price is no more accurate than flipping a coin.

Messing up with martingale

Remember that in all things finance if you think you've found an invincible risk strategy then you should safely assume that you're wrong — there's no such thing as a sure thing!

The way that smaller and larger positions relate to one another in gambling or betting strategies is referred to as *martingale*. Martingale requires you to increase your position size each time you lose in the hope that an eventual win will recover all previous losses. The anti-martingale approach increases bets after wins, while reducing them after a loss.

The best example of martingale in action is at the casino when you're betting on red or black on the roulette wheel. Each time you lose you bet on the same colour next turn but double your bet. This way you benefit from a big win once you actually win.

Sound foolproof? It's not — the casino has table limits (the maximum amount that you can bet) in place for this very reason because even from the minimum bet you'll hit the table limit very quickly. This is also why you have to bet a little bit more to play colours so that you hit the limit even more quickly.

Following this type of ideal into trading leads to very high risk and very poor risk/reward trades and you should avoid these types of strategies at all costs.

The opposite strategy, anti-martingale, is more sensible because it allows you to add to your position size as you're winning.

I look in more detail at a number of rationales that traders can apply to the thought process of trading in Chapter 15.

The best rule to follow is to place your stop loss order at the point where you know you were wrong about the trade — the point where your *original* reason for being in the trade no longer exists.

The reason I stress 'original' in the preceding paragraph is because, through a combination of technical and fundamental analysis (or gut feeling), you can always come up with a reason for being in a trade. Just take a look at the hundreds of different indicators that exist in charting software. If you want a chart to tell you that you should stick with the trade you'll be able to find one. However, this makes for very poor risk management.

Example: In the chart shown in Figure 8-1 the position has broken through a resistance level (which, to many traders, indicates a buy). It fails to continue to move higher and eventually falls below the old support level. This means that your reason for being in the position no longer exists.

Figure 8-1: A breakout chart showing it's time to close out.

Stop loss order hybrids

Different CFD providers take different approaches to stop loss orders. The biggest distinctions occur between the two main types of CFD providers — the market makers and the DMA providers (for more information on how these CFD providers operate, refer to Chapter 2).

In terms of managing your risk, the market makers offer clients the closest to how most people would perceive a stop loss order to work: When the price in question is reached the position is closed. A DMA provider will use what is called a *contingent* order. This type of order waits for the stop price to be hit and then places a market order for the position to be sold (refer to Chapter 1).

In normal market conditions the two different methods should yield you the same result. The difference occurs at market opening times as well as in very volatile markets.

In order for the DMA stop loss to be executed the market needs to trade at the level of the contingent order. If it fails to do so then nothing happens to your order. This can be a problem if you're away from your trading screen and can't monitor the situation.

Market makers on the other hand will be able to execute your order at what they will refer to as 'the first available price'. This means that if the market doesn't trade at the level you wanted, then your stop is executed at a level somewhere below that. Even though you may not get your exact price, at least the position will be closed.

Allowing for market depth

Market depth shows you how many buyers and sellers are interested in the same CFD that you are. It shows the number of buyers there are in order from highest bid to lowest and on the other side shows you the lowest price seller to the highest. This means that the closest buyer and seller price will be at the top of the list. This way you can easily see what price you can buy or sell for. Not all markets have this type of screen. Share CFDs show this but foreign exchange CFDs don't — you just see the price at which you can buy or sell. To understand how a market maker times the closing of your position, Table 8-2 shows the number of shares wanted at each price and the number of shares for sale at each price, as well as the last traded price (although this may not be shown by your CFD provider).

Table 8-2	Looking at Market Depth to See When Stops are Triggered		
Number to Buy	**Bid (Buyers)**	**Ask (Sellers)**	**Number to Sell**
Last Trade	$9.52		
2,000	$9.50	$9.52	5,000
12,000	$9.49	$9.53	300
6,000	$9.47	$9.55	1,300
2,000	$9.44	$9.56	7,000
3,000	$9.43	$9.57	8,000

In this case, if your stop loss price was $9.50 and you were selling 1,000 share CFDs, then your position would be filled immediately even though the price has not yet traded at $9.50. Why? Well, it happens like this.

CFD providers (like traders) don't know what the market will do next so this means that they will take action as soon as they have to so they have the best chance to execute the stop at the price the trader wants. This may mean that as soon as the bid price matches the stop loss price the client has nominated, the order will be executed. (Although some providers will wait until the instrument actually trades at the nominated level before executing the stop order.) If you waited, then the bid might become lower with the price you receive becoming worse. Sometimes this turn of events will be frustrating if the price starts to move higher, but this is nothing to do with the CFD provider — it's just bad luck.

Allowing for volume shortfalls

If you deal in any product that has low volumes then you'll probably be impacted by slippage. *Slippage* occurs when you can't open or close a position entirely at the first available price because there isn't enough volume to fill your order. This can happen using either market or stop orders. Have a look at Table 8-3 to see what I mean.

Table 8-3	Market Depth with Weak Volume		
Volume	*Bid*	*Ask*	*Volume*
2,000	$9.50	$9.60	12,000
500	$9.49	$9.61	1,100
1,000	$9.48	$9.62	1,567
5,000	$9.45	$9.63	18,000
7,500	$9.44	$9.64	22,000
19,000	$9.43	$9.65	6,700
Last	**$9.60**		

If you have 5,000 share CFDs and you are dealing with a DMA provider, to sell here you wouldn't be able to sell them all at the highest buyer's price ($9.50). Instead, you would get 2,000 done at $9.50, 500 done at $9.49, 1,000 done at $9.48 and the rest done at $9.45.

With a market maker you would receive a 'requote' for a single price (which will likely be a weighted average of all the prices described previously). You should talk to your provider to find out exactly how it deals with this type of issue.

If in the example shown in Table 8-3 you had a stop loss order placed at 9.59 then as soon as the depth screen showed what it does here your stop would be executed — not at $9.59 but at $9.50.

Guaranteed stop loss orders

One feature that some CFD providers offer is the *guaranteed stop loss order* or GSLO. With a GSLO, traders lock in an exit price regardless of market movements. In the section 'Allowing for volume shortfalls', earlier in the chapter, I explain how slippage can impact on the amount of risk that you're actually taking with a given trade. A GSLO allows you to manage this risk very effectively.

The chart in Figure 8-2 shows a significant gap in the price. This could relate to bad company news or just general negativity in the market; whatever the case the share price has been hit hard. If you had a stop loss order in place anywhere in that section where no trades have occurred then you would have suffered slippage. If you had placed a GSLO, however, you would have exited the position at your nominated price because these don't require shares in the underlying market to trade at this price in order for the trade to be executed.

Figure 8-2: Gaps in the market can significantly add to your risk.

Like all things in finance, GSLOs have downsides too. Here are some points to consider:

- ✔ **You need to pay a premium to place a GSLO.** This is more than fair from the perspective of the CFD provider because it is taking on a large amount of risk when it comes to this type of order so the CFD provider deserves compensation for it. This payment may be a fixed dollar amount or payable pro-rata based on the size of the position that you hold. Expect to pay the normal commission on the order being executed in addition to the premium that you pay for the GSLO.

- ✔ **Your CFD will not allow you to place a GSLO very close to the current price.** Generally, a sizeable gap will need to exist between the current price and the closest level at which you can place your GSLO — 5 per cent away from current levels would be a reasonable expectation. Depending on the time frame over which you trade and your position sizes, this may be a lot or a little. (You can make adjustments for any amount of risk through the sensible use of position size calculations. To find out how, see Chapter 9.)

In normal trading conditions you don't really need to use GSLOs. But no-one knows when conditions will change from normal to abnormal. However, if trading using GSLOs makes you feel comfortable, then spend the extra money and use them.

Most CFD providers will only let you place a GSLO after the market opens (and you may have to do so over the phone). Whether your order is accepted or not will be at the discretion of the CFD provider — if you inquire about placing a GSLO on a company that's rumoured to be in financial difficulty, don't be surprised if the order is refused.

A GSLO allows you to manage risk in a similar way to an option because the downside is very specifically capped. The difference is that when the stop price is touched then the position is immediately closed out. Figure 8-3 shows that the price can rise higher in line with a rising share price, but on the downside it will go no lower than the GSLO price.

Some providers allow you to move GSLOs free of charge as the market moves higher, whereas other providers require you to cancel a standing GSLO before placing a new order (which requires you to pay the GSLO fee again). The details about this should be spelled out in the CFD provider's product disclosure statement (PDS).

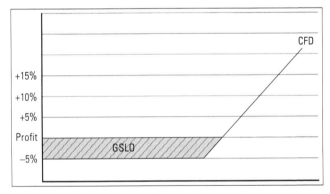

Figure 8-3: GSLOs provide a risk floor.

Reducing Risk on Foreign Exchange CFDs

Foreign exchange (FX) trading has a minimum trade size (almost universally) of US$10,000. So if you're planning on not having more than 3× leverage and have less than US$3,333 in your trading account then you won't be able to trade even the smallest amount. Here then you need to exercise judgement and care. Be sure to take on a position size that has you risking no more than 2 per cent of your trading capital (preferably lower, see Chapter 9) and, as a part of this, ensure your stop loss order is in place. Lastly, regardless of how much capital you have, start with the minimum trade size and go from there — this is a category that can really move. (For more information on trading foreign exchange, take a look at Chapter 5.)

From the perspective of managing risk, you need to take into account some very important features of trading FX CFDs. Most of the tips I present here reduce the risk of the trade that you're taking:

- ✔ **Almost all FX quotes are done to four decimal places.** If you have US$10,000 exposure and the market rises or falls by one increment then you'll receive a profit or loss of US$1. This means that even though the absolute exposure is quite large the incremental movement is quite modest.

- ✔ **FX is a 24-hour market.** The risk of gaps occurring in the price is much lower than something like shares, which may see large swings at the opening of trade each day. Large price swings do occur in FX trades, however, so your stop loss orders will be much more effective. The price can still gap in times of sudden market shocks or at the release of key pieces of economic data, though the high liquidity of FX CFDs does reduce some of the impact. As you can see in Figure 8-4, even the most heavily traded FX pair can move very quickly at the right time. The most active short-term driver of price is economic news.

✔ **Foreign exchange trades far outweigh the volume traded in any other financial market.** Even in turbulent times you can generally get in and out of positions very easily. Something else to consider is the potentially low correlation that FX may have to the share markets of the world, which means that you may gain some additional diversification benefits.

✔ **FX CFDs generally require a margin of 1 per cent, which means that the minimum transaction size will only require an initial margin of US$100.** Keep in mind that a lower margin requirement has nothing to do with keeping your risk lower.

All these points boil down to you being able to give FX some special treatment in terms of the overall leverage that you apply. However, this is reliant on you using stop losses with all of your positions, which allows you to very effectively manage your downside.

Figure 8-4: Big economic news can cause big moves in the market.

Spreading the Load with Diversification

Good, old-fashioned diversification can help you manage the risk of holding your trading portfolio. Although diversification is often thought of as suitable mainly for long-term investors, it also offers real benefits for CFD traders. You can have all of your exposure in one or two shares, but also invest in different products and asset classes that have CFDs available over them.

Diversification offers some real benefits, even on a day-to-day basis, because it can mean that you're less exposed to the ups and downs of the share market. Of course, simply focusing on individual products like indices is fine too — you're more likely to be able to keep a pretty close eye on the whole operation.

A number of very positive aspects about CFDs are glossed over by some traders who focus on things such as leverage and cheap commission. The following points provide some examples of how diversification works when trading CFDs:

- ✔ **You can easily access myriad products and asset classes all from the same account.** Diversification primarily refers to a wide spread of different share CFDs, but if you're looking at diversification to reduce volatility through spreading your exposure around, then you may be able to benefit even more by looking to different asset classes. You'll need to do more work to gain an understanding of these markets, but there can be real benefits from doing this.

- ✔ **You can be very creative.** Perhaps you see a long-term correlation between the oil price and the natural gas price but believe that oil is currently overvalued. Perhaps you could go short on oil and long on natural gas. This way you're keeping your overall exposure to energy small but trading the relationship between the two. This is known as a *pairs trade*, which I look at in more depth in Chapter 12.

✔ **If you study the state of the global economy you can use FX trades as a means of attempting to profit from the economy.** Perhaps you think the Australian dollar will do well due to expectations of strengthening commodity demand but the Euro will fall due to weak expectations of export demand from that area of the world. Perhaps you want additional exposure to copper and oil, based on this same rationale but want to go short on treasuries because you think upcoming interest rate changes will see prices fall.

These examples give you a good idea of the types of exposure that you can take on using CFDs. Keep in mind that you always want to be aiming to do better in terms of performance than you would be able to do by using index funds and cash in the bank.

If you have a portfolio of share CFDs that you've leveraged, you need to monitor your performance based on unleveraged returns. For example, if you have applied an average of 3× leverage, you need to divide your returns by three to get the outcome that is down to your trading skill; otherwise, you aren't deducting the effect of the leverage on your returns. Anyone can increase their returns (positive or negative) by adding leverage, but the true gauge of skill comes from what you can do before you lever your exposure.

Gaining Exposure

One of the best ways of reducing risk is to balance the long and short exposure you carry in your CFD portfolio. The difference between diversification and long or short exposure is that diversification aims to reduce volatility through spreading your money in different areas of the market, whereas the idea of long and short exposure allows you to actively pursue gains from both rising and falling share prices (for more information on long and short exposure see Chapter 3).

Futures contracts are one of the most important (and often misunderstood) types of derivatives. A futures contract enables traders to lock in the buy or sell price of an asset at a set price and a set date in the future. For traders who deal in shares, financial futures allow you to take exposure to a specific index. A good example in Australia is the SPI 200 futures contract. This is a futures contract that closely tracks the value of the S&P/ASX 200 Index. People who buy or sell this type of contract can take on broad and immediate exposure to a broad portfolio.

The Perils of Overconfidence

Overconfidence is a remarkably easy trap to fall into. I firmly believe in listening to the voice in your head that tells you not to get overexcited or overconfident about your trades. I have even said to people that I hope their first trade is a losing trade. I don't mean to be cruel, but I believe that losing trades make the best learning experiences.

'I'm better than average!'

Perhaps you are, but can you bank on it? In any given year you can expect the Australian share market to rise in value by around 10 per cent on average. This means that if you have a wide spread of share investments, 10 per cent is about what you would expect to earn. However, even the average fund manager will have difficulty beating the return of the market on a consistent basis. The average fund manager usually generates an average return. Now, before you begin to mock fund managers keep in mind that some mighty talented and skilled people work as fund managers.

'I don't need to be conservative'

I think you do. Overconfidence brought on by a few wins often leads to over-trading — placing trades for the fun of it, which is a very ineffective way of trading. Only after losing trades will you realise that being conservative and consistent in your analysis and risk management is what will make you an effective trader.

Do you remember the first trade that you ever took and how you were at pains deciding whether or not to take it? You checked your charts again and again before you decided to go for it. Whether you made money or not isn't my only point here. You were being conservative, working to a plan and doing your best to be an effective trader.

You need to develop your trading plan and your own personal discipline to the level that you can remain in control the whole time. I believe that this requires experience and learning from your mistakes (see the sidebar 'Ouch!'). Also, if you keep risk low from the outset you can learn from your mistakes without it costing you too much in capital.

Ouch!

I can remember the best trade I ever had. It happened many years ago and was amazingly profitable — but it was nothing short of a total fluke. However, rather than simply attributing the first outcome to luck I attributed it to my trading skills — a big mistake.

I was in my early 20s at the time and didn't really have a trading plan or much of a trading history. After my 'big win', though, I figured I was on to something and started making more trades.

After another two or three trades I had given back all of the profit and no doubt some of my original capital too. I discovered then that I needed to make a sensible plan and stick to it if I wanted to make a profit from trading.

Chapter 9

Position Sizing

*P*osition sizing involves linking the amount that you're willing to risk with your entry point and your stop loss order, taking on a 'position' that's appropriate for these different factors. Position sizing allows you to manage your risk (for more information on the range of factors involved in risk management, and stop loss options, see Chapter 8). Models for position sizing vary, but all are based on risking a certain amount of capital in a trade and then taking on the biggest position size that you can for that amount of risk.

Position sizing based on your risk tolerance and trading capital is the best way to develop a risk management strategy when you're trading CFDs. The essential rule is that if you risk less on each trade, then you can withstand a lot more losing trades and still survive. Yes, I know that considering the prospect of losing your capital isn't very pleasant, but the more upfront you are about the risks you face, the better you're able to assess ways to minimise them.

In this chapter, I look at the fixed dollar and the fixed percentage models, which are the most popular. Once you understand these key methods you can do your own additional research into others online if you choose. I also show you how to choose the right position sizing for you and how to use an average true range indicator to work out your trading range.

Basic Ways of Integrating Position Sizes and Stop Losses

When many people start trading they begin with a way of sizing their positions so that they can apply them consistently, buying the same dollar amount worth of CFDs each time they trade (say $3,500 worth of exposure in the market they're dealing in) and placing different-sized stop loss orders each time, depending on the perceived risks. Is there anything wrong with this method? Well, in short, no.

Every trader has a unique way of doing things and at the end of the day the really important thing is to understand your own methods and be comfortable with them. However, I don't think that this is the most efficient way to approach trading in CFDs. If you use a different-sized stop loss each time you trade, then you're taking more risk on some trades and less risk on others.

One way to solve this problem is to use the same stop loss magnitude each time you trade. When I say stop loss magnitude, or stop loss size, I'm referring to the distance away from your entry point that you place your stop loss order. In this way you're always risking the same amount on each trade that you take. However, you can run into problems sizing your position this way too, because sometimes you may be better off putting your stop loss closer to your entry point, or even further away.

Example: If you're dealing with a company that trades at a share price of $50 and regularly trades over a range of $0.50 from the high to the low on a given trading day then putting your stop loss $0.20 away from your entry point would not be a good idea because you're likely to get stopped out (see Chapter 3) because of normal market volatility. Conversely, if you were considering a company with a share price of $1.00 and applied the same stop loss size, the closed position would represent a loss of 20 per cent on the share's value — at which point you'd probably prefer not to be a shareholder in that company anymore.

Keep in mind that the closer your stop loss is placed the bigger the position that you can take — but you must take into account the volatility of the shares, otherwise you'll get stopped out on your trades frequently.

More often than not, you need to change your stop loss size to suit the trade. This also applies to trading methodologies when using technical analysis techniques. For example, traders who use chart breakouts are more likely to put their stops very close to the entry point because they can tell very quickly if the trade is going the wrong way, whereas a trend trader who is looking to capture bigger moves in the market is likely to give the position a lot more room to move. (For more information on trading using technical analysis techniques, see Chapter 13.)

If you're comfortable buying a set dollar amount each time you trade, such as $5,000 worth of CFDs (and adjusting your stop loss size to suit the trade), then you only need to be aware that your losses, when they occur, will range in size each time (and hopefully even out in the end). The best way to manage the downside using this method is to keep your exposure to the market conservative because otherwise the losses can become very large. Another option is to apply a more robust position sizing model, like the one I cover in the following section.

Position Sizing Using the Fixed Dollar Model

The *fixed dollar model* focuses on position sizing using a measured means of risk management.

To use this model you work out a loss level (expressed as a dollar amount, say $100) that you're comfortable with. This means that you're willing to lose $100 on each losing trade that occurs.

Example: Using this amount as a starting point, here's how to calculate how many CFDs to buy:

> **XYZ Ltd share CFDs**
>
> Current price: $2.00
>
> Stop loss placement: $1.90
>
> Share price risk: $0.10 ($2.00 – $1.90)
>
> Total $ risk: $100
>
> Number of shares: 1,000

You calculate the number of shares to purchase (1,000) by simply dividing the total dollar risk by the share price risk (your stop loss level). If the share price falls to your stop loss level you know your loss will be $100.

In order to improve the accuracy of your risk calculations, you also need to include commission charges in the equation. In this case you're risking $100 but your CFD provider will charge you $10 commission to enter the position and another $10 to exit the position, for a total of $20. Think of this $20 as risk too because whether you win or lose you'll still have to pay it. To incorporate this amount into the equation simply deduct the total commission from the total dollar risk and then recalculate the equation as follows:

$$\$100 - \$20 = \$80$$

$$\$80 \div 0.10 = 800$$

If you include commission in the equation you may end up buying fewer CFDs, but you'll have a much more accurate representation of your actual risk. Although it may not sound like a lot in absolute terms, failing to include your commission actually skews your risk quite significantly over time.

Applying the Fixed Percentage Model

Position sizing becomes a little more sophisticated using the fixed percentage model. One of the most popular methods of position sizing, the fixed percentage model is reactive to changes in your available trading capital.

To apply this model you work out the percentage of capital you're willing to risk on each trade. Probably the most popular amount is 2 per cent, sometimes referred to as the 2 per cent rule (see the sidebar 'Diverging from the 2 per cent rule').

Diverging from the 2 per cent rule

The 2 per cent rule is designed to keep you in the market for as long as possible even with lots of losing trades. You always risk 2 per cent of your available capital with this method and so if you have had a number of losses you will risk less because you are risking 2 per cent of a smaller amount of capital. Happily, if you have had lots of wins your positions will get bigger because your capital base has grown.

Unless you are very confident and have significant statistical evidence of the strength of your methodology, don't exceed risk per trade of more than 2 per cent. Each percentage extra that you risk will have a dramatic additional impact on your capital if you get stopped out on a number of positions in a row and this makes the chances of your eventual failure that much greater.

First, look at your available trading capital and then calculate what 2 per cent of it is. For example, if you have $10,000 in your account, 2 per cent is $200. Similar to the fixed dollar model this becomes the amount divided by your stop loss magnitude (which is the difference between your entry point and where your stop loss will be placed).

Example: Say you're buying CFDs at $1.90 and placing your stop loss at $1.75. In this case, you'd buy 1,333 CFDs. Don't forget to also include commission in this equation. Normally, commission costs are $10 to enter the trade and $10 to exit the trade, so you need to deduct $20 from the $200 you're risking, making the actual calculation $180 ÷ 0.15 = 1,200.

From this point on, the difference between the fixed dollar model and the fixed percentage model kicks in. The advantage of a fixed percentage model is that as your available capital increases (hopefully through a great deal of successful trading) so too will your position sizes. The percentage that you're risking remains the same at all times, but as the capital in your account grows, the percentage represents more in terms of dollars at risk.

As Figure 9-1 shows, your position sizes change when your available capital falls as well. If you suffer a string of losses and your trading account takes a beating, the fixed percentage model ensures you begin risking less per trade as a result. This method is designed to help you remain in the game.

Figure 9-1: Small risk allows a lot of losing trades.

Of course, you don't have to risk 2 per cent of your capital on each trade; you may decide to risk 1.5 per cent or even 1 per cent. Take a look at the comparative graphic in Figure 9-2 to see how much extra defence you receive by reducing your risk per trade by only 1 per cent.

Figure 9-2: Looking at comparative risk.

Getting Position Sizing Right

You may think that once you start to apply a position sizing model (like the ones I discuss in this chapter) that you can begin trading a large number of positions. In some cases you may actually be safer carrying more positions, depending on the methods you previously used, but don't go overboard. Before you decide which position sizing model to adopt, take a look at Chapter 8, which covers risk management and leverage limits. Keeping your leverage in check acts as a safeguard on the overall exposure that you're carrying in the market.

The overall leverage limits that you apply to your portfolio (discussed in Chapter 8) need to supersede the risk management that occurs as a result of either your fixed dollar or fixed percentage risk rules.

An unpleasant but important way of thinking about whether you can cope with all your positions is to add up what your costs would be if they were all stopped out simultaneously. Although this is unlikely it could still happen from time to time. Take a look at the chart of the S&P/ASX 200 Index in sharp decline in Figure 9-3 to see the kind of circumstances under which this very thing might occur.

Figure 9-3: Never assume the market will turn around quickly.

The chart in Figure 9-3 shows that whether you use wide stops and small positions, or close stops and big positions, at times you're more than likely to see a big part of your portfolio closed out.

When you're using a fixed percentage model, one more decision you need to make is how quickly you change the capital amount that you use in your calculations. Some people choose to simply look at the amount of capital in their accounts at the time of the trade and then base the amount of risk on that. Others review their account size periodically (perhaps once a month) and then base their calculation on that month-end figure. I personally prefer working with the month-end figure to allow for more ups and downs in the market. However, if you see a significant slide in the value of your account you may need to act more quickly than that.

The methods that I look at throughout this chapter can be applied across any type of tradeable product. You simply need to work out where you plan to enter a trade and where you plan to place your stop loss order — just remember to include commissions when dealing in products that charge them.

Some products, however, have a minimum position size, such as FX CFDs (refer to Chapter 5), which may require you to risk more than your chosen percentage under the fixed percentage model. If this occurs I suggest that you simply don't make the trade — you're better off missing out than risking too much on one trade.

Working with an ATR Indicator

Sometimes you may need a slightly different way to work out your position sizes to take into account factors such as volatility in the market or a product in your own portfolio.

Analytical tools, such as volatility-based indicators, can help you decide where to place your stop losses to make your position sizes as effective as possible. The best tool for working out your trading range is the average true range (ATR) indicator. The ATR indicator adjusts itself based on an instrument's recent trading activity. See Chapter 13 for more on using this technical analysis tool.

The benefit of following this type of indicator is that it allows you to place your stops to avoid getting closed out by market volatility factors (as mentioned in 'Basic Ways of Integrating Position Sizes and Stop Losses' earlier in this chapter and in Chapter 8). Generally traders look at the ATR and then multiply it by two or three to ensure plenty of distance between the market and the stop loss. For example, if the ATR indicator reads 28 or $0.28 then a 2ATR stop loss would be placed $0.56 away from your entry point.

Part IV
Trading Strategies

Glenn Lumsden

'I've been searching pork belly futures
and the news isn't good.'

In this part ...

Good trading strategies are creative. With this in mind, the chapters in this part explore some different types of trading methods and hedging strategies, and look at different ways to use them.

To apply trading strategies effectively you need to know how to interpret economic data and use ratios to compare listed companies. You also need to know how to make the most of charting software for technical analysis.

Chapter 10

Making Informed Decisions Based on the Economy

· ·

In This Chapter

▶ Looking at interest rates

▶ Taking a look at economic growth

▶ Watching employment figures

▶ Applying basic fundamental analysis

· ·

*A*lthough many traders focus on charts for technical analysis (see Chapter 13), making informed decisions requires an understanding of what drives prices from a fundamental perspective (that is, the earnings that a company can generate or, in terms of commodities, the surplus of demand over supply). The economic factors that have an impact on the value of your CFDs are

✔ Interest rates

✔ Inflation

✔ Economic growth

Economics, broadly, is the study of the allocation of scarce resources. *Economic drivers* are central to factors such as supply and demand, which drives all prices up and down (whether you're dealing in shares, commodities, foreign exchange or treasuries). When new economic information is announced, the market reacts either by increasing prices (through greater demand) or decreasing prices (through greater supply). This market correction returns the market to something close to equilibrium where all known information is reflected in the price of relevant financial instruments. You see this type of market reaction markedly, for example, in the values of different currencies, which can move rapidly on the release of new economic data.

The interesting thing about looking to economics to determine potential drivers of prices isn't so much in the figures released (which you may or may not find interesting) but, rather, in the interconnection of money, flowing from sector to sector and country to country. So much of what drives the economy boils down to the ease with which governments and companies obtain funds, and where this funding goes in the economy.

In this chapter, I look at some of the key economic releases that can impact both the short-term and longer-term prices of all financial instruments. I also look at some of the issues that traders need to consider at the time data is released so that you can continue to manage your risk in times of uncertainty. And I give you an understanding of major economic information and also some of the key fundamental pricing considerations that you need to make to determine appropriate valuations of different financial instruments.

Understanding the Economic Impact of Interest Rates

Interest rates are an economic factor central to so many aspects of business, from the retail customer all the way through to corporate and government investors. Interest rates determine the cost of borrowing for investors as well as for corporations. The more expensive the cost of borrowing, the more expensive funding an expansion into new areas or funding an acquisition becomes.

Changes in interest rates are often a response to inflationary pressures on an economy. Before embarking on CFD trading, you need to know what inflation is and how this measure of an economy itself is captured. *Inflation* quite simply looks at the increase in the cost of a basket of consumer goods. This measurement is referred to as the *Consumer Price Index*, or *CPI*, and tells an important story about the cost of living changes that people are exposed to.

An increase in the CPI is the *inflation rate*. Movements of interest rates are frequently cited as a response to inflationary pressures.

Note: A product that you buy at the store is just like any asset — the more demand for it, the higher the price goes up. Supply constraints can also drive inflation. An example may be infrastructure constraints that have seen supplies slow down (or be bottlenecked) in some commodities; which drives up the price of what is available.

Different investments become more or less popular in times of high inflation. Possibly the most notable of these is gold, which is seen by investors as an *inflation hedge*, which means the investment often rises in value as inflation increases.

Because the value of currency diminishes in times of high inflation, more stable investments like bonds and other fixed interest products are affected in a negative way because the interest payments are now worth less due to the declining value of the currency.

You can find statistics, information about the state of play with inflation and current interest rates in Australia at the Reserve Bank of Australia's (RBA's) website (www.rba.gov). If you're looking for foreign information, then simply search for the relevant country's site — most of them are excellent at providing information to the public. For example, type into your favourite search engine **England, interest rates**.

Borrowing as a source of funds

Despite the recent economic meltdown doing extreme damage to the popularity of borrowing to fund company investment, it's sure to remain a major component of doing business for all companies.

Interest rates play a lead role at central banks when implementing their monetary policy objectives. Monetary policy is the tool that central banks (like the RBA and the Federal Reserve in the United States) use to control the supply of money in the economy. The lower that interest rates are, the easier it is to borrow, and the more that entities are likely to borrow.

Borrowing isn't the only source of funds that a company can use to expand. *Listed companies* (those that are traded on a stock exchange) can issue new shares to the public. When these shares are bought by investors, the company can use the funds to finance new ventures.

Interest rates and inflation

Low interest rates may sound like the way in which you would want to have interest rates set all the time, but if you do this then spending may start to run out of control and push prices up. Yes, the result is inflation. Higher prices reduce the value of the currency. If inflation gets too high, you end up with what is known as *hyper-inflation*, which is akin to requiring a wheelbarrow full of cash simply to buy a loaf of bread — clearly not something you want to have happen too often. Hyper-inflation can occur in all sorts of economies, with Germany seeing inflation of more than 20 per cent per day in the early-1900s. The most recent example is Zimbabwe, where inflation got close to 100 per cent per day.

Management of listed companies weighs up the pros and cons of issuing shares or borrowing to fund their ventures. The downside of borrowing is that, no matter what, you need to pay the lender back — if you don't you're in default and the whole company can then be in trouble. The upside is that you can pay back and, thereby, retire the debt. Shareholders are much more difficult to get rid of, and if they aren't happy with the way management runs a company, the shareholders can oust directors. However, unlike debt you don't need to pay back shareholders and in fact you can even stop paying them dividends, which adds to flexibility. Nothing is ever easy in finance.

Understanding the link between inflation and monetary policy

The concept of inflation (refer to the section 'Understanding the Economic Impact of Interest Rates', earlier in this chapter) can be kind of interesting to most people who are interested in finance. For the trader though, inflation data is important because an analysis of it provides a view to the future.

Both the federal government and the central bank in Australia (the RBA) play a role in controlling inflationary pressures:

> ✔ **Federal government:** Employs what is known as
> *fiscal policy* — for example, making changes to the level
> of taxation and government spending, which can make

the purchasing or the deferring of purchases relatively attractive to one another.

✔ **RBA:** Employs what is known as *monetary policy*. The RBA has a target rate of inflation (2 to 3 per cent over the economic cycle) and adjusts interest rates accordingly to keep the rate of inflation within this band as far as possible — with a view to making consumption and investment more or less attractive.

The main measure of inflation is called *core inflation*, which excludes volatile items such as petrol and fresh food. Goods and services that fall outside of those few excluded items are those that are monitored for upwards and downwards changes in price.

Keep in mind the following important relationships between inflation and monetary policy:

✔ Central banks around the world want to keep inflation under control because it weakens the value of money, which impacts upon low or no growth investments, like savings accounts, the worst.

✔ Depending on inflation levels, central banks are likely to respond with raising or lowering their level of interest rates.

✔ High inflation equals higher interest rates, which is otherwise known as tightening monetary policy.

✔ Low inflation equals lower interest rates, which is otherwise known as loosening monetary policy.

✔ Of all the financial instruments that you can trade CFDs on, foreign exchange (FX) responds immediately to inflation data as it's released to the market. Ordinarily, if inflation is higher than expected, you see the currency value increase in anticipation of higher rates from the central bank. The reverse is also true.

✔ Traders need to consider comments that come from the central bank because this information gives hints about how aggressively the central bank is likely to attack inflation and inflationary concerns.

✔ Like the FX market, the treasuries market similarly adjusts to interest rate changes quickly. The treasuries market usually doesn't alter much if the inflation data comes out in line with expectation because markets adjust their prices according to expectations over time. If interest rates move surprisingly higher, though, then the value of treasuries is expected to fall as a result, and the converse also applies.

✔ Equity markets adjust to interest rates more slowly than either the FX market or the treasuries market. Increasing rates (or the expectation of higher rates because of inflation data) impacts first on companies carrying large amounts of debt because they have to service a higher interest bill.

✔ Higher interest rates can often weigh on consumer discretionary stocks, as well, because consumers have less discretionary spend. (You see a flow-on effect in the wider economy, too, which becomes apparent in many areas of the share market.)

✔ In Australia, if the RBA is going to move interest rates, it does so always on the first Tuesday of the month (though, of course, interest rates are not always adjusted). To keep on top of what the RBA is thinking, check out its website (www.rba.gov), which is full of good information that can help you to understand what is likely to drive RBA thinking in the future.

Going bananas

When Cyclone Larry crossed the tropical north Queensland coast near Innisfail on Monday morning of 20 March 2006, few anticipated the ensuing connection of banana price to inflation. In fact, a spike in the rate of inflation in Australia in large part was due to higher banana prices. The cyclone wiped out crops in Queensland, which sent the price of this Aussie favourite of fruits higher (as always you can see supply and demand at work). Though this crop is a fairly odd item to have such a profound effect on inflation, that's what happened. Hey, be glad you didn't have to report on banana-driven inflation — I did.

Turning an Eye to Economic Growth

Gross Domestic Product (or *GDP*) is a measure of the rate of growth of an economy. GDP looks at the amount of value added to the economy over a given period. GDP is calculated as the sum of private consumption, government spending, investment spending and net exports. In Australia, household consumption is the biggest individual constituent of GDP. The figure itself is released by the Australian Bureau of Statistics every three months and is backwards looking (a big reason people look to forecasts).

Naturally, economists want this figure to be positive but in the same way that inflationary pressures can have a negative impact on an economy, too high a level of economic growth can also have negative impacts on the overall economy because such growth can become very difficult to control. For example, asset prices can run at huge levels of growth, thereby driving up prices at an unsustainable rate. And a crash in share and property markets is a good example of what this out-of-control market looks like.

Instead of saying one level of economic growth is 'too high', economists look towards signals such as high inflation that comes about due to excessive demand and which may also be fuelled by high levels of borrowing. Then, the main way this situation is controlled by the central bank is to increase interest rates to make borrowing more expensive and therefore less attractive.

To counteract too high a rate of economic growth, Australia's central bank, the RBA, 'tightens' monetary supply for two reasons:

- ✔ To slow the demand for borrowing
- ✔ To make existing borrowings more expensive to service

When analysts sit down to value shares, they estimate the impact that strong economic growth is likely to have on the company. If expectations are quite high, then analysts may increase their expectations of the price that the market is likely to push the share price to. Analysis doesn't stop here though. Imagine that the GDP numbers for an economy are strengthening such that concern develops about inflation getting out of control. If such an outcome is the case, the overall market may start to increase demand for that currency in anticipation of higher interest rate payments. Even this development isn't the end. If a consensus opinion forms, then you're likely to see people selling *treasuries* (interest rate products such as bonds and bills, which are issued by governments — see Chapter 7), which in turn forces down prices and forces yields higher. This theme of interconnectedness is the pertinent fact about the economy: Ordinarily, you don't see one economic factor occurring without another one being affected.

Two things about interest rates are worth covering in a little more detail (especially if you're interested in trading different types of CFD products):

- ✔ **The notion of higher interest rates having a positive impact on the value of a currency:** Though not the only factor, the *interest rate differential* (that is, the rate that one country pays relative to another), is one of the main influences on the value of a currency. If one country has a higher rate of interest, then that country is going to attract investment, which has to be made in the country's currency. This offer of a higher interest rate creates demand from investors buying more bonds that must be paid for in that currency, which then pushes the value of that currency higher.

- ✔ **The value of the treasuries (bonds):** If prices go up, then yields go down. Plain and simple, but the impact isn't as bad as you may think. When a bond is issued, the issuer agrees to pay a rate of interest over the life of the bond (known as a *coupon*). When the bond is issued (usually at $100) the coupon makes up a percentage of the value of the bond. (*Note:* Bonds are issued by a number of groups, but CFDs are generally only available on bonds issued by governments — being the most liquid opportunities.) If the coupon payments are $10 a year, then this means a 10 per cent yield. Imagine though that the market thought interest rates were going to fall. This scenario would see more people trying to buy existing bonds in order to lock in the higher interest rate. Because of supply and demand, this heightened interest by others may push the price up to $110. The coupon payment remains the same; however, an inverse relationship comes in to play. The $10 coupon is now only a 9.1 per cent yield based on the $110 bond price. So what you see is the fact that as bond prices rise, yields fall. If bond prices fall then yields rise.

Economic growth moves in cycles over time. Periods of high growth in asset prices are associated with things like low interest rates and high commodity prices being balanced against the opposite things occurring, which leads towards the low ebb of the economy. These cycles are frequently illustrated using an *economic clock*, shown in Figure 10-1. ***Note:*** While these illustrations of the flow of money provide a neat guide, the cycle doesn't move in such a predictable or ordered fashion as Figure 10-1 implies.

When you study economic figures, the period-to-period data can be very volatile, so I suggest you take a step back and look at the overall trend.

Figure 10-1: An economic clock showing how money flows in and out of the economy over a cycle.

Looking at the Employment Link to the Economy

Another key aspect of the economic picture of a country is the level of employment or unemployment in the economy. The rate of employment in an economy influences a large number of factors, but without going into massive amounts of detail, perhaps just think about how feeling secure in your job makes you feel — hopefully (from an economic standpoint), it makes you feel the need for a new flat-panel television.

Why is making a purchase a good thing? When you buy the TV, your purchase helps to keep workers at the store in their jobs, which gives them an opportunity to go and buy something else from another store, and so on and so on.

Spending in one spot can bounce around and strengthen the economy in lots of other areas. In addition to which, a very strong workforce means good levels of production, which then force up GDP (refer to the previous section) and also help government revenues (which is then either saved for a rainy day — known as a *fiscal surplus* — or, alternatively, ploughed back into the economy to help promote growth in targeted areas).

The Goldilocks Economy

Economists use a term known as the *Goldilocks economy* when referring to the perfect economy — which, rather obviously, means an economy that is neither too hot nor too cold. You can see a perpetual balancing act going on the whole time. You want people to spend but not so much that it drives inflation or is fuelled by debt. You want people to save but not so much that it reduces spending, and so on in a very circular fashion.

One of the ways in which the overall sentiment of consumers is measured is with an index called (rather aptly) the *consumer sentiment index* (which comes from Westpac–Melbourne Institute Survey that you can search for on its website: www.melbourneinstitute.com). This survey-based methodology looks to the positive or negative sentiment of consumers. You may see this sentiment reflected in areas such as retail sales, which provide another important piece of economic data. Retail sales are important for the reasons mentioned in the preceding paragraph but also because the data helps to determine whether people are spending or saving.

Check out these websites for highlights of up-to-date employment figures:

✔ For local information, the best place to look up government data on the domestic economy (including retail sales and unemployment) is the Australian Bureau of Statistics website (www.abs.gov.au).

✔ The global highlight for unemployment figures is the US nonfarm payroll (www.bls.gov). These figures are closely watched the world over because the US economy is the world's largest and can have some spectacular impacts on other financial markets.

These lightning fast price movements are best illustrated with a look at the foreign exchange market where this release of data can have some stunning and sudden effects — like a shift of more than one cent in seconds (doesn't sound like a lot, but its impact is huge). You can find economic data on the foreign exchange market either on your CFD provider's website or a free site such as Bloomberg (www.bloomberg.com).

The copper connection

An example of how wide the implications of economic changes are can be felt locally upon the release of data relating to new home sales in the United States. The question to ask is: 'What companies in Australia might this have an impact on?' The most likely answer may be manufacturers of building products with exposure to the US market. However, if you look beyond the obvious, you can uncover other opportunities that exist outside of categories like home builders. For example, one of the biggest uses of copper is in the plumbing and wiring of new homes; so, if fewer homes are being built in the United States, some of the miners in Australia, too, are affected. This amazing reflection of the economy leads some people to suggest that copper is the only commodity with an economics degree!

Basic Fundamental Analysis

Economic information is one of the key factors that impacts on markets globally. In this section, I focus primarily on fundamental analysis of the share market and listed companies because, if you're like me, the share market is where you're going to spend much of your research time. Why? Because the implications of changes to the economic environment can reach into every product that you choose to trade or invest in and you're likely to want to keep your understanding of the current environment up to date.

Don't worry too much about the merits of fundamental analysis versus technical analysis. Both can be very effective tools when used properly. You can very suitably employ some fundamental tools as a means of determining your short list of potential trades (as covered in Chapter 13) and then use charts for technical analysis to better time your entry and exits.

Exploring company earnings and forecasts

What makes share prices move? Good question. Key economic factors that can affect share price movement include:

- **Risk versus reward:** An investor looks at all asset classes (such as property, shares, cash and bonds) and determines what to invest in based on the expected returns and his or her risk tolerance. Investors tend to seek the best investment on a *risk-adjusted basis* (they aim to invest in the best performing asset for the amount of risk they're willing to take).

- **Inflation:** As I explain in the section 'Understanding the link between inflation and monetary policy', earlier in the chapter, inflation diminishes the value of money. The higher inflation is the greater return the investor needs to generate in order to offset this figure. Returns generated minus inflation are known as *real returns*.

- **Factors of competition:** A company with the best management team, outlook and products is set to attract more investor demand, which can drive share prices higher.

A company's future earnings (rather than current earnings) drive the price of shares. As a result, the market is very interested when companies update their earnings forecasts. Traders especially tune in to these forecasts of company earnings because they give them an idea of what the share price should be right now. Simply put ... if expectations for growth of earnings are high, then people are willing to pay a higher price for shares.

Quarterly earnings forecasts are released and published by most companies as well as by analysts.

You can apply fundamental analysis to find out what you want to know about a listed company. In this instance, *fundamental analysis* boils down to the study of a company's future earnings and what they're worth in *today's money* (see the sidebar 'Today's dollar tomorrow', later in this chapter). This approach means focusing on cash flow and how much it's going to increase in the future.

The questions to ask start to get more interesting: For example, 'If I think this company is going to have growth of *x* per cent a year, then is this company the best option or is there a company with even better growth prospects in the same sector?'

The more cash that the company generates, the better the overall outlook is for the company. You have to offset this benefit against the price that you're paying for the shares. If the company has good growth prospects but a very high share price, then the question becomes, 'Is the growth expectation already "priced" into the shares; if so, are they then "over-valued"?' Great questions, hey?

Analysts are people, too. They can't be right all the time about the value of a company, and a lot of their expectations have to be based on forecasts. For this reason, analysts upgrade or downgrade their valuations of companies as the companies release their results because then analysts have new 'concrete' information to plug into their calculations.

Watch out for when a company revises its forecasts lower, because the share price reacts quickly and negatively. When this revision happens, you see the market revise the price that it believes the company is worth — in this case, lower. In the event of a downgrade, you're best to close out the position immediately if the price moves below your stop and then reassess the position. You're always best to be on the sidelines in times of turmoil. You're not able to sell your position prior to the news so this is just one of those dangers you have to face.

To understand how forecasts can affect a company, take a look at Figure 10-2. When new data is released, the impact on the company earnings is immediately reflected in the share price. For example, as soon as the market finds out the company is forecasted to earn less, the share price falls to reflect this anticipated change in future value. Sometimes, though, the market can overreact and push the price too low, after which the price may recover a little — when the market settles down again.

Figure 10-2: How forecasting affects a company's value.

Why is the share price falling so much and so quickly? Here are two reasons (one of which is inflexible in nature and the other flexible):

- ✔ Primarily, the market makes its assessment of a company's worth based on earnings expectations. For example, say a company is expected to earn $x for the full year. If the company then comes out and says it is only going to earn $x − 10 per cent (that is, just 90 per cent of what the market was expecting it to earn) then this figure is going to be reflected immediately in what the market now believes the shares are going to be worth. (This effect proves to be largely inflexible, because why would the market pay the same amount for a company that is going to earn less money? Of course, it doesn't.)

    The opposite of this scenario also applies but, regardless, it always seems that companies get punished a lot more than they get rewarded.

- ✔ The other factor affecting the company's share price is the general mood of the market at the time. This impact is difficult to quantify but, nonetheless, has a large effect. If you're in the early to middle stages of an aggressive bear market, then profit downgrades are likely to be treated very badly by the market. However, the sell-off may not be nearly as aggressive if the same information were released in the midst of a bull market. You can see in Figure 10-2 (see earlier) how aggressive a sell-off can be when the market is very bearish. (This factor tends to be more flexible, primarily because the market doesn't always react as outlined above.)

Using some simple ratios

Even if you're itching to tackle number crunching, you first need to develop your understanding of some of the rules that go along with the use of financial ratios when dealing in shares (and share CFDs as a derivative of the share price — refer to Chapter 1 for more information about how derivatives work). A *financial ratio* is a mathematical means of assessing specific attributes of a company. Typically, two or more components of the financial statements are used in a formula with the result either being compared to other companies or alternatively compared to common yardstick values.

A ratio on its own ordinarily tells you very little. In some cases, you can apply yardsticks (such as the price–earnings ratio — see the section 'Price–earnings ratio', later in the chapter) but, mostly, ratios rely on comparisons to determine a trend by:

- ✔ Comparing the ratio of one company to another
- ✔ Comparing the ratio of one company to previous measures

Today's dollar tomorrow

When referring to *today's money*, it means that you're 'discounting' future earnings into what they're worth today. Consider *compound interest* (interest earned on interest over time), which accelerates the rate of growth achieved. Discounting future earnings is the opposite of this compounding interest: You work out what the end figure at some point in the future is worth today. Another key point to consider is that a dollar today is worth more than that same dollar tomorrow because today I have the choice to spend or invest but, if I have to wait until tomorrow, I forfeit that choice, so I shouldn't expect the dollar to be worth as much.

Market capitalisation

Market capitalisation (usually abbreviated as MarCap in financial tables) is an important financial tool by which you can accurately compare the size of one company to another. (Many traders want to deal only in the largest companies available on the market — market capitalisation is the easiest way to put these companies in order.) Though not strictly speaking a ratio, you're best to get a handle on this concept if you want to make a go of your analysis of the market.

Using market capitalisation, you can make apples-with-apples-type comparisons of, say, the size of two companies. If, for example, one company has a share price of $10 and another a share price of $1, the first company can appear to be the biggest. This assumption may well be so, but the share price doesn't tell you anything about the size of the company. This point is where market capitalisation comes in — to give you the result of the share price multiplied by the number of shares on issue. To continue with the previous example: If the first company had one million shares on issue and the second company had ten million shares on issue, then both companies would have a market capitalisation of $10 million. This calculation provides a much better comparative tool than just looking at the share price of both companies, which only tells you a very small part of the story.

Earnings per share

The importance of comparing like with like becomes just as clear when comparing the *earnings per share* (EPS) of one company to another. Calculating the EPS gives you the earning for each ordinary share ordinarily over a 12-month period (a 6-month period is also possible depending on the reporting period you're looking at). This ratio is a good way to accurately compare the earnings of two companies because it removes the differences in the size of the companies by getting rid of the difference in the number of shares on issue.

The EPS formula is

> **Earnings per share (EPS) = Net profit for ordinary shareholders/Number of ordinary shares on issue**

In this case you take the profit of the company and divide it by the number of shares. The answer is a much more relevant figure than simply assuming or saying $10 million is a good profit — it might be, but how does it compare on a 'per share' basis?

A good exercise when working out a company's EPS ratio can be to go back and look at the previous EPS figures of the company. From this information, you may also be able to get an insight into whether the company is seeing growth in its earnings and whether it historically has had positive earnings. You can find this information from:

 ✔ Your CFD provider's website

 ✔ The website of the company in question

 ✔ A free site such as Bloomberg (www.bloomberg.com) or Yahoo!7Finance (http://au.finance.yahoo.com)

Price–earnings ratio

When you know the EPS (refer to the previous section) of the company in question, you can then go a step further and work on what's possibly the most popular of all the ratios — the price–earnings (PE) ratio. This ratio is one of the best known ratios because it allows the investor/trader to quickly get an idea of the value of the company relative to its earnings. This figure can then easily be compared to other companies that the trader may be interested in.

You calculate PE as follows:

$$PE = \text{Current market price/EPS}$$

The share price of a company isn't a good reflection of its earnings (but it is an excellent reflection of what the market thinks expected earnings is likely to be), in the same way that the share price isn't good for comparing a company's size (refer to the section 'Market capitalisation', earlier in this chapter). Say that you do this PE calculation and the result you come up with is ten. What is this number telling you? The answer is:

 ✔ At current market prices, you're paying a price that reflects ten years' worth of company earnings. Some analysts interpret this figure to mean that the company is likely to take ten years to repay the investment that you've made.

 ✔ You can very easily use this figure as a comparison of one company to another. (**Remember:** Ideally, companies within the same sector are the most comparable.)

Tempting though it may be, saying that the company with the lowest PE is the best value is a little too simplistic because, typically, companies that the market is expecting strong growth from are going to be trading at a higher PE.

 PE ratios can be based on both historical and future earnings expectations, with the latter being the most common. So, always keep in mind that when you're considering what the company is likely to earn, you're contemplating the future, not the past.

 If you buy into companies at high PE levels, you want to be very confident that the growth is going to be there to support this very high level because, if the market loses confidence and starts selling the shares of the high PE companies and buying lower (potentially better value) PE companies, the share price is going to fall.

Debt ratios

While dozens of ratios are available to you, the amount of debt that the company is carrying has to be an important factor in your decision making. When you look into the way a company finances itself, you're best to consider how much debt it carries because ... drum roll ... it always has to be paid back.

Two important debt ratios are

- *Debt to equity ratio* (which shows how much a company is financed by debt):

  Total debt/Shareholders' equity

- *Debt to assets ratio* (which shows how much debt the company has taken on in comparison to the assets it has — just like with your personal debts, which you don't want to outweigh your assets):

  Total debt/Total assets

Both of these ratios provide an insight into what a company is built on and how high its level of debt is. You may think that you want the company to have no debt, but this approach is a little too simplistic. Debt, when used sensibly, can greatly enhance the growth prospects of the company. However, too much can be a destabilising influence and can become dangerously difficult to service, especially during a market downturn (see the sidebar 'Sitting pretty').

Net tangible assets

One other equation to put to use is a company's *net tangible assets* (NTA), which allows you to look at what a company is actually worth if it were to sell all of its assets and pay off its debts. You calculate NTA as follows:

NTA = (Ordinary shareholders' equity – Intangibles)/Number of ordinary shares

The outcome of this equation gives you the worth of the company on a per share basis after repayment of debts.

Sitting pretty

During very strong bull markets, analysts focus on those companies with what people refer to as 'lazy balance sheets'; that is, those companies carrying little debt and, perhaps, not a great amount of growth prospects either. These companies often come under great pressure from the market to lever the balance sheet (borrow) and try to make the company grow faster. This pressure is often achieved by buying out another company or expanding existing divisions of the company. The market and analysts may use the argument that if the company has no need for the cash they hold, then it should be returned to shareholders. This is because investors would rather invest their own cash rather than have a listed company do it for them.

It was interesting to see the 'love' these companies got during the global financial crisis as the market turned on any company carrying significant levels of debt and rushed towards those that had very sustainable models and faced less impact during the crisis. However, when the market is bullish, it loves debt and can tolerate heaps of it. You have to pay the price though if the economy slows down, which is why you need to look deeper into the story — and your financial ratios can give you quite a bit of help with this scenario, too.

Chapter 11

Understanding Trading Methods

*O*ne of the biggest attractions of trading on the stock market is having a large degree of freedom to find your own way and to make your own decisions. This freedom means that the difficulties that present for anyone trying to catalogue the vast array of methodologies for trading CFDs — over different time frames — are the same for a seasoned trader as well as a novice. However, no matter what sort of time frame you're using and how you choose to approach the market, you're best to incorporate good risk management strategies into the equation.

In this chapter I take you through several of the more popular trading methods you may come across and also look at how you can apply these methods while employing risk management strategies to limit the downside of your positions when you lose.

Trading Methods and You

When you look back in years to come at the ways in which you approached your trading and, with hindsight, realise how your methods altered along the way, you're going to have a better understanding of two things:

- ✔ The kind of methods that most specifically appeal to you
- ✔ How these methods developed into a model that you refined specifically for your own preferences

Realistically, don't be disappointed with the outcomes of your first trading strategies. Knowing how trading methods are going to perform in real time is very difficult, no matter how carefully you test your strategies. Until you mix in a good dose of psychology (read 'greed' and 'fear') you're not going to know where a particular methodology is really going to take you.

Trading Over Different Time Frames

Before making any assessment of the benefits or otherwise of short-term (10 minutes to a few weeks) and longer-term (three months to a year) CFD trading methods, understanding one of the key implications of this marked-to-market settlement system is very important (see Chapter 1 for more on this).

At the end of every CFD trading session (meaning when the market closes for the day), all profits and losses are settled and every trader starts the next day with a clean slate. For the most part, this process doesn't make any difference to traders. However, one key implication is relevant — a trader doesn't have to sell a position (the CFDs that you currently hold) in order to benefit from a rise in its value. For example, if the value of that position rises $100 in a day, you're immediately able to put this money towards new positions or indeed withdraw it as cash from your account. The opposite also occurs if the value of the position falls, with the $100 being immediately debited from your account.

The key point about CFD trades is that unlike most investments you don't have to sell a position to receive the advantage of a beneficial price movement.

The distinction between short- and longer-term trading methodologies needn't be simply about which one allows you to get cash in hand more quickly (because the marked-to-market system takes care of that) but should be about the one that is the most suitable for you.

In any case, you have to work out the balancing act of benefits versus disadvantages that exist for short- and longer-term trading. The pros and cons of each include the following:

- ✔ **Short-term trading benefit:** You're able to lock in profits more quickly.

- ✔ **Short-term trading disadvantages:** You have to deal with narrower risk and reward margins, and your cost of dealing (as a result of more commission and/or spread costs) is higher.

- ✔ **Longer-term trading benefit:** Your profit potential on a per trade basis can be substantially higher.

- ✔ **Longer-term trading disadvantages:** Your financing costs and potential for adverse price moves due to factors such as gapping can be much greater. (Where there are 'gaps' in the price — the point where no trades occur — this can lead to slippage on your stop losses too. See Chapter 8 on managing risk. A *stop loss* is the point at which you exit the position if you make the wrong decision.)

No matter whether your approach to trading is short term or longer term, for each benefit you gain, you're likely to have to give one up.

Understanding Short-Term Trading

A variety of trading methodologies are available to help you decide how best to take advantage of short-term trading. For most of these options, you need to look at a number of different time frames before making your decision to enter a position.

Moving average crossover

A method of analysis known as a *moving average crossover* can determine the relative position of price across a range of different time frames. A moving average crossover occurs when a shorter-term moving average crosses over a longer-term moving average (see the section 'Moving averages', later in this chapter) on each of the different charts, which not only determines direction of price movement but also helps you to time your entry into the position (see Figure 11-1).

Figure 11-1: Moving average crossovers can provide good entry and exit points.

If you're trading based on a 10-minute chart (see Chapter 13 on technical analysis if you need more info), then you're likely to analyse or scan the 30-minute and the hourly charts as well, before making your decision.

For instance, if you're looking for a trending move in the value of a currency and you want to trade using the 10-minute chart, you may first look for the 10-minute, the 30-minute and the hourly charts to all point in the same direction — that is, show the same trend line. When you start to look at different time frames in this way, you can see that the same instrument can look like it's pointing in all sorts of different directions. If this is the case, you may want to look for instruments that are moving the same way in each of the different time frames.

Using swing techniques

Another popular trading method for short-term trading is *swing techniques*. This category of trading is quite broad — so much so that you can use a range of methods including the employment of algorithms and indicators to look for points at which an instrument may be entering a new upswing or a new downswing. Another way in which traders can look to find swings in the market is through the use of price patterns. *Price patterns* allow you to trade using specific rules about when to enter and exit the instrument at both a profit and a loss.

I'm quite a big fan of price patterns as pointers because they don't require the use of any specific indicators or other technical analysis tools beyond being able to recognise important price occurrences (or patterns). I look at how to apply these pointers in a short-term trading situation in the following section on support and resistance (Because this trading method covers a wide-reaching area of trading, I suggest you check out Chapter 13 for more information on technical analysis.)

Working with support and resistance

To recognise price patterns, one of the most important concepts that you need to become familiar with is that of *support and resistance* (see Chapter 13 on technical analysis for more information on what constitutes support and resistance), which gives you some idea as to when price may be starting to move in a wholly different direction.

Waiting for the breakout

As you can see from Figure 11-2, the support line (a line at which a falling price is held up and subsequently moves higher from) drawn has been quite accurate in terms of finding the appropriate support level for the movements in price. You can see though that some minor breaches of support failed to turn into major price moves. This scenario means that you have a choice as a trader. You can

- ✔ Either take the trade immediately after support is broken and place your stop nice and close on the other side of the support/resistance line
- ✔ Or wait for extra confirmation

Waiting for extra confirmation may mean

- ✔ You wait for a move of a certain size past the breakout point.
- ✔ Alternatively, you wait for the price to retrace towards the breakout line before entering.

Figure 11-2: Notice the price finding support repeatedly at the same level.

If you don't wait for confirmation that the breakout is going to hold, then you're less likely to have a successful trade. However, on trades that are successful you're able to generate a greater amount of profit if you act quickly. As you can see, sometimes this strategy is effective and other times, sadly, the strategy fails. Unfortunately, you can't tell which is which until after the trade is completed.

I have seen some arguments in the past about the validity of support and resistance when it is so easily recognised by all market participants — when this happens en masse, people may place a large order just on the other side of a support/resistance line in order to take advantage of larger volume when the level is broken. I agree that sometimes this does occur with the result that you get a failed breakout — at other times, however, the breakout through the price level works perfectly. Sadly, you can't know which will result until after it occurs. This fact may not sound very helpful, but all is not lost because of risk management techniques that you can apply. On average, your aim is to lose significantly less on losing trades than you gain on winning trades. Over time this result can still leave you well ahead overall.

As a general rule, waiting for extra confirmation that the breakout is going to hold makes life less frustrating, so wait for this additional clue.

Getting out with a profit target

When you approach the problem of how to deal with your short-term set-ups, you may want to give thought to setting yourself some sensible profit targets and using them in a disciplined approach. Alternatively if you're able to watch the market closely, then you may be able to employ a method that locks in profit as soon as the market starts to move against you after a positive run. The second of these options is clearly superior but it requires that you be able to watch the market at all times, which isn't feasible for most people.

For very short-term traders, the adage 'cut your losses and let your profits run' isn't an option because you don't want to be exposed to any more volatility than you have to be. So setting the point at which you jump ship (your profit target) in advance can help lock in profits.

Making sure the risk gets you a decent reward

You need to consider what you're risking compared to the reward that you're making. If you're making on average a much bigger reward than you're risking, you can afford to be wrong more often than someone whose profits are about the same size as their losses. This assessment may sound obvious but you don't want to fall into the trap of letting profits burn a hole in your pocket the moment that they appear while letting your losses receive the benefit of the doubt all the time.

 Generally, you need to look for a risk to reward ratio of around 1 to 3 as a minimum (and you want to capture even bigger moves when you can) because, otherwise, the onus of being right becomes too much of a hardship.

Figure 11-3 shows the price oscillating between the lower support level and the upper resistance level.

Figure 11-3: Support and resistance can interact repeatedly with one another.

I cover two ways to approach this situation from the short-term trader's perspective. First, assume that the support/resistance line is going to hold and that the price is going to reverse away from it. You can approach this set-up in two basic ways:

✔ The first and most aggressive approach is to wait until the price moves very close to the support/resistance line and then take on the trade anticipating a reversal. This way means that you go short if the trade is approaching resistance or long if it is approaching a support line.

The principal drawback here is that if the price continues and breaches the support/resistance line, then you need to exit in a hurry — that is, move to the sidelines and preserve your capital.

✔ The second and less aggressive (and also likely more prudent) approach to enter this type of position, is to wait for some additional confirmation that the support/resistance line is actually being respected. If, for instance, you are using a daily candle chart (a chart that shows a new candle each day) you may wait for the price to close above the high of the candle that touches the support/resistance line (as Figure 11-4 shows).

Figure 11-4: The circled areas shown can be good entry points based on support levels.

One of the main benefits of either of these approaches is that you can place your stop loss (the point at which you close a losing trade) nice and close, which helps keep your potential risk to reward ratio nice and high.

Although you may wish to put your stop loss order very close to where you enter the position, you shouldn't put it so close that short-term volatility can knock you out of the position. If you don't have a risk to reward ratio that you're happy with when you place the stop at the price you think is the most sensible, then you have to simply decide not to take the trade. You're best not to risk capital on a bad trade when potentially much better ones are just around the corner.

The second short-term method comes from reading about a trader named John Carter. This methodology is fascinating because it looks for turning points in trends in a way that allows you to place your stop loss nice and close. Carter refers to HOLP (High Of the Low Period) and LOHP (Low Of the High Period). Basic examples of the patterns are shown in Figure 11-5.

Figure 11-5: The method shown here can help you identify and trade turning trends.

Essentially, what you're looking for is a position that shows a nice and consistent trend and, once you've found this, a price point at which you have evidence of the trend beginning to break down. When hunting for a consistent trend, Carter recommends waiting for at least a 20-period high or low as part of a definitive trending movement (see Chapter 13 for more on trends). In an uptrend, the reversal pattern looks for a price level on an individual bar or candle that closes below the low of the highest candle in the trend. These rules are reversed for a price that is in a downtrend.

The real benefit here is that you place your stop just above the high of the highest candle (see Chapter 13 for more on technical analysis) so you're accomplishing two things — first, you're entering the trade based on the earliest evidence of a trend breaking down and, second, you're placing the stop such that you get out as soon as you know you're wrong about the trade.

A lot of the time you may read about placing your stop one tick (the smallest price movement that can occur in the particular market you're trading) above the previous high or something similar — this information is telling you to get out as soon as the price action moves against you in a confirmed fashion. Watch out for a trap here. If you're trading an instrument such as foreign exchange with a spread of say three ticks, then you need to take this into account. This means that if you want to get out at one tick higher than the previous high, then you need to take the spread (the difference between the buy price and the sell price) into account. Essentially, you should place your stop loss at one tick plus the spread above the high. Otherwise, you get out of the position before you even meant to.

The other brilliant factor in Carter's methodology is that the stop is easy to trail up (or down if you're short) in line with the price movements. The basic idea is that as soon as the price moves in your favour for two time periods (say hours), then you begin to trail the stop loss in your favour. The advantage of doing this is that you can gradually lock in your profits in line with the movements of the price. The method calls for you to close out the position only when the price closes below the candle that is two candles back from the current close. If you can't be in front of the trading screen, then you may have to place the stop at this level and be closed out automatically. Sometimes this different stop methodology can work for you and sometimes against you (see Figure 11-6).

If you can be in front of the screen (how often you need to be depends on whether you use a five-minute, hourly or daily chart and so on) you can also keep in mind that you don't move the stop if it moves to a level where you would immediately close out the position. This situation can occur if, during the time period that you're watching, the price moves lower (if you're long) but doesn't close below the stop level, which means you're still in the trade but you don't move the stop loss until the trend resumes. If this occurs, you're likely going to guess that something is amiss. ***Remember:*** Using this rule, you only close positions at the end of a time period and not the beginning.

Figure 11-6: Trailing the stop can help you capture profits and not give too much back.

Carter's style of methodology can work across a range of different time frames so doesn't necessarily always fit only into the short-term methodology.

The shorter the time frame over which you deal, the smaller the profits are likely to be, as are the risks. However, the costs of doing business (either through commission or through the cost of the spread, which occurs when you have to pay more through your provider than in the underlying market) can take up a greater portion of your profits, which is why you need to remember that the benefit of locking in profits more quickly has the disadvantage of profits being smaller in size as well as the trade more frequently incurring costs of dealing.

Looking at Longer-Term Trading

Trading CFDs is more about the longer-term than the long-term. 'A case of semantics?' you ask. The common definition of 'long-term' (around five years or more) doesn't adequately apply in the CFD world. Generally, in the world of trading, three months is around the longest traders are going to hold onto positions — that is, longer than short-term (refer to the section 'Understanding Short-Term Trading', earlier in this chapter). (However, just to keep you on your trading twinkle toes, and because nothing is a given when trades are made, a trader may choose to hold for longer than this time frame as well.)

When trading CFDs, one of the main reasons traders are unwilling to carry positions for an extended period (past the longer-term of three months, for example) is the financing charges that are payable (refer to Chapter 2 for more information). So long as a position moves quite consistently in your favour, the gains comprehensively outweigh the cost of the financing charges. For this reason, it can be quite unwise to close out a good position just because you've been holding it for a while. Instead, be a prudent trader and let the market price be your gauge as to when you exit the position.

When you begin to look at choosing between using short-term trading methods and longer-term methods, you need to consider

✔ Defining which way the instrument is moving in general terms — meaning, is it trending higher or lower

✔ Whether or not now is a good time to enter a position

✔ What methods you're going to use to refine and define that decision

You need to look across different time frames (in the same way as when engaging in short-term trading) to make decisions for the longer-term but, in this case, the weekly, daily and, possibly, the hourly charts are those you need to be most concerned with.

No single indicator or methodology is going to be universally successful when trading CFDs but, when applied sensibly and consistently, they can help you develop a much more measured approach to your trading.

Making Friends with Trends

Pretty much every longer-term trading methodology revolves in one way or another around finding and capitalising on trending movements. The key for a lot of traders is to be able to spot a movement in a trend early and then to run with it for as long as they possibly can. However, the question remains: How does a trader identify a trend movement in the first place? This section looks at some of the indicators that can help you identify trend movements and use them to your trading advantage.

Moving averages

The moving average (the average value of a security over a defined period of time) is one of the favoured weapons of CFD traders in the trend-following arsenal because it emphasises the prevailing direction of a trend by smoothing out fluctuations of price and volume that, otherwise, could easily confuse a trader's interpretation of events. You can find out more about the moving average in Chapter 13 but, for now, I look at some of the ways you can employ this indicator to help you better find and then follow the trend.

Although a moving average is very easy to calculate, it suffers from the same flaw as all indicators — that is, it lags the price movements, meaning the longer the term of the moving average the more it lags. This means accurately pinpointing a trend

movement becomes more difficult and you can potentially miss out on large profits.

As an exercise, I suggest you start with the weekly chart and refine your direction from there. (At the opposite end of this analysis spectrum is the 200-week moving average. And while the application of this broader moving average may give you an excellent idea of the broader trend of any instrument, it lags so far behind the instrument that it offers little in the way of actual timing benefits.) From there, you can start to apply some different moving averages to begin the trade timing process — that is, how to time a trade.

Begin the process with a shorter time frame for your moving average and then add more — and not just one extra time frame but perhaps as many as three, for comparison purposes, because as you take on longer time frame moving averages you get an idea of the broader trend. The shorter-term ones (which track the price more closely) can give you a good idea about when the price trend may be changing direction.

One of the favoured methodologies for using moving averages is the *crossover method*. This system signals an entry point or an alert of a shift in direction when a shorter length moving average crosses from below to above a longer-term moving average (for longer-term trading) or from above to below (for short-term trading).

You're likely to see a wide range of differing opinions related to selecting the most appropriate length of your moving averages to use. Some traders suggest days in the week, days in the month or trading days in the month, for example. The difference of one increment in the length of time over which a moving average is calculated is unlikely to make a vast amount of difference. As soon as you're content with the concepts, you can start refining the numbers. ***Note:*** While a moving average filters out the 'noise' of the market, the more noise filtered (by making the moving average longer) the more it lags the price.

To start with, I recommend you use a simple 5-, 15- and 30-period moving average on the weekly chart. The most useful for the timing is likely to be the 5 crossing over the 15. Having a longer-term moving average on the chart provides an excellent reference point and can often demonstrate the speed and the angle of the trend that you're following after it starts to form.

As soon as you get these moving averages set on the chart, you can begin to use them as a scan for potential trending positions. For example, you may want to look at the close of each trading week for the charts that show a 5-week and a 15-week moving average crossover and then use this analysis as the basis of your short list of potential trades for the following week of trading.

The challenge now is how to refine this scanning process further to the point where you can actually execute a trade.

1. **Look for the daily chart to show the price to be rising away from a trendline or moving average (or at least not falling) which shows that momentum is on the rise.**

    Note that sometimes a chart can easily rise on the weekly and fall on the daily.

2. **Wait for the price to be rising on the weekly chart.**

    For this weekly scan, you may want to reference the daily chart against a moving average such as the 30-period to see whether the CFD price is above or below it.

3. **Wait for the price to be rising on the daily chart.**

    If the price is above the 30-period moving average on the daily chart, it is quite bullish (positive for the price) and if it is below then it is quite bearish (negative for the price).

4. **Execute a trade.**

    As soon as you confirm that the price is moving higher on the weekly chart and that on the daily chart you have probabilities much more in your favour, this moment may be the start of a trade or at least a means of adding to your shortlist. In any case don't forget your stop loss.

 When you're scanning the market using moving averages you sometimes find a crossover occurring on a share price that largely seems to be moving sideways. You can ignore these crossovers because they don't show a shift in trending behaviour. Instead, they reveal an oscillation that's simply part of a sideways movement. You're best served to wait until the price starts trading at a higher or lower level than the current range before examining them again.

Using trend lines

Trend lines are drawn under troughs in the price (uptrend) or above the peaks (downtrend) to determine the prevailing direction of the instrument you're watching.

You may find that a lot of the time when you see an obvious trending movement you can actually draw a trend line under the price seen on the chart (see Chapter 13 for more detail). When you go to make a trade, in many cases, you're going to want to buy as close to the trend line as possible. Though some may argue, for example, that buying at this trend line level is 'cheap', it's not the best reason. Rather, getting a trade in close to the trend line is an effective approach because it allows you to place your stop loss nice and close to your entry, which means that it can become a very good risk–reward trade for you to take on (that is, for each dollar you risk, you may be able to generate three or more dollars in profit).

You can opt to use trend lines in two main ways:

- ✔ You can wait until the price moves back and touches the trend line (or nearly touches) and then make your entry.

    This option is more aggressive because you're not getting any confirmation that the trend line is being respected (that is, the price has only moved back to the trend line and touched it), which is the whole reason that you're making the trade in the first place. However, this is the time that you're closest to your stop loss point so there is a good chance of making a decent risk–reward trade out of it.

- ✔ The alternative is to wait for the instrument price to bounce away from the trend line and then make your entry.

    You may wish to wait for a certain percentage movement or a specific period of time holding above the line as your threshold decision point. This approach may give you a lesser risk–reward trade but at least you get extra confirmation that the trend is still in force, which should increase the probability of a successful trade.

When using trend lines as a tool to help you decide when to make a trade, you need to consider the trade-offs. Either you can have an early entry, which is a lower probability trade, or a later entry with a potentially reduced risk–reward opportunity.

Scaling and pyramiding

A prudent trader neither enters his or her full position all at once nor gets out of a profitable trade all at once. This approach is known as *scaling in* and *scaling out* of a position.

Pyramiding is similar in many ways to scaling but may be something that you do over a longer time frame. Pyramiding is a process whereby you add to your position (invest more in the trade) as the price runs in your favour.

You may sometimes hear traders say that they make 90 per cent of their money from 10 per cent of their trades. For this scenario to be the case, pyramiding needs to be part of their trading approach. When you have a trade that runs for an extended period of time in your favour you're really taking fullest advantage of the situation. So rather than just taking a single, you're looking for extra runs.

Here's how to use scaling in and scaling out of positions:

- ✔ **Scaling in to a position:** If you're scaling in, you can respond to trend line touches by both trading immediately and waiting for confirmation. For instance, you may choose to put in one-half of your position at the touch of the trend line and then the other half as soon as the position rises for two days subsequent to the trend line touch.

- ✔ **Scaling out of a position:** Consider aiming for three times your risk as a trading strategy (3R). What you may wish to do is to take one-third of your profits at 3R, take maybe another third at 4R and then leave the remaining third and see what happens — perhaps closing it out if profits slip back to 2R or 3R. *Note:* While losing money is irritating (but part and parcel of the business), closing out a position only to see it continue on its merry way can be really infuriating. By following an idea like this, you can take some profits but leave some money on the table with a view to seeing how far it goes.

Here's how to use pyramiding to your advantage:

✔ **Adding to a trade:** Pyramiding (see Figure 11-7) is similar to scaling but revolves less around spreading the entry point and more towards really hammering those winning positions home. You have a large number of alternatives for timing your entry to each phase of a pyramid. In essence, you're likely to be looking for set-ups that stand on their own as separate trades when you pyramid. This may mean that you add to a trade each time that a trending position retraces to the trend line.

✔ **Adopting a sensible strategy:** You need to follow some rules in order to keep your pyramid strategy sensible:

• The first thing to consider is where the pyramid strategy gets its name from — not surprisingly, the shape of a pyramid — but how does this shape apply to positions? Well, each position should be smaller than the one before it. This means that you put the biggest position on first and then, subsequently, you put on smaller (or at least no bigger) trades thereafter (see Figure 11-8). You may rightly ask why each trade has to be smaller when surely the right thing to do is to buy more as the trend continues. The problem with going about using a pyramid strategy in this way is that when the position eventually turns against you and the final additional trade is the biggest position, it can eat up all the profits from your previous trades.

Figure 11-7: Trend line retracements can be good pyramid points.

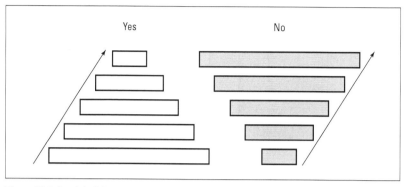

Figure 11-8: Don't build your pyramid upside down.

- You need to be sensible with your money management. You should only take on a new/additional position if the subsequent position is in a decent winning position. Ordinarily, you're likely to add one position at a time but when the time comes to close out you sell them all at once. Accordingly, when you make your first pyramid you should have enough profit in the first position that if you get stopped out you end up no worse off than at break-even. After your second and subsequent pyramid trades you want to be locked in to a profit if you get stopped out of the trade.

When you pyramid into a trade, you're more likely to have to give up the profits you've already made if the position reverses direction on you. This result is likely because if the second tranche (the first trade that you added to your initial position) reverses, the losses that it makes are eating quickly into your existing profits. In order for a pyramid trade to be worth your while, you need to take the fullest advantage possible of the positions that do move strongly in your favour.

Trading ain't gambling: Here's why ...

Some people consider gambling and trading to be one and the same but that assessment isn't really the case — or at least not in the way that many people think.

Gambling means that you're risking money on an uncertain outcome (for example, whether you're at the casino, trading, investing in shares or investing in property, the outcome isn't assured). When you gamble at a casino the odds are always against you because the casino has to make the odds in their favour — they certainly don't want to lose money over time and it's their house. Trading has some similar elements in that aspects such as commission and spreads tilt the game against you and make it harder for you to win over time. Compared to casino gambling, though, a trader has some real advantages:

✔ First, if the trade you're making is going against you, you can close it out. Yes, you lose some money but at least you can preserve the majority of it — try asking the blackjack dealer for some of your money back after a losing hand. (I should point out some games like poker do allow you to 'fold' if you don't like the cards you get dealt but most gambling games don't offer this option.)

✔ Second, you can add to a trade moving in your favour (which you can't normally do when you're gambling — although, again, poker is one of the exceptions). This advantage means that you can alter your exposure as the trade unfolds so that in the end your losses can be small when things go poorly and can be large when things go well.

✔ Third, most casino gambling places no value on skill — with the vast majority of outcomes being luck. If you keep playing long enough at the casino the house always wins — the odds are certain. However, a hard-working and disciplined trader can make the odds work for him or her over time, thus taking the winnings beyond short-term luck. This point of difference is what allows the trader to be profitable over time where the casino gambler just cannot be.

Chapter 12

Taking Lessons from Hedge Funds

*A*s I became more interested in CFDs, it occurred to me that retail traders have a lot of possibilities that simply wouldn't exist were it not for hedge funds. The good news is you can, to a very large extent, run your own hedge fund, if you're so inclined (that is, if you're prepared to put in the time).

Hedge funds use a variety of different methods in an attempt to generate strong returns, which may include trading on both the long and the short side of the market as well as incorporating leverage. One of the aims for many hedge funds is to generate positive returns whether or not the market they're dealing in is rising or falling.

In this chapter, you discover some of the principles of hedge funds and some of the ways in which you can work out how to develop and then apply this investment strategy to your own portfolio.

Hedge Funds: The Traditional Approach

One of the main things that a hedge fund trader traditionally does is to take on *hedged exposure* — this approach means the trader devises a low-risk strategy and then employs large amounts of leverage (that is, increasing the amount of market exposure that the fund carries primarily through borrowing and the use of derivatives — refer to Chapter 3) in order to make the hedge fund profitable.

Although many CFD traders focus their energy on employing leverage and cheap commission, the more savvy traders focus their energy on clever market exposure; that is, not tying themselves to all long or all short portfolios, and not having exposure to only a single market (for more information on dealing on the long and the short side of the market, refer to Chapter 3).

 Hedge fund strategies offer you the power of combining a long portfolio with a short portfolio and the concept of spreading your exposure throughout different markets.

Adopting a Long/Short Balance

Most traders show a predisposition towards focusing their energy, initially, on the long side of the market. Why? Because the first words that most traders hear when it comes to share investing relate to 'buy and hold', and 'buy low and sell high'. However, while these adages may be solid, an approach that includes just investing in the long side of the market doesn't really take into account the product qualities and benefits on offer when it comes to CFDs.

Many CFD traders ask the question: But what if I'm perfectly happy dealing in share CFDs on the long side? Looking at some statistics (I know, I know — stats ... but before you roll your eyes out of their sockets, wait, these are good figures to consider) helps to illustrate why this fairly one-sided approach may not be the best way to go. Over the ten years of trading on the S&P/ASX 200 to June 2009, the market rose on 52 per cent of trading days. It fell, naturally enough, on 48 per cent of days (this excludes days when the market did nothing), and the average gain and loss was around 30 points a day. Surely this straightforward analysis presents evidence that the short side of the market gives you a lot of possibility, too. In fact, if these figures are anything to go by, you may need to be thinking about having roughly one-half of your share market exposure on the long side and the other half on the short side of the market.

Before CFDs (for most traders), the options were pretty much either be long or be out of the market. Since CFDs, tools such as the charts of shares (or any investment product) allow you to look at a trade entirely on its merits of whether you believe you're best to go long, short or doing nothing with it at all. (Chapter 13 gives you more information about how charts can help you to develop your trading method.)

Wising up to weighting

Looking into the concept of long/short portfolios in more depth, you need to realise one simple fact — on a day when the market falls, having short exposure doesn't necessarily protect you from the losses on your long positions. If market analysis were that easy then everyone would be a trader — sadly, working out that balancing act is far from easy because such a trade isn't just about taking on half long exposure and half short exposure.

In hedge fund terms, a fund that is closely balanced in long and short exposure is referred to as *market neutral*. The idea here is that you're not too worried about the rises and falls of the underlying market because you're evenly weighted to benefit from these rises and falls in the short term. But hang on, the downside is that you're unlikely to get returns as good as a rising nor as bad as a falling market, which means you're giving up your equity return profile to some extent.

You need to develop a portfolio that can carry long and short exposure but one that is also weighted by the ebbs and flows of the market — a weighted portfolio. You can consider one of two strategies:

✔ **Make a judgement of the strength and direction of the market:** For instance, if the S&P/ASX 200 Index is above its 200-day moving average then you're generally trading bullish and, if the index is below, then you're ordinarily bearish.

However, this approach is a lagging methodology and, so, doesn't allow for much in the way of protection from a sudden shift lower in the prices of shares.

✔ **Scan the market for both long side and short side exposure at the same time:** If your basic scan of the market is to look for something like the 5-week moving average crossing the 14-week moving average (to try and determine a trend), then you're best to start your scan by looking for the 5 crossing from below to above the 14 for long side position and the 5 crossing from above to below the 14 for the short side exposure. You can see then that this charting methodology isn't a matter of what the market is doing but, instead, what the individual shares are doing; that is, you're trading your portfolio based on the direction as determined by your scan of the charts.

Using beta

Another way to consider your market exposure is by looking at your *beta*. Beta is a statistical measure that gives you an idea of how much the share price of a company is going to move in relation to the underlying market.

Example: If a company has a beta of 1.05, you can expect it to be 5 per cent more volatile than the underlying market. If a company has a beta of 0.95, then you can expect it to be 5 per cent less volatile than the market.

WARNING!

Scan the man ... and correlation

While scanning charts is a strategy that works well for the share market, you can easily incorporate similar scans into different markets, including CFDs, and apply similar rules each time — if something is trending down then you go long and, if something is trending up, then you go so short.

Easy? Not quite. The next thing that you need to be aware of is the correlation that your portfolio has in terms of its different constituents. For example, if you hold CFDs over three different gold stocks and you buy some gold bullion CFDs, then you're not diversifying your portfolio — you're simply adding to the amount of exposure that your portfolio has to the gold price.

You can also determine the expected volatility of your portfolio using your beta measure. You can work out your portfolio beta by multiplying the beta number by the percentage that the individual holding makes of your portfolio. You can sum this calculation and get an idea of how wider market moves impact your portfolio.

Beta numbers are available from your CFD provider or, if not, you can visit a free news site such as Bloomberg (www.bloomberg.com).

If you're short a given position, then its beta number becomes a negative. You still sum all of the figures together in the same way but, depending on the coverage of your portfolio, you may actually end up with a portfolio beta of zero. This result means that movements of the market at large cancel out (at least on a statistical expectation basis).

You don't need to aim for a particular beta number but by having awareness of these figures you can get an idea of how your portfolio may behave.

Beta figures aren't a guarantee of share price movement. They're a look at how the individual shares move relative to the market historically. This glimpse means then that over a period of weeks, for instance, the beta expectation may be very accurate, but day by day you end up with all sorts of anomalies.

Incorporating Different Asset Classes

Hedge funds offer traders opportunities across a range of different asset classes in order to generate profits. One of the most exciting aspects of trading CFDs is your ability to incorporate different strategies to join different asset classes together as part of a working trading portfolio in much the same way. One of the most interesting aspects of this approach is the fact that you can feasibly integrate different methodologies across different time frames to take advantage of different market movements that you see.

The greater the variety of asset classes of CFDs you trade and the more methodologies that you apply means the more time consuming the researching and monitoring of your portfolio is going to be.

Throughout different trading cycles, conditions can change very quickly, so you need to be aware of the risk that you're exposed to at any given point in time. (Be sure to check out Chapter 8, which considers risk management because you're best not to over leverage your trading account no matter how well diversified it is.) This section looks at some methodologies that you can consider when building a portfolio of different asset classes into a reality.

When you're scanning for trades and making decisions about whether or not to hold on to them, one tool you have available is to look at methodologies that include different time frames.

Looking at short-term time frames

Two of the most popular areas of the CFD world for short-term trading are foreign exchange (FX) and indices. Depending on the time frame in which you're looking, you may want to set up your trading method so that you have a stop loss order linked to a take profit order (known as an OCO or One-Cancels-Other). This way you're working out ahead of time the complete parameters under which you wish to trade and you're moving in the market accordingly.

In the short-term time frame, you're best to have a profit target in mind and then to put the order in to close the trade as soon as this target level is reached. If you're trading in this way, the downside is that if you look away from the screen for a little while you may miss out on a successfully closed trade. To counter this disadvantage, and depending on the CFD provider you're using, you may be able to set up your orders well in advance so that your entry order and your profit and loss exit orders are placed automatically.

Even in a short-term trading situation, for example, where you're trading on a chart such as the hourly (refer to Chapter 13), you may wish to plan ahead as far as you can. This option is a good short-term time frame because it doesn't require constant watching from you, which means you can plan the trade further in advance. Keep in mind though that some trade set-ups may take hours (or even days) to establish, so you're best to be ready for them when they occur — which is even more reason to place your entry trades in the market so they're automatically triggered.

Using longer-term time frames

On a longer-term time scale, you may wish to look at trend following of share CFDs (and, potentially, on other instruments like foreign exchange), if you believe that it is going to trend consistently and you're willing to deal with the volatility attached to trading it.

The benefit that you can potentially derive by trading longer-term is one associated with diversification not only of products but time frames. Here's why:

- ✔ On the one hand you can take advantage of trending movements that require you to ride some ups and downs of the market — with the benefit of capturing some potentially large market movements.

- ✔ On the other hand is the ability to capture some short-term movements in the market and then move to the sidelines. While the upside of this type of strategy isn't going to be as great as that seen from a trending move, at least you can lock in the profit that you make and then move on to the next position.

Advanced Strategy Concepts

A group of traders who are particularly defensive of the way in which they make their trading decisions are those who manage the hedge funds. Unlike most conventional managed funds traders, who are reasonably detailed when outlining their strategy, the hedge fund traders remain very tight-lipped about the details of how they do business. Hedge fund traders fit into some broad categories (such as macro-economic and trend following) and stick to that approach for the most part. Other methods such as pairs trading (see the next section) are now quite well known as well.

Some hedge fund traders have been around for a while and can provide a really great education for you regarding some creative and in-depth ways to use CFDs in a more advanced fashion. Naturally, you don't have to go into this depth, but you may use some details to develop new ideas that create something uniquely your own.

Understanding pairs trading

Pairs trading is about looking for two instruments that are highly correlated with one another over the longer-term (see Figure 12-1 for an example of this).

Pairs trading is probably the most commonly discussed of the hedge fund strategies because it does all the things that you like to see in a hedge fund:

- Use of correlations
- Minimal market exposure (though potentially large dollar exposure)
- Exploitation of a perceived market mispricing

Figure 12-1: High correlation levels are key to making good pairs trades.

Here's how to identify your pair of instruments:

- ✔ Look at companies from a very homogenous sector — often the banking sector is a good example.

- ✔ Look for a breakdown of this correlation where one company is trading relatively expensively to the other.

- ✔ Anticipate that the two companies are going to have their prices converge once more and that the longer-term correlation is set to begin once more. This means that you go short the relatively higher priced company and long the relatively underpriced company. The expectation is that you are going to see a convergence in price but be largely protected from market movements by the high level of correlation. You can see the convergence occurring in Figure 12-2.

The word 'relative' is important because whether the company has a higher or lower share price has nothing to do with a company's relativity. Instead, you're looking for companies that have broken out of their correlation. You tend to take a short and long position of the same dollar value.

The idea is that on top of the convergence, while the trade is on, you have limited exposure to the market because the positions generally offset each other to a large extent. What you may also tend to do is monitor the two positions as one because you're interested in their relative combined movements and not the individual movement of the companies.

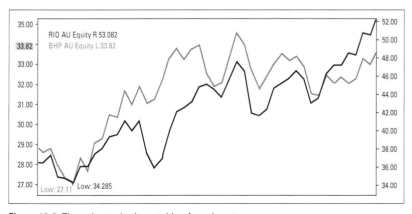

Figure 12-2: The pairs trader is watching for prices to converge.

Knowing when these two companies are correlated and when they break out of their correlation is important. Here's how to identify this step:

- ✓ One way is to overlay the charts of the two companies on the same scale but this is a fairly poor method.

- ✓ You're best to get the raw price data and place it in a spreadsheet and run a correlation formula over it — this way you know for sure how tightly correlated the companies have been.

- ✓ The next thing to look at is how far apart the prices have moved and whether they're stretched to the point where they're likely to move back together for you.

To help your analysis of price movement, you can examine some historical measurement but the better way is to head back to your spreadsheets and analyse, historically, how far the companies have been apart. You can then calculate standard deviations of price spread — you may find that historically every time the spread goes beyond two standard deviations that the prices converge quickly after that. To help with this calculation, check out the Investopedia website (www.investopedia.com) and type into the search box **standard deviation**. *Tip:* Use a spreadsheet, like MS Excel, to do the calculation itself.

Don't be surprised if only one of the 'legs' of the pairs trade is a winner. As long as it makes more than the other 'pair' loses, you're going to be ahead overall.

Correlations that don't work have been the undoing of some very smart traders in the markets, so don't assume that a correlation must be respected because such an approach isn't always going to make the grade.

You don't want to be holding a pairs trade forever. Because you have one long and one short position, it helps to offset the financing somewhat but the tendency to take on larger positions can mean that you end up with a hefty finance bill, so be mindful of that possible outcome in your planning.

Tapping into index stripping

Index CFDs (CFDs that track an entire index like the S&P/
ASX 200) are a very popular hedge fund product because they
give you exposure to a wide range of the market, which allows
you to benefit from broad market moves. However, if your
plan is to carry this exposure for some time but you believe a
certain market sector isn't going to be a great performer, then
you may not want to carry as much exposure in that sector. The
strategy here is called *index stripping*. The methodology includes
removing this underperforming component of your exposure so
that you only have exactly the portfolio you want.

Example: Say you're bullish on the wider market but you think
the finance sector is going to be something of a lead weight
on the performance of the overall index. If you're long on an
Australian share index CFD, then you're going to likely shed this
weight and remove it from your portfolio. Here's how:

1. **Work out how much exposure you have to the market
   with your long index position.**

   If these contracts are worth 5,000 points at $1 a point
   and you have five of them, then you have $25,000
   exposure to the market.

2. **Work out exactly how much exposure the financial
   sector makes up of the index.**

   If you say this exposure is 20 per cent (check the
   website of an index provider such as Standard &
   Poor's — www.standardandpoors.com — or your CFD
   provider), then you need to gain short exposure worth
   $5,000 on the finance sector.

   Depending on your CFD provider you may be able to use
   a *sector contract* (a CFD that tracks an individual sector
   of the market such as the mining sector or the finance
   sector) here or, alternatively, you have to go short the
   finance sector stocks. Ordinarily, you need worry about
   going short only the companies that make up significant
   weighting in the sector — smaller companies have very
   small weightings and have an almost negligible effect. If
   you're dealing in small amounts you may worry about
   going short only the top three or four constituents,
   which likely gives you a quite similar overall effect.

If your weightings are chosen correctly, you can see that you aren't really taking a short position in the finance sector — in fact, you're taking no position at all. Why? Because you're long the sector in the index exposure that you have and short the sector using the short share or sector CFD position that you have. This strategy, in effect, leaves you net neutral to the finance sector. This means you're hoping that the finance sector indeed underperforms and your index position is going to do better overall due to not having that type of market exposure.

Myriad strategies are available to CFD traders. While you need a bit of creativity to come up with them, the main point to take on board is to work hard on the testing of your strategies before applying them in real-life trading. By looking at ways to apply both short-term and longer-term exposure to the market (and not necessarily one market but potentially several), you can consistently direct your exposure such that you generate positive results.

Chapter 13

Ah! Technical Analysis

*T*echnical analysis has gone from being seen as something akin to tea-leaf reading to an essential tool that all short-term traders are familiar with. Even for longer-term investors, technical analysis can provide an important bridge between making a fundamental determination about the underlying quality of an investment and actually making the trade based on sensible timing factors.

Like any type of method that you choose to employ to determine what positions to trade, technical analysis isn't foolproof, nor is it 100 per cent accurate. Technical analysis tools, or charts, give you the opportunity to get on the right side of the price movements occurring at a point in time and, specifically, allow you to isolate points where you can safely say you're wrong about the trade that you're making and exit while the losses are minimal.

In this chapter, I describe some of the key technical methods that you have at your disposal as a trader.

Using Technical Analysis to Predict Patterns

Technical analysis is based on the premise that price change is determined not only by new information but also by how humans respond to news and are influenced by fashion and 'herd' behaviour. Why? Because these human responses form repeatable patterns that can be predicted by analysis of price itself.

A range of technical analysis tools (in three broad categories) are available to the trader:

- ✔ **Trend indicators:** Indicators and methods that look to determine whether an instrument is trending, and which you can then use to decide on the strength of the trend and whether or not it's likely to continue. This type of methodology can also help determine whether your timing to enter the market is good or not. Trend indicators include items such as moving averages, the lowest low value (LLV), the parabolic stop-and-reverse, and the average true range (ATR). (For each of these methods, see the section 'Applying Useful Indicators', later in this chapter.)

- ✔ **Chart pattern analysis (which may also fall under broader swing trading):** Involves looking for patterns that occur within price movements over time, such as rectangles, triangles, breakout patterns and symmetrical triangles. Through study of past prices, traders know specific ways in which to trade instruments that have a price chart that falls into these types of patterns. (For each of these methods, see the section 'Getting into Swing Trading', later in this chapter.)

- ✔ **Momentum oscillators:** Attempt to give the trader a view as to whether an instrument is overbought or oversold (where a price has moved too fast or too far in either direction). By analysing how the market ebbs and flows, this method allows the trader to better determine whether it may be a good time to buy or sell. This category of technical analysis tools includes indicators such as the Relative Strength Index (RSI) — see Chapter 14.

Identifying Trends

One of the core ideals that underlie technical analysis is that the market (and individual instruments such as a CFD listed company) moves in trends, and trends persist. An instrument in a trend is more likely to remain in that trend than it is to break down and move in the opposite direction.

Although sticking with a trend for its entire duration isn't for everyone, identifying the direction of a trend and then following it can help you to determine when best to get into a trade (or out of one).

Identifying three kinds of trend directions can get you started:

- **Uptrend:** Where price is moving in a generally upwards direction.

- **Sideways trend (or trading range):** Where price is moving in a generally sideways direction between two levels (*support and resistance* — lines where the price has repeatedly been unable to move above or below).

- **Downtrend:** Where price is moving in a generally downwards direction (that is, the opposite of an uptrend).

A trend can show plenty of upwards and downwards movements and still quite clearly highlight whether the instrument is trending or not. The most common approach taken by traders that highlights this movement is (for an uptrend) to take the time to trace a straight edge trend line underneath the prices that are shown on the chart, as shown in Figure 13-1 (and, of course, the opposite for a downtrend).

If you're drawing a 'dictionary definition' uptrend, you need to be able to draw a straight line that connects three price troughs together; for a downtrend, this should be three price peaks. If the price breaks through the uptrend line it may be a good time to sell. On the other hand if the price touches this level and then starts to move in the other direction, you may have unearthed a good time to buy (or sell/go short in a downtrend).

Figure 13-1: An uptrend line, making you really, really rich.

The drawing of a straight edge trend line is one of those simple and under-appreciated skills of technical analysis. Not only does this trend line help to define the broad direction of the instrument, but the line itself serves as a good point of reference to help you with your buying decisions (refer to Chapter 11 for more information on trading methods). You're best to strengthen your ability in this effective type of charting before making forays into other more complex methods.

Being able to draw the trend line as neatly as in Figure 13-1 is great, but it doesn't have to appear like this in order for there to be a trend in place. More specifically than the trend line, you're actually looking for a series of higher peaks and higher troughs (see Figure 13-2) in order for a trend to be in place.

In some cases, you can also draw a second line parallel to the trend line above the price action and engulf the price in a channel, as shown in Figure 13-3. A channel can be quite useful in determining when a price may have extended to the maximum away from the trend line. The only downside of relying purely on neat channels is the relative rarity with which you're able to neatly fit a channel around the price action.

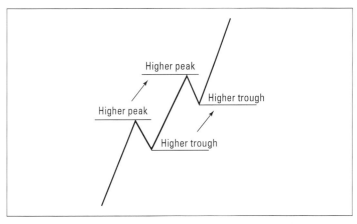

Figure 13-2: Looking at the peaks and troughs is the way to find trending moves in price.

Figure 13-3: A channel trend line, showing rising support and resistance.

Applying Useful Indicators

Indicators are another tool in the trader's arsenal of methodology with which to decide market entry and exit points. For the most part, *indicators* involve applying a mathematical formula to the recent trading price of the instrument that you're trading to give you information about where the price is, relative to where it has been.

Determining overbought and oversold levels can be one of the great strengths of using indicators, but is also one of the things that can lead new traders to ruin because of their deceptive simplicity.

In this section, I look at some of the key considerations that traders need to be aware of for stop loss placement.

Always approach new technical analysis tools with great caution because nothing, especially tracking price movement trends, is ever as easy as it seems.

Getting the most from moving averages

The *moving average* is the first mathematical-based indicator that most traders come into contact with. Like the trend line, this simple indicator can go a long way to helping you determine likely entry points on any instrument that you choose to trade.

Here's how to calculate the moving average:

1. **Take the average closing price value over a certain number of time periods** — for example, 30.

2. **The next day, add the next time period and remove the first** — in this case, add day 31 and remove the first day.

3. **Recalculate the average.**

4. **Repeat steps 1 through 3 every time period from then on.**

This process makes a moving average. This type of calculation results in a line that follows the price of the instrument but which has some of the *market noise* (meaning volatility — the daily ups and downs) removed. The longer the period over which you calculate the moving average, the more market noise you remove (see Figure 13-4).

You may find that using a moving average (say a 21-day average) is a good way of determining which way price is trending. If price is above the line, then it's trending up; if it's below, then it's trending down.

Traders often use moving averages to determine an entry point. The method traders most commonly use is referred to as the *crossover*, which occurs when a shorter-length moving average crosses over a longer one: For example, a 5-day moving average crossing a 15-day moving average, as shown in Figure 13-5. A combination of shorter-term and longer-term moving averages allows the trader to reduce the noise of the market while continuing to see changes in trends quite quickly.

The downside of a long moving average is that the direction of the average becomes less responsive to changes in price.

Figure 13-4: Moving averages show the market with less 'noise'.

Figure 13-5: Shorter-term and longer-term moving averages at crossover.

Marking the lowest price

A useful indicator for placing a stop loss is the lowest low value (LLV). The *lowest low value* is an excellent tool for trend following because it allows the trend to give a good sign of a breakdown before you exit the position and is a means of trailing your stop upwards as you move further into profit. The LLV marks the lowest value that the price has traded at in the last *x* number of periods. You can then place your stop loss on the other side of this value and, hopefully, watch your profits climb. Have a look at Figure 13-6 and you can see the way in which the LLV trails the price, which provides you a good place to put your stop loss orders. (***Note:*** Like most things in CFD trading you can look at this issue from the flipside, too — traders on the short side of the market are able to use the *highest high value* (HHV) as a means of managing positions that they hold.)

You can adjust the number of periods over which you calculate the LLV depending on your needs but, for the most part, you're best to choose a value between 5 and 20. If the charting application you're using doesn't have this adjustment available, your option is to draw one by hand. You can work out where the LLV goes simply by counting back the relevant number of time periods.

Weekly, daily, hourly

A trend on the weekly chart trumps a trend on the daily chart. And this in turn trumps a trend on an hourly chart. Strange, isn't it?

Many short-term traders neglect weekly charts reasoning that they're too long-term to be of any use to them. However, they can be highly effective at pointing out the broad direction of companies (or any other tradeable instruments).

Looking for a moving average cross-over (of prices) on a weekly chart is usually an excellent scanning tool. These weekly trends can bolster your trading methods, helping you to identify a short-list of companies to look at more closely on daily and hourly charts.

Although the LLV indicator seems very easy to follow, you should keep in mind that you're going to have to give some of your profits back at the end of the trending movement because the LLV always sits below the price. And, the larger the number of periods in the LLV, the bigger this give-back is going to be. The benefit of this scenario, however, is that it gives the trader a much better opportunity to let the trend keep running in their favour rather than cutting it off short.

Figure 13-6: The LLV is a very useful method for determining stop loss placement.

Stopping and reversing a trade

The *parabolic stop and reverse* (PSAR) is designed for use only in trending markets as a means of looking for turns in price for entries, and even more for exits.

When price moves from below to above the PSAR, this movement is considered a bullish (or buy) signal — the opposite of this applies, too (that is, when prices move from above to below the PSAR, this movement is a bearish, or sell signal).

The PSAR allows a level of automation that is like music to a trader's ears. Why? Because, for each time period, this charting application adjusts itself and moves closer to the price. The reason the PSAR can do this is because it contains an *acceleration factor* — the longer the price keeps moving higher (or lower), the faster the value of the PSAR changes, thereby moving the stop closer and closer to the current price, which means that when price eventually reverses you are quickly stopped out and hopefully have locked in a large profit. Figure 13-7 shows how this indicator generates potential entry and exit signals for the trader depending on the prevailing direction of the market.

Figure 13-7: The PSAR helps the trader identify shifting trends in the market.

This PSAR indicator was created (by renowned technical analyst J Welles Wilder) to enable a trader to respond to being stopped out of a position — to reverse the trade and continue. The problem with this approach, though, is that eventually you end up holding a long or a short position in everything. In this case, when I say 'everything' I mean that literally, because if you use the PSAR as your only indicator it tells you to either buy or sell on every chart that you look at. To counter this effect, you need to filter the indicator more carefully. For example, why not look for a trending instrument (that is, something that is moving consistently higher or lower in price) and then test the behaviour of the PSAR as a trailing stop loss indicator.

Although you can change the settings of the PSAR on your charting application, the creator of this indicator was clear that it should be left programmed to its default settings.

Spotting the average range

The *average true range* (ATR) — developed by technical analyst J Welles Wilder — uses volatility in the movement of an individual instrument as a means of working out potential stop loss points.

Like the moving average (see 'Getting the most from moving averages', earlier in this chapter), the ATR allows you to look at price in a different way. The ATR looks at the trading behaviour of an instrument and expresses it as a value that describes the likely range over which the instrument is going to trade over a certain time period.

To find the ATR, the first thing that you need to work out is the *true range*, that is, the maximum value out of:

- ✔ The high for the current period minus the low for the current period

- ✔ The high for the current period minus the close from the previous period

- ✔ The close from the previous period minus the low for the current period

Using the software, you then take a 14-day exponential moving average of the results and you have your ATR. While you don't have to make this calculation yourself (because most charting applications will be able to do this for you), you're best to understand exactly what the numbers all mean. You can see that the value of the ATR rises and falls in line with the volatility of the instrument's price in Figure 13-8.

To enable you to absorb more than the recent amount of instrument price volatility in your placement of a stop loss, you can employ a multiple of the ATR as your stop loss placement level — for example, 2 × ATR. The logic behind this approach is that you're waiting until the price moves outside of a reasonable range (determined by the ATR) before closing out your position. This will help you avoid getting closed out unnecessarily.

The ATR (or multiple of it) can be an ideal stop loss placement solution when other options such as using support or resistance levels (horizontal lines where the price has repeatedly been unable to move above or below) may not be available (see the next section).

Figure 13-8: The ATR tells you a lot about the trading behaviour of any instrument.

Getting into Swing Trading

Swing trading is a methodology that allows you to look for patterns in share price charts (which can include rectangles, triangles, breakout patterns and symmetrical triangles) that point towards a certain type of outcome being probable. This form of trading gives you opportunities to take measured approaches to your trades with precise rules for the placement of stop loss orders as well as take profit orders. The idea of the swing is that you're getting in at the start of a new upswing and getting out (or maybe going short) at the start of a downswing. Like everything trading related, though, saying is much easier than doing.

Much of what swing trading is about falls into the category of what traders refer to as *breakout trading* — where you're looking for some type of support or resistance to build up, at which point you make the trade when the price breaks out, or when the pattern of support or resistance is broken.

When swing trading, one of the main skills that you need is *pattern recognition* (although you can use this skill in other forms of trading, too), which considers the way in which an instrument is trading and then isolates how you can deal with it (based on your trading rules or perimeters). (**Remember:** Moving averages are also very useful for helping you to find changes in prevailing price direction.)

One of the key benefits of this type of trading is the option it gives you to apply it across a range of different time frames without changing the rules that you use.

For example, the chart in Figure 13-9 shows a formation referred to as a *rectangle*, which is a continuation pattern. You can identify this pattern by the price being arrested in its movement — that is, by the price moving in a sideways movement between a support and a resistance level. Typically you're looking for two peaks hitting the resistance line and two troughs hitting the support line before calling it a confirmed rectangle. The pattern is eventually confirmed by the price breaking out and continuing in its previous direction, which is what the trader is waiting for before entering a new position. This chart is a daily time frame.

Figure 13-9: Rectangles show a wonderful interaction between support and resistance.

A popular and powerful swing trading pattern is the *ascending triangle* (see Figure 13-10). This pattern is intuitive in the way it unfolds, so much so that you can see the market psychology lying behind it.

Figure 13-10 shows the price striking a resistance point and then being repelled to lower levels as the rally is greeted by heavy selling. Each time the price falls, though, it is supported at progressively higher price levels — which is what gives the pattern its distinctive shape.

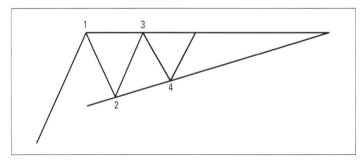

Figure 13-10: Triangles show prices being squeezed between two trading levels.

The way that you approach this trade from an entry point is to buy as soon as the price resistance level shows signs of breaching. Then, you can place your stop below the resistance level because, if the price slides below this level, you're not likely to want to hold the position anyway.

You can see on the ascending triangle chart (Figure 13-10) that the target for the price breakout is measured by the height of the triangle in the build-up phase. The fact that you have a price target (a common feature of most swing trading methods) means you can be very clear from the outset where you're likely to sell out for a profit — if you have a successful trade.

Another important trading pattern is the *symmetrical triangle* (see Figure 13-11).

Figure 13-11 shows the price movement moving closer and closer, together with the peaks becoming lower and the troughs becoming higher — which is something of a sign of uncertainty for the market.

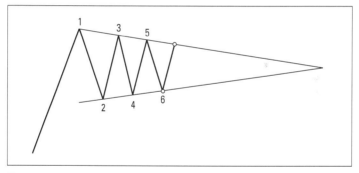

Figure 13-11: The symmetrical triangle has rising support lines and falling resistance lines.

Minimising losers

No matter what sort of methodology you're using, you're best to make sure that the reward you anticipate making is likely to be significantly greater than the risk you're taking.

A 1:3 risk–reward ratio is the ideal minimum to aim for. Otherwise you're in a position where you have to have significantly more winners than losers in order to remain profitable over time.

Like the case with the ascending triangle chart (refer to Figure 13-10), you can see in Figure 13-11 that the symmetrical triangle chart measures to the height of the pattern and then extrapolates this measurement forwards as the target for anyone buying in.

If a swing trading pattern begins to fail in the build-up phase, you're best to consider it void and ignore the pattern.

Understanding General Rules on Technical Stop Loss Points

When you see a support and resistance level in the price chart, you can be sure that the rest of the market can see it too. So remember that if you're placing your stop loss points just on the other side of these levels you may be disappointed with the result that occurs if the price trades at this level.

If you're looking at a foreign exchange (FX) chart for instance, and the price breaks through a level and continues briefly in that direction, and then quickly reverses, you're best to assume that a big buyer or seller is using the momentum that occurs at the breakout level to trade a large amount in the opposite direction. It isn't that the buyer or seller is trying to ruin everyone's fun but that the trader needs to position their order in the market. This scenario isn't always going to unfold this way, but you should realise that you're not the only person out there who can identify these types of patterns.

When you're trading an instrument that has a spread, such as FX, you need to take the spread into account when placing your stops. What this means is that if the price is between 1.2345 and 1.2348 and you want to close the position if it reaches 1.2320, then you need to take the spread into account. If you simply place your stop at 1.2320, you're going to be stopped out as soon as the bid price touches this level — not the offer. So this means that if you want to be sure that the price has indeed broken this level then you would place the stop at 1.2316. This is one pip below the nominated stop level, plus the spread. In this way, you're sure that the level of your stop is properly breached.

Stirring the Software Pot

These days, you can't flex your technical analysis wings without software ... charting software.

Your CFD provider is likely to supply you with basic software, usually free of charge. At the other end of the spectrum are charting applications that allow you to create original indicators completely from scratch. If you want this type of advanced functionality, you have to pay for it. (For more information on the range of software available, see Chapter 14.)

Advanced functionality doesn't improve trading capabilities, however. Little correlation exists between the quality of different types of charting software and the traders who use them: If you're a new trader and spend $3,000 on a charting application, you're still likely to be less successful than an experienced trader who's using a $100 piece of charting software.

Regarding your choice of charting software, you're best to start your journey with something cheap and then upgrade as your ability begins to expand beyond the limitations of that software. Don't buy the software with the expectation of one day using all of its tools. The most advanced software allows you to program your own indicators and scans (which may look across entire markets for instruments that satisfy a number of technical criteria), but this functionality isn't very useful for beginners.

For more information on charting software, see Chapter 14.

Chapter 14

Charting CFDs with Software

*T*echnical analysis, or charting, is the core method that CFD traders use to determine when to open positions, close positions, and to explore ways to manage risk.

A large range of charting software (with varying functionality) is on the market. The range in price and features available and, in some cases, the options in terms of customisation, scanning and program indicators based on your own requirements can be mindboggling. Ordinarily, though, for each new feature that you do need, you're going to find lots more that you don't need, so you're best to be sure of exactly what you're after before spending your money.

Remember, spending heaps of money on software doesn't make the process of improving your trading ability any easier. You're best to assess the different software based on your requirements and then determine whether the price is fair for you. Your first charting software purchase should cost you very little — you work up from there. If you make your trades based on fundamental factors (see Chapter 10), you're going to likely need only reasonably basic software, but if you use only technical analysis, then you may find making an extra investment well worth your while.

In this chapter, I look at some of the key considerations you should take into account when looking at charting software. I also describe particular pieces of software that are available.

Introducing Charting Software

Some of the problems that traders face when choosing software are

✔ How to decide what charting software tools are going to be the most effective for them

✔ How extensive a set of charting software tools needs to be to meet their CFD trading goals, for example:

- How powerful it needs to be

- Whether a particular software's functionality is, in fact, the most suitable for the trader's experience level

This section takes a look at the progressive functionality available to traders — from the most basic of charting software to the top of the pops.

Before I get into a large amount of depth in the world of available software, I want to point out that any list of available software that I give in this book is far from exhaustive due to the fact that a great many options are available.

You can get access to charting software applications from:

✔ **Your CFD provider:** Generally, the most basic charting software is available online and offered by your CFD provider. The great advantage is the cost to you — free! When internet trading was developing, you had access to free charts but they were quite rudimentary. Now, however, traders are a more demanding lot and want things like live streaming charts to be offered for free as well, which in turn means lots of competition between providers that eventually gives them and you more of the fancy stuff. Be aware, though, that you get what you pay for (or not, so to speak).

✔ **Search engine websites:** Interactive charts are available from websites like Google Finance, Big Charts or Yahoo!7 Finance. The only downside for this category of online software resources is they often don't provide charts on some of the indices and commodities that you may be interested in.

✔ **Hybrid installed software:** The first step that you may make into more advanced charting software is to use hybrid software installed on your computer. First, you install a program on your computer, and then you go online to use it. The good thing about this kind of software is that it allows you to save all of your work so that all your analysis is there waiting for you next time.

✔ **Offline/standalone:** This is the point where the expense starts to get interesting — remembering, of course, that there is no automatic correlation between the expense of the software and its success. Basically, the more expensive the software the more flexibility you have to make the software do exactly what you need by doing things such as modifying, combining and creating technical indicators. In addition, you can have the software scan the market for many more criteria. (You can even take it further — custom indicators allow you to scan based on a combination of criteria built into a single indicator.) Sounds great — and it is — but there's a downside too. You need to pay a data provider for the data that the software needs to run, and to get into the advanced scanning you need to learn a programming language. This is far from impossible to do but it's something you need to keep in mind. (See the section 'Top Ways to Scan' later in this chapter for more on scanning.)

Another thing that sets high-end software aside from cheaper options is the ability to backtest. Backtesting involves programming a set of criteria for entry, exit and risk management and then testing how it would have performed over time. Although it's a wonderful feature, the programming can be very time consuming and the more advanced pieces will require you to learn a programming language in order to use them.

A lot of programs will have a basic backtesting functionality built in but you may have to buy an add-on for the really fancy stuff. For instance, for Metastock you can buy TradeSim (from www.compuvision.com.au), which can set you back anything from around $200 to $1,500, depending on the version you buy — naturally the more expensive, the more complex the work it can do.

Picking up where you left off with hybrid software

Sometimes you can look at a chart and make an assessment about where you think stop losses should go, the likely direction of the trade, and where you think you might take profits. If you leave the chart unmarked and come back to it in a couple of days, you may make a totally different assessment of what's going on. This new assessment can be influenced by things such as changes to prevailing market conditions and even by your own mood. More importantly, you can end up missing important patterns that may otherwise have been very plain to you on a different day.

Hybrid installed charting software allows you to get around the problem of missing evolving chart formations by allowing you to

✓ **Draw all the points that you can identify when you see them at first glance.** Even if the pattern isn't complete, you lay the groundwork for more easily identifying a more complete pattern in the future. If you mark up charts as you go, you can see many tradeable formations occurring over time.

✓ **Regularly mark all the interesting points that you see.**

✓ **Write notes on your charts to remind yourself.**

The extra features offered by standalone software are very important to some people but totally irrelevant to others so you are wasting your money unless you are planning to do quite specialist work. Not only does it require significant effort but there is a lot of extra learning required to properly understand the test results that this type of software generates.

Choosing the Charting Software That's Right For You

This section looks at some more-specific attributes that you can consider when choosing charting software options. Unfortunately, there are too many software options for me to cover them all individually — otherwise the title of the book would be *Charting Software For Dummies*. However, some examples of software are included.

Ordinarily, one software application is more appealing than another kind because of its:

✔ **Availability of charts:** Once upon a time (when dial-up internet was the norm) it was a real pain to have to turn your internet on in order to get access to charts. For the majority of people though those days are past so connectivity isn't the issue that it once was. Unless you have a laptop and you are planning to do a lot of analysis on the go, then having to connect isn't really a problem. The one thing that can sometimes be a little bit of an issue is that each chart has to load individually — adding only a second or two of waiting time but it's something to be aware of.

One of the real benefits of using your CFD provider's charts is that they will likely provide real-time intra-day charts, which can help with short-term timing of the market. These charts can be quite expensive when you're paying for them yourself. It's interesting that in the time that online trading has been available (not much more than 10 years) traders have gone from being happy with any old charts to demanding free streaming charts — which goes to show the benefits of competition for consumers.

With free and hybrid software, up-to-date charts are available as soon as you go online.

With standalone software you'll have to download data — generally daily — so that your charts remain up to date. This extra downloading is not a big drama as the software that comes from your data provider will generally prompt you to do it all with just a few clicks of the mouse.

✔ **Features:** The free charting software offered by your CFD provider isn't going to be the best software in the world but it should offer a good range of different charts such as line, bar and candle — if it doesn't, your analysis will be pretty limited. Many programs offer more specialist types of charts too, such as 'point and figure' and 'renko' charts, so for no money you do get a lot. Most also offer drawing tools (straight lines) for trends and support/ resistance marking, as well as a number of indicators such as moving averages, the parabolic stop and reverse and the average true range (see Chapter 13 for more information on indicators). Lastly it is not unusual for the program to offer a reasonable amount of price history — going back at least a few years — and viewable over intra-day, daily, weekly and monthly time frames.

Depending on the CFD provider, the free software offered may or may not include volume on the charts. Finally, free charting software will rarely save your chart settings automatically, and some won't allow you to save your chart settings at all. Check with your provider to find out whether the software they supply offers this feature.

Hybrid software can offer all of the above features, with the added feature of you being able to save the settings, marks and comments you have added to the charts.

Offline or standalone software can also provide all of the above features — and a whole lot more. With this software you can do things such as modify, combine and create technical indicators, as well as scan market data based on defined criteria. A lot of these types of programs also allow you to backtest your trading strategy (for very advanced testing you will often need add-on software). See the section 'Introducing Charting Software', earlier in this chapter, for more on the features of offline or standalone charting software.

✔ **Functionality:** This is a bit tricky to define based on the type of software because I have seen really cheap software that does things better than really expensive software — so you don't always get what you pay for. However, you will want to look for more flexibility the further along you go.

Any level software should allow you to modify the indicators that are available, making the software useful across a wide range of different situations.

Any software type should also allow you to scan the market for different criteria. Free software may only offer basic scanning, like looking for share prices that are hitting their 52-week high. Standalone software should allow you to do things like combining several different indicators and finding CFDs that fit all the criteria that you need.

More advanced software also allows you to custom write your own indicators, which pretty much limits you only by your ability to write the program code to tell the software what to do.

✔ **Price:** The price for software can differ enormously. To give you an idea, I've included examples for each level of software, and what you'd expect to pay. (Naturally I don't need to talk a lot about the cost of free software so I've started with hybrid software.)

One of the better pieces of software in the hybrid software category comes from Incredible Charts (www.incrediblecharts.com.au). At the time of writing, this software cost $18 per month and actually offered a wide range of features for the price, with charts available for Australian shares and for shares from a number of foreign markets. The software saves any drawings and indicators you add to the charts for the next time you view the charts and also offers some decent scanning options. One of the real benefits of this type of software is that you don't pay extra for the data. Australian data provider JustData (www.justdata.com) charges $230 for their cheapest annual package for Australian shares data so you can see that it's a reasonable cost saving.

Some data providers allow you to pay less if you access the data only after specific times — for example, after midnight of each trading session. You need to consider whether it is appropriate for you but if you only look at your charts in the morning before the start of each day's trade then this may be just what you need.

✔ Once you move on to standalone software, the price for a mid-range product is about $400. A good example in this range is EzyChart, which at the time of writing was being sold by local vendors Moneybags (www.moneybags.com.au) for $429.50. The good thing about this software is that it's easy to use — according to Moneybags, the average Windows user can get the software under control in 30 minutes.

✔ One of the better options in the higher echelons of software is Metastock, which is US-based software that can be purchased through local vendors Paritech (www.paritech.com.au) or directly from Equis (www.equis.com) in the United States. The reason that I mention buying directly from the programmer is that, depending on the exchange rate, this can sometimes save you a lot of money — just make sure that you check out the alternatives first. At the time of writing, local vendors, Paritech, were selling the standalone software for around $700 — data will be extra. There are several other packages out there for around the same sort of money. By the time you want to buy this type of software you will have a decent idea of what you are looking for, so keep these requirements in mind when comparing products.

✔ If you're really enthusiastic, even more advanced software is available. The purchased software that I have mentioned so far has end-of-day data but you can also purchase software that provides real-time charts. Of course, these added features come at a price. There's an easy rule to remember and to illustrate I quote from one of my favourite films, *Lock Stock and Two Smoking Barrels*: 'It comes with a gold-plated Rolls Royce ... as long as you pay for it.' The same goes for charting software. Sticking with Metastock, their real-time version (Metastock Pro) will cost you around US$1,400 for the software, with Equis selling annual data for the Asia–Pacific region for US$1,300 per annum on top of that (www.equis.com.au) — quite a bit of money so be sure you need it! You can also look at alternatives like Bull Charts (www.bullcharts.com.au) or something extra flash in the form of Trade Station (www.tradestation.com).

✔ Lastly, there is specialty software out there that looks for very specific features in the technical analysis environment. These programs can run to several thousand dollars and I don't cover them in this book — by the time you need them you will be able to find them on your own.

Before making any investment in software be sure that there is enough support and education available to help you learn how to use the software effectively — if it's complex you may need quite a bit of help! Some providers will offer standalone packs that go with the software and may have a help line that you can call. Also, check online to see if you can find any forums on the software you are interested in — these can be invaluable as people are often keen to give advice and support.

Incorporating Indicators

These days, most technical analysis software has a pretty comprehensive suite of indicators available, so this level of functionality isn't going to be a factor when deciding which software package to buy. The ways in which you can apply them and use them to find trading opportunities, though, vary from package to package.

Technical indicators are available in technical analysis software to scan the markets and these are likely to make up a decent portion of your overall set-up. The main time that you would need to look at more advanced options on the indicator front is if you want to program your own or combine several into one, which requires some decent software.

While overlaying several different indicators at the one time is easy in terms of the functionality of most software options, being able to do so doesn't mean they're going to be more effective. For example, indicators that fall into the oscillator category (such as the Relative Strength Indicator and the Stochastic Oscillator) may give quite similar results at similar times to one another. So, rather than overlaying several similar indicators that are going to give you roughly the same signal, you're best to look outside of that family of indicators when determining your scan.

Imagine how difficult it is to prepare a scan that uses five different indicators; trying to then manually reconcile the result gets even harder. Instead, a good starting point for putting together tests that you can more easily debug is to start by using the moving averages indicator (which helps you determine likely entry points to a trade). For lots of traders, using moving averages is appropriate because they're looking to trade trends anyway. The reason these may be particularly useful is because you can easily see where trends such as moving average crossovers are occurring on the chart, which means you can work with your scan to ensure the results are those that you're looking for. (See Chapter 13 for more on moving averages.)

Writing Your Own Indicators

If you type **J. Welles Wilder** into a search engine such as Google, you can read about a technical analyst who is responsible for coming up with many of the most popular technical indicators that traders use today. You can also enjoy the rationale he applied to create them, which may just bring on a flurry of creativity of your own — hopefully enough to develop some of your own indicators. (See the sidebar 'Building your own bit of genius'.) Before you get too excited about designing your own indicators, though, you need to realise that the new skill set you're about to learn is going to take plenty of patience and perseverance because you're going to take longer than the first attempt to get the process right.

Here's a suggested method for creating your own indicator:

1. **Take a selection of indicators you like.**

   For instance, you may like trading based on companies that have a certain value RSI and maybe a crossover of two moving averages.

2. **Join them together as one big indicator.**

   This step may sound complex but, ordinarily, it isn't too much of a drama in terms of the overall interpretation. The single indicator usually takes on the form of a binary indicator, which means you get a yes (that is, all the criteria are in place) or a no (that is, one or more of the criteria is missing) answer. This can only be done on more advanced standalone software but can be very useful as a means of finding instruments that fit the characteristics that you are looking for in a trade.

3. **Check that all the criteria you're looking for is in place.**

   If so, your custom indicator tells you to buy and if not, it tells you to do nothing at all.

4. **Start your trade.**

   When you're satisfied that the time is right to trade, go ahead — just don't forget your risk management and your position sizing rules (see Chapters 8 and 9).

Building your own bit of genius

J. Welles Wilder's work allows you to peruse the Relative Strength Indicator as an example of the kind of equation you may be looking at when planning to build your own indicator.

The Relative Strength Indicator is built with the following:

UPS = (Sum of gains over N periods) / N

DOWNS = (Sum of losses over N periods) / N

RS = UPS/DOWNS

RSI = 100 − (100/(1 + RS))

This indicator can then have a *smoothing average* applied to it to reduce visible market noise.

You can see that the overall equation isn't overly taxing, which isn't to say that developing the idea from scratch for what you want to examine isn't going to be, so you're best to be very mindful of the complexity of what you're taking on. Then all you have to do is work out what the result is telling you and how you can apply the indicator in order to make better trading decisions.

Top Ways to Scan

Scanning is informative; scanning is fun (at least for some people). You discover all sorts of information about what's happening on a given day. The following roundup offers some great ways to scan the market using charting software.

- ✔ **Price and volume:** If you're a new trader, start with price and volume scans. This approach may mean that you're likely to want to look only for shares that have turnovers well in excess of one million shares a day. On the price front, you might want to look for prices that are at the highest level they have been at in the last 52 weeks. Alternatively, you may want to look for prices that have increased more than a certain percentage (a figure determined by you) in the last week.

  The general rule when it comes to using software to scan share CFDs is: The more volume (amount traded over a given period) the better, because you can get in and out of a trade more easily.

  Foreign exchange (the value of two currencies, or the exchange rate) doesn't have volume displayed because there is no official market for it — the rate is simply determined by the prices banks are paying one another for currency at any given point in time. So it's not possible to scan FX CFDs using volume as a criterion.

- ✔ **Price breakouts:** A very popular way to scan charts is to look for price breakouts. When you look at charts from the swing trader perspective, you're looking for price breakouts in price patterns such as the ascending triangle (refer to Chapter 13 for more on swing trading patterns).

  You can look for price breakouts that take the form of a *highest high value* (or *lowest low*). This kind of scan looks for a chart that reaches the highest or lowest level seen in *x* number of periods. You can use this scan as part of an entry or exit set-up or as a means of short-listing trading opportunities on the long side (52-week high) or the short side (52-week low).

When looking at the results of your scanning, also consider:

- **Number of trades a day:** As you develop your scanning, you quickly come to the conclusion that you need to balance your desire to scan with your need to create scanning results that don't present you with too great a number of opportunities. As a trader you're naturally going to want as many returns as possible from your scans but this approach isn't a very efficient way of trading. Why? Because every time you trade you're up for trading costs, plus the simple fact is that not every trade is going to be a winner.

    If, for instance, you're holding positions for several weeks trying to capture trending movements, you don't want your scanning software results telling you to take on 30 new positions a day — you end up with so many that you're unlikely to have sufficient capital to carry them all, let alone carry the risk tolerance. Really, then, taking on one or two positions a day is the likely maximum you're able to tolerate.

    If you get one or two of the good trades a day, you're doing okay, and if you're getting 10 or 12, then they're probably not that great a prospect — or if they are, you're putting yourself up for a win for the Nobel Prize somewhere down the track!

- **High-probability CFDs:** Certainly, trading on a shorter time frame enables you to carry more positions for a shorter period of time, but you need to be able to balance out the equation of length of trade and number of positions realistically. More important is the quality of the scan that you come up with because you only want to be entering into trades that you consider to be 'high probability'. These are CFDs that you're very confident are going to turn into successful trades. You don't want to waste your time (and more importantly your capital) on trades that you don't feel confident about.

On the hunt for market momentum

A good way to shortlist share CFDs for trading is to scan for those that are making new 52-week highs. The reason for this approach is that you at least know that the company has some market momentum on its side. As a trader, you want to resist the temptation to look for companies that are trading at very low levels (and are trending down), thinking they represent good value. Always be aware that value is a relative interpretation and that shares may be very cheap for a very good reason. Ordinarily, you're best to look for a share that is heading in the direction that you want to trade in.

Part V

Knowing Where You're Going

Glenn Lumsden

'Let's try some word association. If I were to say "Eurodollar versus USD", how would that make you feel?'

In this part ...

*I*f you don't understand the factors that can influence your trading mindset or you simply trade without a plan, you'll never understand why you win some and lose plenty more.

In this part, I tackle the mental aspects of playing the money market, then I show you how to create your own trading plan from scratch. I also look at ways to track and assess your progress, so that you always know whether you're moving forwards or backwards, and to help you improve and better understand your performance.

Chapter 15

Analysing Your Trading Behaviour

*Y*ou need to keep analysing and assessing your approach to trading and take responsibility for the outcomes that you generate from the market. The study of trading behaviour has revealed that an individual's natural tendencies actually work against successful outcomes. People who make rational decisions in everyday life start acting strangely when money's on the line!

In this chapter, I talk about the way you behave as a trader. Who is responsible for your gains? Who is responsible for your losses? You are, of course. Another question you need to ask yourself is how much time you want to spend trading. Giving up your day job to go full-time may not be the wisest move when you're just starting out.

I discuss how to recognise the problems common to traders, such as making decisions because you're afraid to lose money, which will help you manage the mental side of trading, and how frequently assessing your trading behaviour will help ensure your success as a trader.

Avoiding Common Trading Pitfalls

At least half the battle of trading goes on in your mind. Your self-esteem can plummet after you've lost money, compared your own failures to someone else's successful trading, or sold a position in profit too early because you were afraid of it reversing even though this was contrary to your trading plan. Do you sometimes think of the market as an entity that's out to get you? Why can you stop thinking about the losing trade but not the winning trade? Why do you follow your trading plan when you're winning but abandon it when you're losing? Well, you're only human …

Being aware of the mental traps traders can fall into can help you stop and assess your trading behaviour and stay on top of the game. Following are pitfalls you might encounter on your trading journey, with tips on how to avoid them.

Personalising the market

A dangerous trap that people fall into is treating the market almost like a person; sometimes one who is out to get you! Some people take this further and say that a certain stock owes them money; they might say, for example, 'I lost $500 trading XYZ and I'm going to keep trading this company until I get my money back from them.' If you've ever felt this way or actually focused on a company or instrument in order to exact your 'revenge trade' then it's time to move on. The company itself extracts money from shareholders when it lists (and during corporate capital raisings), but other than that the ups and downs of the share price don't make the company directly wealthier or poorer. And there certainly isn't a vault over at the company's headquarters labelled 'Gains from unwary shareholders'.

The market doesn't feel that you're a good trader or a bad trader whether you lose money or make money. It doesn't feel anything. In Australia the share market isn't even run by a person; it's just a computer that matches buyers and sellers with one another. This means that the sad reality is that you aren't going to get praise or acceptance from the market — you need to find this within yourself.

Hoping and waiting instead of taking action

Like most people, you're probably not particularly good at taking losses. Through a combination of hope or plain old denial many traders let a position run against them for a long time before eventually doing something about it.

Have you ever heard or used the phrase 'I'll wait until it gets back to break-even and then sell it'? Just how long are you willing to wait for this to happen? You can see from the chart shown in Figure 15-1 that you may be waiting an awfully long time. And this is based on the assumption that a stock moving lower will bounce and return to its former glory, which unfortunately is not always the case.

By waiting you're creating a goal that potentially risks a lot of money in order to give you the satisfaction of not having a losing trade.

Make a decision and act to clip the loss early and then move on to the next trade. This way you're at least taking active control over your positions rather than simply hoping that they'll come good for you at some stage in the future.

Figure 15-1: Long-term price movement back to break-even.

Exploring prospect theory

Lots has been written about *behavioural finance* — the study of the psychology of trader behaviour and the resulting effects on the money market — because it helps explain why and how markets operate.

A major concept of economics is referred to as *rationality*, which says that people will act in such a way as to make the best choices — about consumption, saving and so on. But it seems that many people don't make rational decisions when they're trading on the share market.

Prospect theory looks at how people make different types of decisions when posed with risky situations. Research has found that people give different answers to the same or similar questions depending on how the questions were framed: Whether the outcome was a loss or

profit they had to take immediately, and depending on what was going to happen next. Examples of trading behaviour that defy rational thinking are:

- A willingness to take a risk to get back to break-even, even when the alternative is an even greater loss if the risk doesn't pay off.

- A willingness to lock in a profit rather than take a risk to gain an even bigger profit.

- An aversion to loss that makes traders employ strategies and defences to avoid losing money that actually prevent success.

You've probably heard the expression 'cut your losses and let your profits run' — behavioural finance studies have found that maybe we're actually pre-programmed to do the opposite.

Starting from scratch instead of adjusting

Some traders are quick to throw their hands in the air, tear up their trading plan, sulk for a while then decide to start from scratch every time they have a string of losing trades.

Trading has the potential to be an extremely frustrating activity because you are trying to predict movements of prices that are very difficult to predict. Having said that, your experience is one of the best assets you have and it can only be developed through actual trading. You can test using old data all you like but once you actually start trading you will learn things that you never thought of. If you start from scratch every time something goes wrong you aren't using your experience to the fullest because you are going down entirely different paths again and again.

You need to keep modifying your trading plan, strategies and methodology — making fine adjustments and moving closer and closer to the ideal method for you. (I discuss developing your trading plan in Chapter 16.)

Forgetting to monitor what you already have

A common problem for traders is focusing too much energy on finding the next trade and less on monitoring what they have already. New trades are exciting and full of potential, but remember that your prime determinant of profit is not your entry but your exit. You need to spend more time thinking about the optimal exit strategy for what you already have instead of thinking about what you might do next because the positions that you already have represent genuine capital at risk. Potential new trades don't. I discuss managing your existing trades in Chapter 17.

Keeping your own counsel

You need to learn to trust your own judgement and trading plan and be wary of other people's advice. One of the most damaging things to your self-esteem is hearing how well someone else is trading when you're having a bad run of it. It doesn't cost other people anything to tell you how wildly successful they are with their trading, but it could cost you plenty. People can tell you they haven't had a losing trade in a year. You may think to yourself, 'Wow! I haven't done anywhere near that well'. But maybe they haven't closed any paper losses and are deluding themselves, or maybe they're flat-out lying to you (and themselves I might add). I advise you to wish them well and get back to your own planning. You should feel lucky if you get one or two people in your life that you can talk shop with and believe that what they're telling you is a pretty close version to reality.

Closing out too early

When a position has moved in your favour for a good period of time you'll probably start feeling edgy and want to close out. But you only want to get out when your trading plan tells you that it's time to, not just because the profit is burning a hole in your pocket.

If you get out too early you might regret your decision when the price rallies higher. Let me tell you that this will happen, in the same way that sometimes you'll get stopped out on a trade only to see it rally. Have a look at the Average True Range indicator in Chapter 13 for more help with dealing with this problem. You can't blame anyone in these circumstances; it's just one of those things.

Your trading diary (see Chapter 17) can be really useful to track whether you're getting out of positions too early on a regular basis. If you can see that this happens regularly, you can then make a modification to your trading strategy.

Don't drive yourself nuts over making mistakes like closing out too early, though, because annoying things like this will happen all the time over the course of your trading career. Remember that sometimes the market goes in your favour, too, so don't chop and change your methods all the time to try to catch lucky moves.

Asking Yourself Whether Working at Home Is for You

One of the best (and scariest) aspects of trading is that you don't need anyone's permission and you can approach your trading in any way that you like. How much you trade and whether you do well or not is up to you.

A lot of advertisements for trading courses and the like push the idea that people can give up their day job and trade full-time. You know, telling the boss to shove it and getting out of bed late and then spending your days in a bathrobe. But do you really want to give up the social aspects of your job to sit by yourself in front of a computer screen all day?

You may need to make some shifts in your wider life in order to adapt too. Although you may not have thought of it, going in to work each day provides you with a large amount of social interaction. If you trade from home there will be no clients and no co-workers to keep you company. You may not think this sounds like a big deal but it's probably worth thinking about how you can replace this interaction in another way rather than trying to cut yourself off from the world altogether.

Without things to keep your mind active you may be tempted to trade for amusement rather than follow your carefully formulated trading plan (see Chapter 16). You could trade 24 hours a day with your CFD provider, but you need to be disciplined and stick to your trading plan, otherwise you aren't trading, you're gambling — without even the spectacle of the horse racing to amuse you.

I suggest you keep your full-time job and trade part time, especially when you're first starting out. Imagine the extra mental pressure that you put on yourself if you have to earn a living from trading alone; each trade that you make will help to determine the sustainability of your newly chosen profession. However, if your regular pay cheque is still rolling in then there's less pressure to perform.

Perhaps further down the track you can consider full-time trading if you have a long history of consistent profitability and your job is actually interfering with your ability to go to the next level.

Fighting the Fear of Losing

Fear is something that you probably would like to remove entirely from your emotional repertoire but you do need it. Fear reminds you to stick to your trading plan: Manage the downside, keep your positions small and employ stop losses on your trades.

One of the negative aspects of fear is hesitating to make a trade when the opportunity arises, but this is a relatively minor problem. The biggest problem is when the fear of losing allows you to deem a losing trade to be acceptable because there's a chance that it will come good at some stage in the future.

Some traders though may have a very good reason to be afraid of losing — if you are carrying positions that are too large for you based on your available capital then you might be risking all or more of your capital in a single trade which is very dangerous. This type of behaviour may arise as you become emboldened after a string of winning trades — the thing you aren't considering though is the fact that one loss on a highly leveraged trade can be your undoing. Good risk management plans should help you avoid terminal losses even in the worst of circumstances, which can help remove a lot of the fear element from trading and let you take a big step towards success. This happens because a lot of the fear is removed, making the whole decision-making process more clinical and objective and your trading more enjoyable.

Accept the fact that you're going to lose sometimes and fight against the fear of losing. Once the position has moved outside the parameters of your trading rules then you have to give it the chop and not find ways to justify holding onto it a little while longer.

Remove the expression *paper loss* from your vocabulary. This term refers to a position that you hold that's worth less than you bought it for but which may come back to profit. This is just a way of thinking that everything will be okay if you just hang on long enough. Be clear in your own mind about what the risk is before you place the trade.

A sure sign that you're feeling the fear too much is sitting and staring all day at the trading screen. I call this the 'intra-day stares'. You feel that if you keep a very close eye on the market then nothing bad can happen. The opposite is in fact the case because the more you stare at the market the more you can convince yourself that the market is at its top or at its bottom, or that you have to sell out because it's as high as it can go. This is the fearful side of your personality whispering lies in your ear. Again, be clear on your plan and be sure to stick to it.

Every trade that you take is a risk and no matter how clever you are you aren't going to know what the outcome is going to be before you place the trade. Giving into fear and getting stressed while carrying the position isn't going to help you. The best that you can do is to follow your risk management rules. Ask yourself:

- ✔ Is my position size based on an appropriate amount of risk for my capital?

- ✔ Do I know where my stop loss will go?

- ✔ Am I sure that the position fits my entry criteria?

If you can answer yes to all of these then there is little more that you can control. The market will rise and fall but not because of you hoping that it will. See Chapter 16 for more on developing your trading plan.

You'll overcome your fear once you grow comfortable with your method and when the actual process of trading becomes quite mundane because you're simply following the rules you've set for yourself. Over time you may have a hit rate of little better (or indeed worse) than 50 per cent, but as long as your average win is bigger than your average loss you're still doing okay.

Chapter 16

Developing a Trading Plan

. . . .

In This Chapter

▶ Looking at a trading plan's key components

▶ Understanding what trading plans are all about

▶ Knowing how you want to trade and how to set goals

▶ Testing your trading plan

▶ Keeping your risk levels down

. . . .

Some people say that 'failing to plan is planning to fail'. Nobody plans to fail, but many people don't put nearly the work into their trading plan that they should.

CFDs offer you a vast world of trading opportunity. However, without a trading plan you subject yourself to not understanding what you're doing right and what you're doing wrong. Your trading plan helps you to better understand yourself as a trader.

In this chapter, I show you why time spent on planning is never wasted. Answering some simple questions about your motives will go a long way in determining what you want from your trading, which you can then incorporate into your plan. Whether your goal is to generate extra income for yourself or to trade full-time, you can craft this into your trading plan. Once you put your plan into practice, you can then start to finetune it as real-world experience helps you better understand the world of CFD trading.

Putting First Things First

In order to take full advantage of the flexibility of CFDs and to create a trading plan that works, you need to be able to answer these questions:

- ✔ 'What type of CFDs am I going to trade?' This may include domestic share and index CFDs with a small portion of FX. Or you may focus your energy on international share CFDs and commodities.

- ✔ 'What time frame am I interested in?' This can be anything from intra-day trading through to trading over several weeks (medium-term trading) or months (longer-term trading). There's no best answer, but whichever time frame you choose requires a specific skill-set. Remember that the shorter the time frame, the more time you will need to dedicate to watching the market.

- ✔ 'What set of conditions will I use to determine when I enter and exit a position?' For example, you can choose to wait for a specific technical analysis formation to help you best time when to open and close your trades.

- ✔ 'How much am I planning to risk on each trade that I make?' You only want to risk a small percentage of your overall capital. A good rule is to never risk more than 2 per cent of your capital on any trade.

These are the key components that make up a trading plan. If you can't answer each question, then you're leaving the world of trading and getting results that might as well be generated by the flip of a coin. You need to know how you'll respond to a range of market conditions and not leave outcomes to chance.

To make a success of your trading you need to keep moving your capital into positions that are moving in your favour, and quickly dispense with those that are moving against you. How long you hold positions is determined by your strategy and the market conditions.

Getting Started

When you start developing your trading plan, you need to sit down with a piece of paper and decide how you're going to approach the situation. Write down the reasons you want to trade as well so you're clear on what it is you want to achieve.

The key thing you want to work on initially is deciding how you plan to enter the trade and, in particular, the way in which you plan to exit the trade.

Note: When I talk about exiting a trade, I mean quitting a trade either after making a profit or after a small loss. I've heard people say (when talking about a losing trade) that they get out when they feel the position has moved far enough against them. This type of behaviour isn't based on a plan. This reaction is simply following gut feeling, and won't help you become more consistent with your approach to trading.

When you know where you want to get into a trade and where you'll want to get out, you can then work out your position sizing very easily (for a rundown on position sizing, refer to Chapter 9).

Evaluating an example plan

In order to better understand what a plan should look like, you need to be able to define the key characteristics, such as time frame, entry and exit rules, and your risk management methods.

Example: I'm a medium-term trader aiming for a holding period of between two and three weeks and I like to follow trends. I'm a conservative trader, so if I'm carrying more than 3× leverage I only take a new trade when the previous trade has either had its stop loss moved to break-even value or higher, or it has closed out at a small loss. My trading plan is outlined below.

I'm going to buy share CFDs on the opening of trade after the 5-day simple moving average crosses the 30-day simple moving average. I will confirm the strength of the trend with an ADX indicator with a minimum threshold value of 30. I will risk 2 per cent of my trading capital (including commission). I will close out my position when the share price falls below the 20-day moving average, or trades below its lowest value in the last five days. I will place my stop loss with my CFD provider. If I'm carrying more than 3× leverage on my account I will not take on any new positions until I've closed another one out.

In this example of a trading plan you can see that I suggest not taking any new positions until the stop orders on my old positions are at break-even or better, or until the previous position is closed out for a small loss. This is a good idea because it helps prevent me from making 'boredom' trades, which can occur when your portfolio hasn't done much in a little while. Also, this strategy ensures you're preserving your capital as best you can, and not adding losing position after losing position to your trading portfolio. (All of the technical indicators I mention here are described in much greater detail in Chapter 13. See Chapter 8 for more on keeping leverage under control.) By using this method, you generally won't have more than one losing position at a time.

These points are important and answer the major questions I list earlier in this chapter and that you as a trader need to ask yourself when determining your trading plan. In the example above, you know exactly when you'll enter and exit your trades, and you've kept your risk nice and conservative. You want to do the same with the trading plan you develop.

Understanding why you need a trading plan

A trading plan separates average traders from great traders. That's because those with a trading plan know where they're going and those without one, don't. (In Chapter 15, I provide some helpful information on understanding some of the mental challenges that trading places upon you.)

The main reason you need to trade with a plan that you follow to the letter is so that you can easily work out what you're doing wrong. Don't believe that the first trading plan you come up with is going to be completely successful and remain unchanged over the course of your trading career. You'll need to finetune your plan over time and consider doing so to be part of the process (I show you how in 'Finetuning Your Trading Plan' later in this chapter). When you get into trouble is when you trade without a plan because then you have no way of knowing what you're doing right — or wrong.

When you become interested in trading, you're inundated with different possibilities. These possibilities include using methods such as:

- ✔ Trading price breakouts
- ✔ Using oscillators and moving average crossovers
- ✔ Trading based on company and market-related news

You can find these terms in Chapters 10 and 13, which relate to fundamental and technical analysis.

These are just a few of the different methods people use to trade — none of the methods is right or wrong, but you're spoiled for choice, that's for sure. The trouble starts when you try to take the sampler option, and have a bit of a go at all of them. The problem with doing this is that sometimes you'll win and sometimes you'll lose; because you've chosen methods largely at random, you won't know whether a win was good management or good luck. The best traders are consistent with their methods and also consistently profitable. This is what is required if a trader wants to make a living from their trading or indeed make a worthwhile improvement to their income.

To see how charting software works (see Chapter 14, which contains a section on software selection), you can take different indicators and use them over different time frames, simply by changing their calculation values. I suggest that you spend time in front of your charts and try out the different functions that are available. After you see how long the different values will keep you in trades, and how much you'll need to risk, you'll have a much better idea of the methods that suit you.

Keeping things in check

How many indicators should you use? Well, there are hundreds of different technical analysis indicators available, but don't try to use them all. Start with two or three and become comfortable with them. Adding more doesn't always increase your chances of success, but it will make your life more complicated. I like the envelope analogy: If you can't fit it all on the back of an envelope, it's too complex!

What you always need to keep in mind is that creating the plan is relatively easy, but *sticking to it* takes an incredible amount of discipline.

Looking at Your Individual Needs

I mention throughout this book that there's no ideal way to trade CFDs, but whichever way you choose must suit you. Regardless of your requirements, even making small amounts of extra regular income can make a huge difference to your overall financial position over a long period of time.

One of the best places to put extra income is into your mortgage. You may not think that an extra $100 a week would make a lot of difference, but if you put this amount on a mortgage that charges 8 per cent per annum over 10 years, it adds up to almost $80,000. So, don't believe that small amounts of income won't help your financial position.

Working out what you want from your trading

The scale of reward that you hope to generate from your trading should be your guide to the amount of effort that you need to put into developing your trading plan. For example, if you're looking to generate some extra income, then you need a trading plan that allows you to review your trading portfolio less regularly than people who get all their income from their trading. This also means that you should be aiming to hold positions for a longer duration to help keep the time commitment down (Chapter 13 contains a guide to short- and long-term trading methods).

When you begin trading, I suggest that you start with trend following. You can look at several different CFD products, including share CFDs (both domestic and international), and even foreign exchange (FX) and commodities if you have a higher risk tolerance and you're interested in day trading. To track these higher risk products, you'll want to focus on daily and weekly price charts, and indicators like the RSI and moving averages, which you may find helpful (see Chapter 13 for more information on trend following, price charts and indicators).

Don't fall into the trap of thinking that the faster you turn your portfolio over, the more money you'll make. Trend following involves holding your positions for a longer period of time, but the rewards can also be significantly greater, so be sure not to disregard a method just because it doesn't sound exciting. In addition, even though CFDs offer low commissions, the fees will still add up if you're turning your portfolio over frequently.

The person who makes the most frequent trades is the *day trader*. Day traders open and close all of their positions on the same day, which means they carry no overnight exposure. If day trading is something you have time for, then you need to focus your energy in products that have high degrees of volume and volatility. A real favourite in this area is FX (which has the greatest volume of any market). You can also consider share CFDs and commodities (though the big markets of the United States are probably the best for this, so you may need to be prepared for some late nights). With day trading, you'll be focusing more of your analysis towards the hourly, 30-minute and even 5-minute charts. Also, in most cases you'll start to add indicators, such as the RSI and Bollinger Bands, to better time your trades (for more information on these indicators, see Chapter 13).

If you're planning to trade full-time, then you should be looking at a minimum of a three-year time frame in order to build up your skills and experience. When you're starting out you should be working on methods that fit in with your current career path, rather than ones that try to replace it.

Taking trend following to its heights

One of the world's foremost traders and advocate of trend following is Ed Seykota. He was also a pioneer of computerised trading in the 1970s. Some people may consider trend following to be dull, but Seykota has been able to grow his wealth to such an extent using trend following that he's been able to pursue other passions in life, which have extended to things such as challenging generally accepted concepts in science. Although trend following certainly isn't for everyone, I believe Seykota's success highlights what the real attraction in trading should be — being able to achieve your own goals.

The advantage of part-time trading is that you aren't placed under additional pressure due to trading being your sole source of income. I believe that you only need to consider going full-time if your current job is hindering your trading from moving up to the next level. See Chapter 15 for more on deciding whether trading part-time or full-time suits you best.

You don't want to consider any type of trading a hobby or something that you do for a bit of fun because the effort and time commitment required and potential financial risk are too great for that to be an effective way of dealing with your trading. You're making a serious commitment, so you need to be looking for some decent reward.

All CFD providers allow you to place stop orders (see Chapter 3) so that your position can be closed out automatically after a price target is reached. This means that you don't have to sit and stare at the computer screen all day. The only people who need to do this type of thing are very active intra-day traders (see Chapter 13 for more information on trading time frames).

Setting realistic goals

In the preceding section I state how important it is to consider trading a money-making exercise and not a hobby, but the question remains: How much should you be aiming to make?

Some people are very *goal-oriented* and need to have a specific target that they're always aiming towards. Others are more *absolute* (or unrestricted) in their nature and are simply looking to take the fullest advantage of whatever opportunities come their way. Your 'style' is a very personal decision and only something that you can determine for yourself.

If you're aiming towards a specific dollar target, such as $1,000 a month of income, you'll have times that this can't be achieved because there are no trading opportunities available to you. When you have constructed your trading plan you only make a trade when it satisfies your rules, otherwise you have to sit on the sidelines. You need to follow your rules rather than make your target.

One of the most common CFD products people deal in is share CFDs, which are CFDs that follow the price of listed companies. With share CFDs, your absolute minimum return (that you'll be targeting as a return in a one-year period) will be to match the return of the underlying share index. In Australia, the main index is the S&P/ASX 200. The reason why this is your minimum is because it's a return that could be achieved with no effort on your part whatsoever (by dealing in an index fund). By doing this you can generate the same performance as the index, so if those returns are enough for you, then this is where you want to put your money. Then you don't have to lift a finger.

An *index fund* is a managed investment that attempts to replicate the returns of an underlying index, such as the S&P 500 in the United States, or the S&P/ASX 200 in Australia. These index funds are attractive to investors because they have relatively low management fees, low capital gains tax (due to low holding turnover) and long-term growth potential. Probably the best known funds manager in this category is Vanguard.

Trading with CFDs enables you to far exceed the returns that are generated by the index, but you need to remember that the more leverage you apply, the more risk you're taking to achieve these returns. (For more information on managing risk when employing leverage in your trading strategy, refer to Chapters 1 and 8.)

The other big question that you need to ask yourself when setting goals relates to what time frame you plan to trade over. Traders employ methods that can see them holding CFD positions anywhere from a few minutes to more than a year. I provide more information on some of the methods traders use in Chapter 11, but here it's important to understand the broad issues related to trading using different time frames.

For example, the idea of very short term trading is often very attractive to people as they embark on their trading journey. This isn't surprising, because the idea of opening a position in the morning and closing it in the afternoon for a nice profit is a very attractive one. But remember, this type of trading is the most difficult to master, because you're relying on relatively small moves in your favour from the market in order to capture a winning trade, so your losing trades on average have to be smaller still.

Although *trending movements* (followed in trend trading, covered in Chapter 13) take longer to unfold, they can be very profitable for you. Trend trading requires you to absorb more market volatility, but it also means that you save money on commission.

If a position is running in your favour, you should take full advantage of it — let the market do the work for you.

In your first year of serious CFD trading, a reasonable goal would be to break even. I know that this sounds less exciting than making a fortune, but you need to be realistic. If you keep yourself steady, you'll gain a lot of experience and not lose any of your precious capital, which will make your next year of trading a lot easier.

If you want to set a profit target for yourself, you can get started with something moderate like $100 per week. Depending on your account size, this may be more or less than the index rate of return, but it's a nice round figure to work with. This doesn't mean, though, that you need to stop trading for the week after you've made the target as you always want to do the best that you can over any given period of time.

Another goal that I particularly like is to avoid experiencing losing months. This means not putting a dollar target on your profits, but simply aiming to do the best that you can.

Avoid making daily goals for yourself. Some days the market is not going to move in your favour at all, which means that you have no chance of making your target. This subsequently means that there's added pressure on you the next day to earn even bigger returns simply to catch up.

A lot of traders will find that the vast majority of their profits come from a small percentage of their trades (say 90 per cent of profits from 10 per cent of the trades). You might want to aim for an annual profit target instead. This way you can allow for a lot of ups and downs in your trading but still focus on coming out ahead in the end and being consistent in the medium to long term.

Using your individual needs to create your trading plan

In the financial markets, the level of risk that a person is able to tolerate is frequently attached to their age and the number of years left until retirement. Younger people are seen as more able to tolerate risk because they have more working years ahead of them to recover losses they may make. This is reasonable to an extent when looking at CFDs; however, because the average time frame of investment in CFDs is usually quite small, the time factor is less relevant. In any case, the amount of your total assets that you expose to CFDs should only be a small percentage — for example, less than 5 per cent.

A trading plan helps to further reduce your exposure to risk. But remember that you need to stick to it.

Time factors and amounts invested aside, your trading plan needs to help you determine *your* individual level of risk. Most new traders put all their focus on the upside, and put little or no focus on what happens when things go the wrong way. Make sure you know when you will exit a trade if it doesn't move in your favour. You should also know that if you exit the trade at a loss how much it will cost you. Remember that any losing trade should only cost you a small percentage of your total capital.

Most position sizing methodologies (see Chapter 9) require you to know the placement of your stop loss in order to properly work out the position size. Determining your stops this way also ensures that you're focused on controlling losses at a time when you have no money at risk (that is, before the opening trade is executed), so you're likely to be at your most sensible and rational.

For more information on managing your individual needs, see 'Balancing Risks with Your Goals' later in this chapter.

Finetuning Your Trading Plan

As you begin your CFD trading journey you're likely to find that your plan needs to change. This is normal, but generally you want to keep changes minor and not make frequent overhauls.

Effective ways of taking a detailed look at your trading methodologies can help you finetune your trading plan. In the following section I outline two of the most useful methods, which are backtesting and paper trading.

The major difference between backtesting and paper trading is that backtesting looks at the past and paper trading is done in real time and so is forward looking.

Backtesting

Backtesting is a means of making a very deep analysis of a trading strategy by looking at each and every trade that a set of trading rules would have made, based on past data, and then looking at the outcomes it would've generated. Backtesting tests a strategy in a comprehensive manner by considering not only how profitable the strategy would have been, but also its rate of wins and losses and other information, like the longest string of winning and losing trades.

This type of method is used very heavily by non-discretionary or system traders. Backtesting, though it sounds rather simple, also involves dealing with a unique set of emotional challenges. As a wise academic once said, 'When it comes to finance, if you think you have found a risk-free trade, you have done something wrong.'

Whether you backtest on paper or on computer, the process requires you to spend vast amounts of time looking at historical data and considering ways that you can exploit the information to your advantage. The data that you generate from your backtesting allows you to probe your trading plan for weaknesses.

After you've completed your backtesting, don't be put off if your first trading plan fails to be profitable. Discovering this early is always better because you don't have any capital riding on the outcome. You should be relieved that you found out when you did that you were heading down the wrong path.

Trading is only judged by one thing — your profitability. Backtesting is a great way to test a trading methodology; however, it won't help you improve your methods if you can't be completely honest and thorough in your testing, so you must record all the profits as well as the losses.

These days, backtesting is done primarily on a computer and generates large amounts of data.

Paper trading

Possibly, the most common first step that any trader or investor takes when they get involved with the markets is to undertake *paper trading*. This simply involves determining what positions you 'would' have bought and then monitoring their progress on paper, checking to see whether your strategy would've been a successful one.

To make the most of your paper trading, the main thing you need to do is be honest with yourself (just as you need to be when backtesting, described in the preceding section). If you look back on a losing paper trade and then come up with a reason why you wouldn't have taken it, then you're ruining a potentially valuable lesson about your method. A good rule to follow is this: If you have more than 80 per cent winning trades on paper, then you're not properly monitoring your methods because this would be unlikely in real-life trading.

Paper trading is usually the final step you take before putting a trading plan into action with real capital on the line. You're simply following your method in real time to test the outcomes. It's very important to have already clearly defined your method and then follow it to the letter. By doing this you can highlight some of the negative and positive aspects in your plan that you may not have thought of otherwise.

Either on paper or in a spreadsheet, keep a list of all the positions that you would have taken had you been following your plan. Don't forget to include all commissions and financing charges, because these can make a big difference to your bottom line, particularly if you're trading frequently. You need to monitor this list for several weeks or more to get an accurate assessment of how your plan is behaving.

After you complete the test phase you can then digest the data that you've recorded. Ask yourself questions about the size of the losses of your test trading, and the number of losses you record in a row. Consider these points:

✔ Am I comfortable with these losses?

✔ Could I make changes to minimise these losses?

✔ Am I letting my profits run to a reasonable level?

✔ Could I change my stop loss levels?

✔ Are my commissions taking up a huge percentage of profits? If so, would I be better off with a plan that gives me trade signals less often?

When you answer these questions honestly and you're happy with the results, you can proceed knowing you've given yourself the best chance at a successful start to your CFD trading. Although it's very tempting to simply 'have a go', without paper trading (or backtesting), rushing right in will only sour the experience that you could have in trading CFDs.

Paper trading, when done diligently, provides an illustration of how a set of trading rules might behave in real time. The process is informative if done honestly and accurately. However, paper trading is not a means of building prowess as a trader, and is in no way a replacement for real-life trading experience.

Balancing Risks with Your Goals

If you've read the rest of this chapter, it should be plain to you by now that no matter how you approach your CFD trading, you're in for a lot of work. The main thing to remember is that you need to focus your energies first and foremost on keeping your risk level low. This means that whatever your trading plan, it should feature small position sizes and the continuous use of stop losses. Chapter 8 goes into detail on managing risk when you're trading CFDs.

No matter what you do, you're going to make a lot of trades that are losers. This doesn't mean you can't be profitable, but you won't make any money at all if the size of the losses on average begins to outweigh the gains. Having losing trades is just part and parcel of the business that you're getting involved in, and the real difference between a winning trader and a losing trader is how you deal with these losses.

I've seen a number of trader surveys in my time, and one thing I find most unnerving is the number of traders who say that their trading strategy is based on gut feeling. If you wonder why people seem to have difficulty trading, then this factor is a likely reason.

Begin your endeavour by trying to find a combination that signals when a trend is in existence and then when the trend is beginning to break down. In the early stages, focus your energy on the daily and even the weekly chart. These time frames determine the dominant direction of the price movement.

Even if you plan to trade over a very short time frame you should still know the direction of this dominant trending movement, and should plan to trade only in the direction of this prevailing trend.

As you become more advanced in your trading you may choose to do some countertrend trading, but I believe that this is usually a lower-probability strategy (see Chapter 14 for more information on this strategy).

Chapter 17

Tracking Your Progress

In This Chapter

▶ Managing existing trades — time well spent

▶ Staying focused on making a profit

▶ Keeping records of your trades

*I*f you don't plan your journey how will you know when you've arrived? This question is often asked in trading circles, and it means that if you don't keep track of your trading you can't measure your success (or failure!).

In this chapter, I discuss how it's wiser to spend time watching the trades you already have rather than becoming obsessed with finding the next trade. You need to stay focused on what you have and make sure that you're making money; I show you how to set financial goals and measure your profits.

Keeping good records of your trades can give you a much better understanding of your own performance — and not just the dollars and cents. Making daily notes can be tedious and dreary, but it gives you an insight into your performance in the market. You can start to look at things like your trading behaviour, your win–loss ratio, and the dollar amounts of winning and losing trades. I cover what to include in daily entries in your trading diary, how to analyse the data and then act on it.

Monitoring Your Existing Trades

Managing the trades you hold is an important part of tracking your progress. As you become more experienced with your own trading behaviour you'll start to know how many positions you can manage.

If you're dealing in share CFDs and not trading full-time, then eight to ten positions (and probably less) are likely to be the most that you can manage at any one time.

You might think you can manage more, and maybe you can, but remember that for each position you have you need to monitor the charts, amend the stops regularly and exit the position when required. CFDs are not a set-and-forget investment so you need to set aside plenty of time to monitor positions.

In Chapter 14 I look at different ways that software can assist you with managing trades. The more automated your methods become, the more positions you can carry. The ability to automate your trading, though, comes with trust in your method and this can only be built over time and with experience.

Try to spend as much time monitoring your trades as you do finding new ones (for more information on monitoring, see Chapter 14). Every day, you need to decide whether you want to keep a particular position or replace it with something else. Follow your trading rules carefully because you need to keep your portfolio moving forward as best you can.

If you don't keep a close eye on your positions, leaving them in your trading portfolio but outside of your direct focus, you can very easily end up in a position where you take a significant loss on a trade that could have been avoided with some active monitoring on your part. Don't let the first thing you hear about it be your CFD provider demanding more money as part of a margin call.

Relying on a trading robot

In the trading world, and particularly in foreign exchange, there's growing interest in 'robot' software. This software scans the market using programmed criteria, opening and closing positions automatically based on rules it has been set.

I don't know many people who could tolerate giving over control of their trading to a piece of software, but this would be the ultimate test of confidence in your method.

Perhaps you could add to your list of things to do when setting a trading method: 'I must have enough confidence in my rules that I would let a robot trade for me.'

When you're building your trading plan you may want to consider the idea of a 'time stop', which is put in place to get rid of positions that aren't going down, but aren't going up either. Even if a position isn't falling it's tying up precious capital so you're better off replacing it with something that's got some wind in its sails. And even if a trade isn't losing value, you opened it because you thought it was going to move higher in value so it's not doing what you thought it would.

Measuring Your Financial Success

You need to keep tabs on whether you're making a profit trading because basically if you're not making money there's no point — you can find lots more fun things to spend your time and money on! You need to focus on measuring your success simply in dollar terms.

Determining how much profit you want to make trading and focusing on achieving that goal ensures you're not drifting on the trading sea without a rudder. Setting realistic goals to be achieved in a certain time frame helps you keep track of your trading progress. A good way to establish financial goals is to follow the **SMART** rules. Goals need to be

- ✔ **Specific:** Establish a goal that you can clearly define. You might decide that your goal is to become a full-time trader. You could also say that you plan to design a foreign exchange trading strategy that is expected to win on 60 per cent of trades that you make.

- ✔ **Measurable:** Make your goals measurable. 'I want to get rich trading' isn't a measurable goal. Something that is measurable, though, would be to say, 'My goal is to make $200 a week from my CFD trading.'

- ✔ **Attainable:** As in the previous example, a goal of $200 per week will likely work for most people if they put together a reasonable plan and have a decent capital base. To become a millionaire in your first year with starting capital of $1,000 is on the low end of the attainable scale.

✔ **Realistic:** Set a realistic goal, like $100 profit per month, and then ratchet things up from there. Avoid setting a goal of $1 million in your first year (although I seem to remember Martin Schwartz making his first million in his second year ...). Just try to be profitable at first and go from there.

✔ **Timely:** Set a deadline for when you want to achieve your goals.

Remember to keep adjusting and adapting your goals as you gain confidence and experience in trading. You can set progressively higher goals for yourself when you have your methods and trading plan down pat.

If you're trading index or foreign exchange CFDs, you may want to set goals in terms of pips (or points) movements; for example, 50 pips a day. The amount of money that you make is just a multiple of the number of pips you make times the size of the position you take. If you have a small trading account it may be $50 a day on average (50 pips × US$1, which is the minimum exposure) or it could be $500 or more. So you can see that the dollars you make are only a multiple of how many pips you can make.

Focusing on the bottom line

The reason behind your trading must be to make money; you must be in it to win it. If you're looking for an interesting hobby or pastime you should probably go with model building or stamp collecting because at least they won't gobble up your money and leave you with nothing.

If you're lucky enough to find trading a mentally challenging activity, that's fantastic because it will make the arduous and tedious times more rewarding. But finding the whole trading business exciting can be dangerous. You may want to keep reliving the heady excitement and adrenaline of that first successful trade, which was a trip into the unknown. The way you conquer this urge is by following a carefully constructed and tested trading plan (Chapter 16 shows you how). Step outside of the rules of your plan and you're back in the realms of chance.

As boring as it sounds, you'll experience the best outcomes when each trade is as dull and unexciting as the last because if you get to this stage you know that, win or lose, you're sticking to your plan and managing the trade as best you can.

Keeping a Trading Diary

Keeping a trading diary sounds simple but it can be difficult to keep up — you may need to exercise some good, old-fashioned discipline to maintain it. You need to write down all of your potential trades, your actual trades, any thoughts that you have about the market at that point in time and the decisions you made. Do this every day so that you have a record of the thought process behind each trade you've taken as well as the profit and loss.

You can then go back and check on the decisions that you've made. You may find regular recordings of 'placed my stop order too close' or 'too quick to take profits' and then you can take steps to modify your trading plan (refer to Chapter 16). Traders can talk at length about their best trade and their worst trade but probably not in much detail about the vast majority that lie somewhere in between the two.

Filling in your trading diary is hard to do for an extended period of time, especially if you're doing badly. When the market is moving consistently in your favour it's a great pleasure to write the fine details of your success and reflect on what a brilliant trader you are — you could do this for years on end. But you deserve a huge pat on the back if you can write in your diary every day for a week after ten losing trades in a row and still record the events in vivid detail.

Figure 17-1 shows a basic template for what your trading diary might include. You can put whatever you like in your own diary but be sure that the contents are relevant. Every month you should go through and see if there are things that are consistently going right and consistently going wrong — then do more of the former and less of the latter.

David's Trading Diary

Date	Code	Entry	Stop Loss	Exit	Units	P/L $	P/L %	Reason for Trade
17/05/09	RETA	$4.57	$4.42	$5.31	1200	$888.00	16.19%	The share price broke resistance at $4.50, which confirmed an ascending triangle formation. The trade was held and closed out as soon as the projected profit target of $5.31 was reached. I risked $0.15 and made $0.74 — giving me a risk–reward ratio of just under 1:5, which I am very happy with.
18/05/09	DRNE	$6.10	$5.80	$5.80	1000	–$300.00	–4.9%	This was an inverse head and shoulders trade that I had followed for a while waiting for the correct set-up. Unfortunately it didn't continue higher after the breakout and was quickly stopped out.
21/05/09	WDET	$9.98	$9.50		250			I have entered this trade based on a breakout from a rectangle. It is quite a wide range, which means I have a large stop loss placement and a small position size.

Figure 17-1: A trading diary lets you record all the details of your activity to help refine your trading.

All of the costs of CFD trading need to be accounted for to make it profitable and to give you an accurate picture of exactly where you stand. You also need to be able to extract certain details from your recorded data:

- ✔ **Profit and loss:** You can use a spreadsheet to calculate this simply by working out the start value (entry price × number of CFDs) and deduct it from the exit value (exit price × number of CFDs). You only need to do a small modification to make this into a percentage calculation.

- ✔ **Financing charges:** These can be calculated using your CFD provider's formula for financing and then applying this to your spreadsheet.

- ✔ **Commissions:** These are simple because they are an easy percentage formula that you apply to your initial exposure and then again when you close out the position. For many CFDs you won't be paying commission anyway. Remember that there is likely to be a minimum amount of commission payable so be careful applying just a basic percentage formula if the position size is quite small (for example, less than $10,000 exposure).

Making the most of Microsoft Excel

You *can* keep handwritten records but in this section I focus on using your computer and how you can increase its functionality in regards to your trading. I don't want to limit your flexibility by giving you specific formulas to use in your spreadsheets. In the help section of modern spreadsheet software you will find examples of all that you will ever need for a trading diary so if you aren't familiar with spreadsheets then this should be your first stop.

Using a spreadsheet like Microsoft Excel is the best way to record your trading data because you can use formulas to automate commissions, financing, win–loss ratio averages on days a position is held for, track your accounting costs, and easily work out your average profit and loss. You may need to invest in a book to help you with Excel — *Excel 2007 For Dummies,* Wiley Publishing Inc, is a good one!

Set up your file so that it includes all the entries, such as commissions, that I specified earlier in the chapter in 'Keeping a Trading Diary', then record away. Yes, you still need to manually enter all the details of trades, but think about the upside of doing this — you're forced to keep thinking about the open positions you have at any given point in time, which is good because losing sight of leveraged positions is financial Russian roulette.

Microsoft Excel makes life easier because with one press of a button you can activate a formula list. Here you can search for what you need to do and then you just either plug in the numbers or better yet refer the formula to the cells that contain individual details of your trades such as the number of CFDs and entry price which you use in your calculation. Use these formulas to

✔ **Count winners and losers.** To do this, create a formula that looks for whether the Profit & Loss is positive or negative and returns a 1 or a 0 (or indeed a blank cell if you like) depending on what you're looking for. Then all you need to do is count them up to find out what your winning and losing trades are.

✔ **Keep track of the financing (the account costs of CFD trading).** You can create your own formula or you can choose to add the charge each day from your CFD provider's daily statement. This latter option takes more time but at least you're always on the same page with your provider. Check your provider's product disclosure statement (PDS) for how they calculate their financing so that you can replicate their formula.

✔ **Note where you placed your initial stop losses.** Then you can work out your average returns for each dollar that you risk, known as *expectancy*, which is useful for working out how strong your trading is. Seeing at a glance where your stop losses are helps ensure that you're getting out where you planned to, and if you aren't you need to work out why.

✔ **Total the profit and loss for all of your positions in a gross and net form.** This way you can see what the effect of costs is on your overall profitability and find out your average profit, average loss and your win–loss ratio.

If you don't have Microsoft Excel you can always download Open Office, which has a very respectable spreadsheet program included in it and contains most of the same functions as Excel. You can also buy Excel-based spreadsheet software designed specifically for use with CFDs; have a hunt around on the internet to see what you can find. As an example, the people at Trading Lounge (tradinglounge.com.au) do a very useful spreadsheet that you can download.

Using off-the-shelf software

Even though CFDs are relatively new in the financial world, savvy programmers have already developed CFD record-keeping software that can calculate all of the things that you can do in a spreadsheet in a much simpler to use and pleasing-to-the-eye set-up. These programs are either custom-made for CFDs or have functions to help with them.

Before buying a program, make sure the software works out your financing and commissions for you and that it provides a statistical breakdown of your trading activity. You don't want something that's designed for share investors and has been lightly modified to adapt to CFDs so don't be afraid to email the provider of the software and ask them.

This software is really good for beginners because it sets you up in the right frame of mind for recording and analysing the trades that you make. I strongly suggest, though, that you spend no more than $200 on CFD-specific software and that you search for the program that will suit your needs the best.

Like any software it should be easy to use and come with good instructions as well as some form of support if you need it. The program itself should work out things like number of winners and losers, average gain and loss, total gain and loss, and it should also be able to help you determine where you are doing well and where you are doing poorly so you know what you need to work on. In the end there isn't much that software like this can do that a diligent Excel user can't, but it comes down to what you prefer and what you are willing to spend.

Keep in mind that simply spending big money on record-keeping software won't do the work for you. You still need to be diligent and disciplined because this is where you can get a real idea of your strengths and weaknesses.

Part VI
The Part of Tens

Glenn Lumsden

*'I was just showing him how leverage
works both ways.'*

In this part ...

1n this traditional serve of *For Dummies* top ten lists you discover the mistakes that people frequently make when they begin CFD trading. You also get tips on the best ways to stay on top of leverage and — my personal favourite topic — why you need to plan each trade before you lay down your money.

Chapter 18

Ten Common Mistakes Beginners Make When Trading CFDs

- -

In This Chapter

▶ Underestimating the power of leverage

▶ Failing to make proper plans

▶ Taking your eye off the market

- -

*I*n this chapter I look at some of the most common issues that people fail to fully comprehend when dealing with CFDs. A big part of this is the way in which most people approach the problem of trading and then add fuel to the fire with leverage. Many of the major problems people have when trading relate to a lack of contingency planning for unforeseen events. When you're dealing with a leveraged product like CFDs you need to focus a lot of your energy on working out how you'll deal with negative outcomes as they arise. You must be prepared with a solution if a problem arises.

Being Unfamiliar with the Product

Being unfamiliar with CFDs can cause problems when trading them. CFDs are powerful and very highly leveraged trading instruments. They have the ability to let retail traders get closer to running their own hedge fund. CFDs allow you to access the markets of the world from a single trading platform, and allow this access very cheaply in terms of your commission, which is very low compared to dealing in products such as shares. CFDs also enable you to lose more than your initial investment, which is your margin payment. You can also lose more money than there is in your account, which means you have to come up with the rest.

Providers are required to give you a copy of their product disclosure statement (PDS) that explains all the ways your chosen CFD product works. Read it. Although the PDS may be a huge document, all of the answers about what the provider will and won't do are in the PDS, so be sure to familiarise yourself with it.

Being Careless When Executing Trades

All CFD providers have differing software through which you execute your trades. The software may even let you deal with only a single click of the mouse, which means that you can deal quickly but also increases your opportunities to make a mistake. For this reason I suggest that you act like a stockbroker and read your order back to yourself before you execute it. It's worth an extra few seconds.

I have heard stories of kids in the house jumping onto a live dealing platform and having a costly play around. You're still responsible for the trade even if you didn't mean to make it, so be sure to lock the computer when you're away from it.

At some stage you're likely to make a trade in error — going long when you meant to go short, buying too many or selling too many. I suggest that when you trade in error, close out the position and start again. You still need to pay commission on both your entry and exit, but you shouldn't be thinking about the commission at this stage because you didn't want this trade and didn't mean to be in it so why would you stick with it?

Forgetting about Outstanding Orders

When you place a stop order or a limit order (both of which are often referred to as pending orders) over a position you have open, that order may remain in place even if you close the position that you put it over in the first place. This means that if the price subsequently falls or rises to that order level you're left with a new position that you didn't want. Regularly check outstanding orders and be sure that you don't have any in place that you no longer want. Repeat this procedure whenever you manually close out a position.

Opening a Position without a Stop Order

Sure, you want to be right all the time but the reality is that you won't be — and this is especially true when it comes to trading. You should know in advance of opening a position when you're going to get out of a position. One of the best ways to be sure that you get out of a position is by placing a stop order with your CFD provider. This means that as soon as the price where you know you're wrong is reached, the position is closed out straightaway. It's better to be wrong and preserve the vast majority of your capital than to be wrong anyway but lose a lot more money.

Never move stop orders away from the direction you want the position to move in; that is, if you're long, stops only go up, and if you're short, stops only go down. A stop is only worth something if you allow it to be executed because cancelling and leaving the position open means you're flying totally blind.

Trading Too Often

You can trade all you like but be sure that you're trading because your plan says to do so, not just for entertainment value. Every trade costs money in spreads or commission. Keep costs to a minimum because they're another impediment between you and profitable trading.

On this same note people often feel that the more often they trade, the more money they can make. I think that, realistically, trying to capture trending moves of decent size is more profitable because your costs are kept significantly lower.

Failing to Keep an Eye on the Market

CFDs are by no means a set-and-forget product. By trading CFDs you are making a huge commitment in time and effort because you need to regularly watch the performance of your positions. Using stop losses can go a long way to reducing the requirement to watch the market like a hawk, but you need to be mindful of movements that are occurring all the time. I am talking here much more about defending the downside and not so much about cashing in on the upside.

Don't let a winning trade turn into a losing trade. Once you've managed to make some good gains in the market don't give them back because you're not spending enough time watching the market.

Trying to Be Too Big Too Fast

Lots of people prefer to know how they're performing compared to others and whether they're doing well. Should you be trading bigger sizes?

Just being profitable is something that should please you. You may hear about someone making $10,000 on a single trade and think that you would like to do the same. However, keep in mind that for a person to make a large profit she must also be willing to risk several thousand dollars in the same time frame.

Nothing in the market is going to be given to you easily. There's always a risk and reward trade-off, so unless you're willing to risk thousands in a day then you aren't likely to make thousands in a day. Don't believe that someone else is applying some sort of risk-free method to the market because such a method doesn't exist.

Be very careful who you accept counsel from when it comes to trading. Keep away from most public discussions on the market because you'll end up feeling that you should be doing something differently, better, or not at all, which doesn't help you with your trading.

Failing to Preserve Your Capital

However you approach the market you need to be very focused on keeping as much of your capital intact as you can. Always remember how many hours have to go into earning $1,000 and you'll be less likely to risk the money lightly. Of course, you can't make money trading without risking some of your money, but this doesn't mean you want to give your money away through carelessness.

Another thing to remember is not to add to losing positions. It can be tempting to add to positions that have fallen in value so that you can get a lower overall average entry price. This is called *averaging down*, or even worse, *doubling up*. Averaging down puts you in a position where you're risking more capital on a position that has done the opposite to what you had anticipated. Averaging down is a dangerous strategy and encourages a dangerous mindset because it can empty your account very quickly. Save the capital for adding to positions that are moving in your favour.

Confusing Paper Trading with Real Trading

Most people do some paper trading before they start to trade for real. Interestingly enough, nearly everyone does very well as a paper trader because almost everything that is difficult about trading is taken away when you're dealing only on paper. You can also conveniently leave out whatever results you don't like the look of.

When you trade for real all of the challenges are added back into the equation, making things a lot more difficult. Paper trading can be very effective for final testing of a carefully constructed strategy but isn't a substitute for actual trading experience.

Blaming Someone Else for Risky Trades Gone Bad

When you lose money on a trade (and you will) there's a great temptation to try to push the blame onto another party rather than look inward for responsibility. Sometimes the market moves against you just enough that you're stopped out and then it goes back the other way. A lot of people want to blame their provider, but this type of market movement is one of those annoying things that happen. I suggest that for your own self-development you look to yourself for responsibility before pointing the finger at someone else.

By the same token, having a losing trade doesn't mean you should feel bad. You'll have lots of losing trades. You can't win all the time so don't crush yourself with self-criticism every time you have a loss.

On rare occasions, your broker or CFD provider may quote you a bad price and this can hopefully be rectified with a call to your provider. The provider can resolve problems for you the fastest, so make the provider your first stop if something does go wrong. Program the number for your provider's dealing desk into your phone, and be sure you know your account number and any passwords that you need to deal.

Chapter 19

Ten Lessons for Dealing with Leverage

*I*n this chapter I look at one of the aspects of CFDs that people find most attractive — the leverage inherent in CFDs. I suspect that people feel that if they take on really big positions then they need only a tiny move in their favour to make a decent profit. The opposite is also the case, of course — it takes only a tiny move in the wrong direction to lose money — but it's human nature to gloss over the bad when you want to focus purely on the good.

This dynamic makes for an interesting combination, where traders are excited by the most dangerous aspect of the product that they are dealing with. It means that you must work to appropriately control the amount of leverage that you use to remain in control of your overall trading outcomes.

Leverage Doesn't Have to Mean Massive Positions

Using leverage doesn't always have to mean you take on huge positions with a view to ultra short term profits in the market. Traders can employ diversification in order to get more diverse exposure than they might otherwise have been able to. For example, a trader could choose to take the $10,000 he has in his trading account to take on a $30,000 position, or he could build up six $5,000 positions that he believes are going to trend quite consistently over the next month or so.

Diversification is generally seen as the focus of long-term investors, but only taking exposure to one or two positions may be dangerous because the outcomes you have on a day-to-day basis are very heavily focused on a narrow end of the market. While you don't want to take on dozens of positions, a decent spread of positions may help to smooth your equity curve.

Just Because You Can Doesn't Mean You Should

Different CFD providers offer different margin requirements on their CFDs. Providers who offer the most liquidity generally have the lowest margin requirements, which may be as low as 1 per cent (or even lower in some cases). Based on a margin requirement of 1 per cent you could turn $10,000 into $1,000,000 worth of position if you wished. If you did, however, a very small move in price would immediately put you in a position where you'll receive a margin call from your CFD provider.

The key is that there's nothing stopping you from doing a trade like this, even though the trade makes no sense from a risk management point of view.

Keep the Leverage Conservative

Even though you won't generally be able to nominate how much margin you pay, you can control the amount of leverage that you employ. For example, if you had $30,000 worth of share CFD exposure and the margin requirement was 5 per cent then you would need to provide $1,500 in margin. If you had $10,000 in your account you have levered this by three times (3×). If you had fully levered up the position, you could have gone to $200,000 or 20× leverage.

You can see that this margin tells you the maximum amount of leverage that you can take on, but you're in complete control of the minimum.

A 3× leverage is pretty reasonable as a conservative maximum for most people, so try putting a self-imposed cap of a similar amount on your trading.

Different CFDs Suit Different Leverage

When you are dealing in share CFDs the CFD provider places a higher margin on them than they would for a product like foreign exchange (FX) CFDs. A big part of the reason for this is because you need more exposure to FX to make US$1 per tick (a tick is just another way of referring to the smallest increment movement of price) than you do with share CFDs (where 100 share CFDs will do it). In FX you have a general minimum trade size of US$10,000 and that means it carries an inherently higher level of leverage.

Keep in mind that the amount of margin required gives you an indicator of the risk of gaps in the market. A gap in the share market is common because the market is closed overnight and prices adjust for news releases that have occurred while the market is closed. In the 24-hour FX markets, gaps are less common and are likely to be of a smaller magnitude.

One dollar per tick on shares and FX is not the same thing because FX pairs can move quite a lot further in a given session than shares. You may think $20 per tick isn't too bad on shares; however, it may prove to be more than you bargained for with FX.

Let Your Account Have Plenty of Room to Breathe

The more leverage you use, the less room you have for the market to move against you before you receive a margin call. If you use only conservative leverage you may go your entire CFD trading career without ever receiving a margin call, which is something to aspire to because it shows a sensible approach to your leverage management.

Focusing on the upsides of taking on a very high amount of leverage reduces the number of times that you can be wrong and survive to trade another day.

Know What You Stand to Lose

Calculating the likely downsides of trading precisely may be difficult, but you can make some good estimations for a day-to-day basis. If you have a decent spread of share CFDs you may feel that if a big slide took place in the United States overnight you could be in for a fall of 5 per cent, which would mean a loss of all of your margin if the share CFDs require a 5 per cent payment. The difficulty is to work out what effect a crash similar to 1987 is going to have and how concerned about it you should be. Clearly a fall of 20 per cent is going to be very costly to anyone holding long share CFD exposure, but happily this is a very rare event.

If you are leveraged to only a low level then you can withstand this type of fall. Alternatively a trader who is very highly leveraged may be totally wiped out. A crash similar to 1987 may be a rare event; however, you only need to be wiped out once.

The Long and Short Advantage

You may find that carrying long and short exposure in the same market (particularly share CFDs) reduces your risk at any given point in time. This may mean that in a sharp downturn losses on the long side are offset (to some extent) by gains on the short side.

Carrying long and short exposure can be very effective in the event of a sudden widely distributed fall in the market. However, a sudden fall in the market won't happen every day, so you need to pick your short positions as carefully as you do your long positions and not just carry short exposure as an attempt at insurance.

A Close Stop Doesn't Make Over-leveraging Alright

A lot of position sizing methodologies let you take on a bigger position the closer that your stop loss is placed to the market. The temptation for traders is to place their stops really close so that they can have a much bigger position for the same apparent amount of risk.

The big downside occurs if a big gap in the market happens so your stops are gapped over, leaving you with a much bigger risk than you calculated. There isn't a safe way to leverage in an extremely heavy way, so use smaller sizes and focus on the defence of capital.

Even Small Amounts of Leverage Make a Big Difference

If you could make 15 per cent per annum trading shares without leverage (which would be very good), then simply by doubling your exposure to the market using CFDs you are miles ahead of where you would otherwise have been, with only a small use of leverage. Keep this in mind before you implement a strategy that sees you taking out vast amounts of leverage.

Leverage Your Returns and Your Volatility Too

Returns are increased directly by leverage and so too is volatility. When you look at your expected performance don't just think about where you would like to be in one year. Instead try to think about what the journey is going to be like.

Making a positive return is one thing, but you must be prepared for dealing with the negative trading sessions and the drawdowns that your trading account faces. The more leverage you apply the bigger the peaks and troughs, so try to prepare yourself as much as you can. The more that you trade, however, the easier the peaks and troughs are to cope with.

Chapter 20

Ten Ways to Plan Your Trades

*I*n this chapter I look at some of the major advantages that arise from putting extra effort into planning your trading in as much detail as you can. Thinking about solutions to problems you're likely to face helps you be prepared.

You can't predict the outcome when you trade, so you need to build in risk management tools. Keeping good records helps you to remember the details of trades. You can't be right all of the time, so devise a strategy that keeps your risk low and minimises damage to your portfolio from losing trades.

Spend Time Building Your Strategy

If you're building a technical analysis strategy then there's really no substitute for looking at lots and lots of charts to determine what works for you. If you're looking at something fundamental you'll need to master the relevant formulas and analytical methods and/or secure relevant research for your analysis. You can find any number of trading strategies out there to use and a lot of them are very good. The weakness isn't necessarily in the strategy but in the trader using the strategy. You can't shortcut the process of deciding what works for you by opening an account and grabbing another person's strategy.

You can test different strategies for nothing by being diligent with your work with the charts. If charts are your primary means of selecting and managing positions then you need to be sure of the way in which the trades that you take are likely to behave when you open positions for real.

You need to undertake comprehensive testing for several reasons. If you undertake comprehensive testing you'll get a good idea of how likely your trades are to be successful, a likely win–loss ratio, and reasonable estimates of likely drawdowns that you'll face on your capital. Once you get underway you need to give your strategy time to work. Throwing your strategy away if the first two trades don't make money isn't sensible because it isn't a proper assessment of the strategy you've employed, so you need to stick with it. As you find problems you can finetune them, but don't undertake massive overhauls to your plan on the fly because it wastes a lot of the testing that you've done.

Write Down Your Plan

I speculate that for every trader who writes down her plan, ten or more traders don't. Writing down your trading plan doesn't need to be a complex issue at all. In fact I've heard a very sensible recommendation that your written plan should fit on the back of a coaster.

Your trading plan should specifically deal with your reason for buying and selling and how much you plan to risk on each trade. A plan is only as good as the following two things:

- ✓ The plan's profitability
- ✓ The trader's ability to follow it

Your Plan Helps in Uncertain Conditions

If you're explicit in your planning you can comfortably respond in a range of market conditions. Of greatest concern is a large and sudden move in the market, when you must be able to respond quickly. Can you hold on or are you going to sell out? Will you be left in a bigger losing position than you originally anticipated? You must be able to answer these questions and respond to all market conditions so you can act quickly in times of uncertainty.

Don't put yourself in the position of knowing that you need to do something but then doing nothing.

Record Your Results

You can refine your planning in even more detail by being diligent with your records of winning and losing trades. Don't try to forget about your losing trades because they can point you towards problems you're having with your planning. One of the worst things you can do is become frustrated and do the 'trading plan tear down and rebuild' routine.

Unless you've cobbled your plan together parts of it are sure to be correct. Throwing away your plan is a waste of the effort you put into it. No plan is going to be right straightaway, so keep refining.

Psychology forms a huge part of a trader's success or failure. When you modify your plan be sure that the plan is at fault, not you.

If You Don't Know Your Stop Loss, You Don't Know Your Risk

All traders want to think about how profitable a trade may be, but you can't do so at the expense of not properly managing your risk. Before you open any trades you should know exactly where you're going to get out if the trade doesn't go the way that you hoped it would. If you can't say exactly where you're going to get out then you haven't managed your risk. Not managing your risk is one of the worst things you can do because you're not properly defending your capital.

Planning an exit at a small loss is one thing, but for some people executing the exit can be quite another.

Stop losses should only move in the direction of the trade, not away from it. Moving away from the direction of the trade increases your risk.

Be True to Your Plan

If you're asked, 'Is it better to follow your plan and lose money or ignore your plan and make money?', what would your answer be? Answering 'Yes' to the first part of the question is tempting because everyone enjoys a profit; however, this is the wrong answer — but you guessed that already! If you ignore your plan then you may as well not even have one.

One of the hardest times for traders is when they're having a profitable trade and decide that they want to cash it in, even though their plan says to let the trade keep running. You can convince yourself of anything if you want — all you need to do is recall the adage that 'you can't go broke making a profit' and you're set. Stick with your plan, even when you're tempted not to.

There is an exception here and that's not to follow your plan until you have no money left. You may want to put a 'circuit breaker' in your plan where you stop trading and reassess your plan. A good rule would be when you have lost a certain amount of capital (for example, 15 per cent) you stop trading and work out whether your plan should be modified or whether you should scrap it and go back to the drawing board.

Test All New Set-ups

One of the negative impacts on traders is the law of small numbers. People see a small sample size and make an assessment based only on that sample. In trading circles this may mean that you look at a couple of similar set-ups on some charts that look successful and decide that this set-up is worth trading in the future.

Remember that just because the sample worked once or twice, statistical probability isn't necessarily in your favour. Every new set-up you consider needs to be rigorously tested, otherwise all you're doing is gambling.

Don't Spend All Your Time on Your Entry Plan

One thing that gives people a feel-good experience is opening a trade and having it run quickly in their favour. This is about as close to instant gratification as trading is likely to get. Remember you only get to keep the profits you've made when you close the trade. Don't just focus on the first part of the trade; remember to focus on the part that dictates how the trade will end. This means that you need to have a very clear plan about the conditions that will trigger an exit from your trade at either a profit or a loss.

Include Targets as Part of Your Plan

Some people are very keen on setting goals for themselves, which is a useful way to improve monitoring of your progress. Remember the idea of setting SMART goals (see Chapter 17 for more on SMART goals). SMART goals are those that are Specific, Measurable, Attainable, Realistic and Timely. If you can fit your goals into all of these categories it gives you a good set of targets to work towards. New trading opportunities come along every day, so you don't need to move too far too fast.

Include targets as part of your plan so that you keep modifying your strategy to deliver better results.

The Plan Tells You When To Pay Attention and When to Ignore the Market

Your CFD provider probably offers thousands of CFDs for you to trade. Do you want to trade them all? Few people have that much capital to play with and those who do know trading thousands of CFDs isn't an effective use of their capital.

Your trading plan acts as a market filter so that you focus on looking for a very specific market set-up and ignore anything that's not an opportunity to trade. A detailed trading plan makes sorting market opportunities from market noise easier.

Glossary

2 per cent rule: A risk management technique in which traders vary the size of each new position so that it will not lose more than 2 per cent of their trading capital assuming the *stop loss order* they place at the same time they enter a trade is triggered. This technique does not guarantee that no loss will be greater than 2 per cent of your trading capital as there will be some cases where there is *slippage* on a stop loss order.

ascending triangle: A chart pattern in which a horizontal *trend line* can be drawn across peaks of at least two separate trends and an upward sloping (or ascending) trend line can be drawn across at least two separate troughs in those trends. The two trend lines thus form the shape of a triangle. A common trading strategy involves entering new positions in the direction of a breakout of the triangle pattern.

auction: A process in which prices are discovered through parties entering competitive bids and offers. This is often done via electronic trading systems that match bids and offers to determine sale prices.

average true range (ATR) indicator: A widely used technical analysis tool that is designed to indicate the level of price volatility in a market over a given time. It is often used to set a trailing *stop loss order* once a position has been entered.

backtesting: The process of testing the profitability of a trading strategy against historical price data or charts. At least 30 to 100 past examples are normally required before the test results are regarded as statistically significant.

beta: A statistical measure of how volatile an individual security has been compared to the whole market or to an index over a given period. The market's beta is defined as being 1. So a stock with a beta of 0.8 has been 20 per cent less volatile than the market while a stock with a beta of 1.2 has been 20 per cent more volatile.

breakout traders: Traders who use *breakout trading* strategies.

breakout trading: Trading strategies based on entering trades once price breaks through a defined *resistance* or *support* level. New *long* positions are entered on a break through resistance while new *short* positions are entered on a break through support. The strategies are based on the view that once price breaks through support or resistance a new trend is likely to be established.

capital: The wealth (whether monetary or in assets) owned by an individual or company.

carry trade: An investment strategy that involves temporarily selling or borrowing an asset with low yields in order to buy a higher yielding asset. The investor is attempting to make a positive return (or 'carry') holding the higher yielding asset compared to the return on holding the lower yielding asset or compared to the cost of borrowing that asset. However, in this type of trade you are exposed to the risk that the market value of the high yielding asset that you now own will fall compared to that of the low yielding asset that you have to repurchase in the future. Large-scale carry trades have been made in currency markets in recent years — for example, borrowing Japanese yen to invest in Australian debt securities.

charting: A range of techniques that use charts of past prices and other indicators to anticipate future price movements.

close out: Selling a *long* position or buying a *short* position so that you no longer have any exposure to changes in market price.

commodity: Physical substances that are exchanged without any quality differentiation and for which a general market price is established — for example, a pound of copper or a bushel of wheat. This differs to the price of a house, for example, which is likely to be unique and based on individual factors such as location.

commodity CFDs: *Contracts for difference* in which the underlying instrument is a *commodity*.

commodity currency: The second currency quoted in a foreign exchange pair. A foreign exchange pair price depicts how many units of the commodity currency are needed to buy or sell a single unit of the first currency quoted in the pair. (Confusingly there is another common usage of 'commodity currency'. In this sense it refers to the currency of a nation that derives a large amount of its export revenue from *commodities*. The value of these currencies can be heavily influenced by fluctuations in commodity prices. The Australian and Canadian dollars are the best known examples.)

compound interest: Where interest is rolled over into the following period's investment principal. The interest that has been added therefore also itself earns interest.

consumer confidence index: An index based on a survey of consumers that asks a number of standard questions, such as whether they expect their financial position to improve or deteriorate over the next year and whether they think now is a good time to purchase major consumer items. The results of the survey are collated into a single index number designed to reflect overall consumer confidence. Consumer confidence indices are widely used to predict future changes in consumer spending.

Consumer Price Index (CPI): A measure of the quarterly changes in the prices of a 'basket' of goods and services commonly purchased by metropolitan wage and salary earners. CPI is the most common method of measuring the rate of price *inflation*.

contracts for difference (CFDs): An agreement between a buyer and seller which allows them to make a profit or loss due to fluctuations in the price of an underlying instrument such as a share, index, *commodity* or *currency pair*. If the price of the underlying asset rises between the time a CFD is opened and the time it is closed, the seller must pay the difference in value to the buyer. If the price falls, the buyer must pay the difference to the seller.

core inflation: A measure of *inflation* that excludes items that are subject to volatile price movements — for example, vegetable prices, which fluctuate widely based on seasonal conditions.

countertrend trading: The practice of trading in the direction of 'corrections' or 'countertrends'. These are minor trends in the opposite direction to the longer-term trend. They are typically smaller and last a shorter time than minor trends in the same direction as the longer-term trend. Many trading strategies therefore seek to avoid following countertrends

as they are often considered poor risk–reward opportunities.

coupon: The periodic interest payments governments make to holders of bonds. Prior to the days of electronic registration, bond owners would tear a coupon off the bond each six months and present it at an agent of the central bank to receive their interest payment.

cross rate: An exchange rate between two currencies other than the US dollar.

crossover method: See *moving average crossover*.

currency pair: A price quotation of the relative value of one currency in terms of another.

data releases: The release of economic statistics usually by a government body such as the Australian Bureau of Statistics. Releases are typically made at regular dates on the basis of a predetermined schedule.

debt to assets ratio: Total liabilities divided by total assets. This ratio shows the proportion of a company's assets that are funded by debt as opposed to equity.

debt to equity ratio: The amount of a company's debt divided by the amount of its shareholders' equity. This is a measure of a company's leverage. A high ratio implies greater risk and may make it difficult for the company to meet interest payments in the event of a downturn in earnings or an increase in interest rates.

delta: The ratio of change in the price of a derivative compared to the change in price of an underlying asset, such as a share. Where a derivative has a delta of 0.5, a $1 change in the share price will cause the derivative price to change by $0.50.

diversification: To vary an investment or a trading portfolio so as to limit exposure to any single instrument. For example, the entire portfolio may be allocated across a range of different asset classes such as shares, CFDs, property, fixed interest and cash. Within each of these classes, assets may also be varied. For example, a share portfolio may be allocated across a range of industry sectors.

earnings per share (EPS): A ratio determined by dividing a company's after-tax profit by the number of ordinary shares it has issued.

economic clock: A diagram in the form of a clock that depicts what is likely to be happening to the prices of various assets (such as shares, property and interest rates) at different stages of the economic cycle as the economy moves between periods of contraction and growth in output.

economic drivers: Changes in the economy that lead to changes in the market price of investments such as shares, commodities or property.

economics: A discipline that studies the production, distribution and consumption of goods and services in human society.

ex-dividend date: The first trading day on which the buyer of a share is no longer entitled to payment of the current dividend.

exiting: See *close out*.

exposure: Refers to a situation where you have a current or open position. This means you are financially exposed to the consequences of a change in price of the instrument you have open. The larger the size of the position, the greater the exposure to the possibility of financial gain or to the risk of financial loss.

financial ratio: A measure of the relative size of two items in a company's accounts — for example, its debt and equity. Financial ratios are widely used by securities analysts and investors to compare different companies, to assess changes in a company over time and to assess companies against a standard benchmark for risk.

fiscal policy: A government's financial policy covering the amount it earns (for example, through taxation), spends, borrows and invests. Fiscal policy impacts on the overall level of economic activity. Where a government runs a deficit (spends more than it earns) they are putting more into the economy than they take out and so adding to *Gross Domestic Product*.

fiscal surplus: A surplus of government income over expenditure in a given period. A fiscal surplus has the effect of reducing the overall level of *Gross Domestic Product* as the government is taking more out of the economy than it is putting in.

fixed dollar model: An approach to risk management where the size of every position a trader enters is calculated so that if the *stop loss order* is triggered the resulting loss will equal the same dollar value.

fixed percentage model: A risk management technique such as the *2 per cent rule* in which traders vary the size of each new position so that it will not lose more than a fixed percentage of their trading capital if their *stop loss order* is triggered.

foreign exchange CFDs: *Contracts for difference* where the underlying instrument is a *currency pair.*

fundamental analysis: Analysing and valuing financial assets based on factors such as financial statements and earnings forecasts, company strategy and risk assessment, demand and supply forecasts, projections of future economic growth, industry developments and government policy.

Goldilocks economy: An economy that is able to sustain reasonable levels of economic growth without creating too much inflation (that is, it's 'not too hot and not too cold'). In the late 1990s and early 2000s many developed economies had sustained Goldilocks periods where they were able to achieve relatively high growth rates with little inflationary pressure due to the large amounts of excess capacity (that is, unemployed people) created by the severe recession of the late 1980s and early 1990s.

Gross Domestic Product (GDP): The total final value of goods and services produced by a country's economy in a given period of time (usually a year or a quarter).

hedge funds: An investment fund that is only open to high net worth or professional investors and has a large minimum investment requirement (for example, $1 million). These requirements mean that the funds are exempt from much of the regulation applying to retail investment funds and they often have very flexible investment mandates allowing them to hold both *long* and *short* positions, to invest or trade in a wide range of financial assets and to use considerable leverage.

hedged exposure: Where a position is opened in one instrument that is opposite to an investor's or trader's exposure in another instrument — for example, you may open a *short* position in 1,000 BHP share CFDs to hedge a *long* position of 1,000 BHP shares. Any loss of value resulting from a fall in the price of BHP shares will then be offset or hedged by a profit on the short CFD position.

highest high value (HHV): The high of any chart candle or bar that is the highest of all the highs in a given period covering multiple candles or bars. For example, each candle in a one-minute chart shows the price high and low in a one-minute period. Over a given 20 periods, the highest high value will be the high of that one-minute candle that is greater than or equal to the other 19 candles.

hyper-inflation: Very high inflation that is out of control. When hyper-inflation is present the purchasing power of money falls rapidly and large losses result from holding money assets such as cash or debt securities for any length of time.

index CFDs: *Contracts for difference* where the underlying instrument is an index reflecting changes in the value of a group of shares — for example, the largest 200 shares listed on the ASX.

index fund: A fund that invests in the assets underlying an index (for example, the shares in a share index or the commodities in a commodity index). Each individual investment is weighted so that the performance of the index fund tracks the performance of the index itself. These funds allow an investor to obtain a return equivalent to the overall market and claim to do better in the long term than many managers who seek to beat the market through active asset selection techniques.

index stripping: A trading strategy that involves buying an index CFD and selling certain *sector contracts* or *share CFDs* within the index. This is a strategy to use if you believe that an overall index will rise but that certain sectors or stocks within the index will underperform. If you are correct, index stripping will improve the result of a long position in the index.

inflation: An increase in the money value of goods and services over time.

inflation rate: A measure of the extent of *inflation* that occurs in a given period — for example, a year or calendar quarter.

initial margin: The amount of cash or other approved collateral a trader is required to have with a CFD provider in order to open a new position.

interest rate differential: The difference in yield between similar interest bearing assets or benchmark interest rates in different currencies — for example, the difference between the US Fed Funds Rate and the Reserve Bank of Australia's Cash Rate.

intra-day trading: Trading where positions are opened and then *closed out* within the same trading day.

leverage: The use of debt to partly fund the acquisition of an asset. This has the effect of amplifying profit or loss as a percentage of the trader's equity.

limit-move rules: Rules used by some international futures exchanges that place a limit on the maximum price movement in a market between one day and the next. Where a market is up by more than the limit no trading will generally occur that day because no traders are prepared to sell under what is regarded as fair value. Typically no trading occurs until enough daily limits have passed so that trading can occur at the new fair value. The purpose of limits is to create a market breather, avoid panic and allow margins to be called in fast-moving markets. However, they can create a new set of problems by preventing people getting out of positions.

liquidity: A gauge of how readily transactions can be made in a market. The two main measures of liquidity are how far price has to be pushed and how long it takes to complete larger transactions.

listed companies: Companies whose shares are available to be traded on regulated exchanges such as the Australian Securities Exchange. To be listed companies need to comply with listing rules — for example, reporting standards and minimum size requirements.

longer-term trading: In the context of CFDs, longer-term trading refers to strategies where the average duration of open positions would be between a few days and several months.

long trading: Where the initial transaction is to buy and the position makes a profit if price rises but a loss if it falls.

lowest low value (LLV): The low of any chart candle or bar that is the lowest of all the lows in a given period covering multiple candles or bars. For example, each candle in a one-minute chart shows the price high and low in a one-minute period. Over a given 20 periods the lowest low value will be the low of that one-minute candle that is less than or equal to the other 19 candles.

margin: The amount of cash or approved collateral needed to open and then hold a CFD or futures contract. An ***initial margin*** is required to open a new position and after that any losses must be met as they arise in the form of ***variation margin***.

marked-to-market: Revaluing something at market values. In the case of derivatives such as CFDs cash payments are then made between the buyer and the seller representing profits and losses resulting from any changes in value of the underlying instrument.

market capitalisation: The total market value of all shares of a company listed on the stock market, found by multiplying the number of shares on issue by the current market price.

market makers: An organisation or person who makes firm prices to both buy and sell at the same time. Bid and offer prices are made to clients or other market participants without knowing whether that other party wishes to buy or sell.

market neutral: A market neutral investment strategy attempts to carry no exposure to changes in the value of the overall market. For example, you may be long in some shares and short in other shares so that theoretically if the whole market goes up or down by 5 per cent you will have no profit or loss. The strategy is attempting to make money only through the stocks held in long positions doing better than those held in short positions, or vice versa.

medium-term trading: In the context of CFD trading this refers to strategies where the trader is prepared to hold positions open for longer than one day but where the average duration of positions would be no more than a few days.

monetary policy: Policies carried out by central banks to set interest rates and control the amount of money in an economy with the aim of keeping inflation and unemployment at acceptable levels.

moving average: A mathematical technique designed to provide an indication of the overall trend in prices by smoothing out short-term fluctuations in price. In a simple moving average, the average of closing prices over a certain trading period is calculated — for example, 20 days or 20 minutes. Once trading for a new day or minute is finished, the first closing price from the previous average is dropped out and the closing price for the last day or minute is added in. If the new bit of data is higher than the one dropped out, the average will go up; if it is lower, the average will go down.

moving average crossover: When a shorter-term *moving average* crosses through a longer-term one. A cross from above to below indicates a change from uptrend to downtrend. A cross from below to above indicates a change from downtrend to uptrend.

net tangible assets (NTA): Tangible assets are generally a company's physical assets, such as land, buildings and machinery. Intangible assets consist of the value attributed to certain non-physical assets, such as customer goodwill or patents. Net tangible assets refers to the value of all a company's tangible assets less the amount of debt it owes. It gives a view of what may be left over for shareholders if a company is wound up and its assets sold and debt repaid. Intangible assets are excluded because they often have no value if the company is not operating as a going concern.

noise: Small price moves that turn out only to be minor oscillations and can confuse a trader about the overall price trend.

non-advisory product: A financial product where the provider of the product does not provide advice on whether it's a suitable investment for a customer or on whether this is an appropriate time to buy or sell. For example, a CFD provider may offer the service of a platform used to buy or sell CFDs but not provide any advice about whether now is a good time to buy or sell a particular CFD.

order: An instruction given by a client to buy or sell CFDs. The order will stipulate the quantity to be bought or sold and instructions about the price or timing of execution.

oscillating indicators: Mathematical indicators designed to provide insight into whether a market has become overbought or oversold. These are situations where markets are regarded as being more than normally vulnerable to a price reversal because price has moved a relatively long way in a short time or because a trend has been in existence for a long time without correction. The indicators will oscillate within a band of values — for example, 0 to 100, or above and below a centre or zero line.

pairs trading: A CFD transaction in which a trader buys one instrument and simultaneously sells a similar one. For example, you might buy Westpac bank share CFDs and sell National Bank share CFDs. In this example, you're seeking to profit from a change in the price relationship between the two particular banks rather than from an overall movement in bank shares.

paper loss: A loss that has yet to be realised. For example, you will have a paper loss where you have bought shares that have since fallen in value but have not yet been sold. Your statement of assets will show a lower value on paper

but this will be restored if the shares rise again. The loss will not be realised until you actually sell the shares for less cash than you initally paid.

paper trading: Simulated trading where traders record where they would have bought or sold. This can be a useful way of assessing the likely profitability of a trading strategy before actually committing risk capital to it. Paper trading can also be used to practise the mechanics of trading and get a feel for placing orders or what you would be likely to do once you have entered a trade and the price moves.

parabolic stop and reverse (PSAR): A technical indicator designed to show market trends and higher probability points for changes in market momentum. The indicator uses an acceleration factor that often gives it a parabolic shape on a chart. It is often used to set *stop loss orders* that trail behind a price trend.

pattern recognition: A form of analysis that involves recognising patterns such as *ascending triangles* and *rectangles* formed by bars or candles on a price chart. Common trading strategies are often based on the assumption that a break out of these patterns indicates the likely start of a new trend.

pip: The smallest amount by which a foreign exchange quote can vary — for example, .0001 AUD:USD. The name comes from 'price interest point'.

portfolio: A collection of investment assets such as shares, CFDs, fixed interest, property and cash.

position sizing: A risk management technique whereby an investor calculates the size of each new trading position so that the maximum likely loss on the trade does not exceed a certain amount or a certain percentage of their trading capital. Examples include the *2 per cent rule* and the *fixed dollar model*.

post-market auction: A facility under which traders can submit bids and offers for shares for a limited time after the close of ordinary trading on a stock market. Where bids are received that are equal to or higher than the lowest offer price a single weighted average price is established. This becomes the official closing price. Any bids at or above this price and any offers at or below this price will then be executed at the official closing price.

pre-market auction: A facility similar to the *post-market auction* where an official opening price is established from bids and offers placed prior to the opening of the stock market.

price–earnings ratio: A ratio calculated by dividing the market price of a share by the company's earnings per share. This is a widely used method of measuring a company's value. It has the advantage of allowing more meaningful comparisons of similar companies or of a single company's

valuation over time. For example, it makes more sense to know that Bank A has a market valuation of 12 times its earnings but investors are only paying 11 times earnings for Bank B than it does to compare the basic share prices of, say, $27.50 with $24.25.

pricing in: A market price (for example, a share price) should, theoretically, reflect the market's assessment of all the known factors that may affect its valuation, including projected future earnings and likely risks. When a factor like a potential law change affecting a company's earnings is 'priced in', it means that an investor considers that the potential change is already fully reflected in the share price.

product disclosure statement (PDS): This is a document that licensed Australian financial service providers must give to potential clients when they are offering or recommending a financial product to them. The aim of the document is to make sure that the client has all the information they need to make a good decision about whether to use the product. Required information includes an explanation of how the product works and what its benefits and risks are.

pyramiding: This is a staking strategy whereby traders add to the size of their position as price moves in their favour. The strategy aims to increase returns from profitable trades. The increased risk taken is managed by ensuring that any new positions added are always smaller than the previous one. This means the first position at the base is the largest and the final one added is the smallest — hence the name.

rectangle: A chart formation in which a horizontal line can be drawn across two or more trend peaks and across two or more trend troughs.

requote: CFD platforms indicate a bid price at which a client can sell and an offer price at which they can buy. A requote occurs when a client tries to buy or sell at the indicated price but their order is not executed and instead they are quoted a new price. The most likely reasons for this are that the client is trying to execute a greater volume of CFDs than is available at the original price or that the underlying market has moved.

resistance: A price level that the market is unable to rise above for some time. When price rises to a resistance level the weight of selling outweighs the buyers and price is pushed down again. A number of different trend peaks often occur at a resistance level.

scaling in: A staking strategy where traders will gradually build a position with several orders at different price levels rather than entering the whole position with a single order.

scaling out: A staking strategy where traders will gradually exit a position with different orders at different prices. The most common technique is to have more than one profit objective. Some profit

is taken at the first objective but some of the position is left in place to let the position 'run'. These strategies will normally involve moving your *stop loss order* to reduce risk as each new profit objective is met.

scanning the market: Searching charts with different instruments to find those where a certain opportunity is close to occurring (for example, a *moving average crossover* involving a 10- and 20-day average). This is often done by technical analysis software, allowing you to efficiently scan large numbers of charts for opportunities.

sector contract: A *contract for difference* where the underlying instrument is an index over an industry sector. A sector is made up of listed companies on an exchange that fall within a particular industry, such as healthcare or information technology.

share CFD: A *contract for difference* where the underlying instrument is a share in a company listed on a stock market.

short trading: A form of trading where the initial transaction is to sell. The position is closed with a buy transaction. The trader will profit if price falls and lose if it rises.

slippage: This occurs when an *order* cannot be executed at the stipulated price. For example, you may have a *stop loss order* to sell *share CFDs* at $1.00. However, if the market closes one day at $1.02 and opens the next at $0.98 (see *pre-market auction*) then the order will be executed at $0.98 (or less if there is not sufficient volume to execute the order at $0.98). The trader will have suffered slippage of $0.02 or more per CFD.

spot price: The price quoted for immediate settlement (that is, payment for and delivery of an instrument). It is the opposite of a forward price, which is for settlement at some time in the future. Each market has its own convention for what constitutes immediate delivery. On the Australian share market it's T + 3 (three business days after trade day). On foreign exchange markets it's T + 2.

spot rate: An exchange rate for immediate settlement (see *spot price*).

stop loss order: This is an order that aims to limit your loss. A stop sell order is placed at a price below the current market price. It is an instruction to sell at market if price falls to the stipulated price or lower. A stop buy order is placed above the current price and is an order to buy at market if price rises to the stipulated price or above. A stop loss order is a stop buy or sell order that is placed to close an existing position. It prevents (or stops) a loss getting any bigger.

support: A price level that the market is unable to fall below for some time. When price falls to a support level the weight of buying outweighs the sellers and price

is pushed up again. A number of different trend troughs often occur at a support level.

swing techniques: These are techniques that aim to position a trader to sell near the end of a price upswing or to buy near the end of a downswing. Swing techniques involve being prepared to hold positions for longer than a single trading day to ensure the swing has time to complete. However, they are based on relatively short-term swings with trades normally lasting a matter of days or weeks, as opposed to *longer-term trading* where positions may typically be held for weeks or months.

symmetrical triangle: A chart pattern in which a downward sloping *trend line* can be drawn across peaks of at least two separate trends and an upward sloping trend line can be drawn across at least two separate trend troughs. The two trend lines thus form the shape of a symmetrical triangle. A common trading strategy involves entering new positions in the direction of a breakout of the triangle pattern.

technical analysis indicators: Mathematical formulae designed to show whether market prices are trending up or down. Moving averages are probably the best known example.

terms currency: The first currency quoted in a foreign exchange pair. A foreign exchange pair price depicts how many units of the second currency quoted are needed to buy or sell a single unit of the terms currency. See also *commodity currency*.

tick: The minimum amount by which the price of a particular CFD can change.

time stop: A strategy to exit a position at the prevailing market price once a certain time has elapsed.

today's dollar: The value of a dollar today. This may be measured by what it buys — for example, how many dollars it takes to buy a Big Mac today compared to the number required to buy one in the past or the future.

trading plan: A business plan for trading. It may include risk management plans, budgets, operational plans (such as plans for training or backup plans for internet failures) and specific trading strategies (such as rules for entering and exiting trades).

trading price breakouts: A trading strategy based on buying when price rises above a *resistance* level or falls below a *support* level.

treasuries: Debt securities issued by a government treasury, such as treasury notes or bonds.

treasury CFDs: *Contracts for difference* where the underlying instruments are *treasuries*.

trend following indicator: Trend following indicators are designed to provide an insight into whether price is trending up or down.

However, because they are based on mathematical calculations they will inevitably lag or follow the actual trend.

trend line: Lines used to provide an easy visual appraisal of the direction and momentum of a trend. An uptrend line slopes up and is drawn across at least two or three separate trend troughs. A downtrend line slopes down and is drawn across at least two or three separate trend peaks.

trend trading: Trading strategies designed to profit from trading in the direction of price trends. Traders attempt to recognise the beginning and end of trends as early as possible. The ideal trade involves entering the market near the beginning of a new trend and keeping the position open until as near as possible to the end of the trend.

true range: A calculation of the average or 'true' range within which a market can normally be expected to move during a given period. The true range is calculated by taking the average of differences between the high, low and previous closing price of each candle or bar in the period.

variation margin: Payment of profits or losses resulting from changes in market price of the underlying instrument. These are a requirement of many derivative contracts such as futures and *contracts for difference*. Variation margin payments are automatically debited or credited to a client's account before a position is closed or formally settled.

wiggle room: A small amount of leeway that a trader allows before responding to the breach of a significant price level. For example, when trading range ***breakouts*** some traders may not enter new positions until price has moved a small way beyond ***support*** or ***resistance***. They are looking to reduce the risk of being caught out by a false start.

Index

Notes

Notes

FOR DUMMIES®

Health & Fitness

1-74216-946-5
$39.95

0-7314-0760-1
$34.95

0-7314-0596-X
$34.95

1-74031-094-2
$39.95

1-74216-984-8
$39.95

1-74031-009-8
$39.95

1-74031-059-4
$39.95

1-74031-074-8
$39.95

1-74031-011-X
$39.95

1-74031-173-6
$39.95

0-7314-0595-1
$34.95

0-7314-0644-3
$39.95

Business & Investment

1-74216-971-6
$39.95

1-74216-852-3
$39.95

1-74216-941-4
$36.95

0-7314-0787-3
$39.95

0-7314-0991-4
$39.95

1-74216-853-1
$39.95

0-7314-0828-4
$19.95

0-7314-0827-6
$19.95

1-74031-166-3
$39.95

0-7314-0724-5
$39.95

0-7314-0940-X
$39.95

1-74216-859-0
$32.95

FOR DUMMIES®

Reference

1-74216-972-4
$39.95

1-74216-945-7
$39.95

1-74031-157-4
$39.95

0-7314-0723-7
$34.95

0-7314-0909-4
$39.95

0-7314-0722-9
$29.95

0-7314-0784-9
$34.95

0-7314-0752-0
$34.95

Technology

0-470-49743-2
$34.95

0-7314-0761-X
$39.95

0-7314-0941-8
$39.95

1-74031-159-0
$39.95

Printed and bound by CPI Group (UK) Ltd, Croydon, CR0 4YY